CW01020951

Masterworks of
The Jewish Museum

Masterworks
of
The Jewish
Museum

Maurice Berger and Joan Rosenbaum
with entries by
Vivian B. Mann, Norman L. Kleeblatt,
and the staff of The Jewish Museum

The Jewish Museum, New York
Under the auspices of the Jewish Theological Seminary of America

Yale University Press, New Haven and London

This book has been published in celebration
of the centennial of The Jewish Museum, which
was founded in 1904.

The Jewish Museum
Manager of Curatorial Publications:
Michael Sittenfeld
Publication Assistants: Ivy Epstein and Beth Turk

Offsite: Publications, Planning, Projects
Project Director: Mary DelMonico
Editors: Sheila Schwartz and Janice Meyerson

Yale University Press
Publisher, Art & Architecture: Patricia Fidler
Assistant Editor, Art & Architecture: Michelle Komie

Designed and typeset by Katy Homans, New York
Printed in Italy by Conti Tipocolor, Florence

Front cover: Andy Warhol, *Sarah Bernhardt* (detail),
from *Ten Portraits of Jews of the Twentieth Century*,
1980.

Frontispiece: Line drawing of the expanded Jewish
Museum, 1990.

Back cover: First row: Israel Dov Rosenbaum,
Decoration for the Eastern Wall *(Mizrah)*, 1877 (left),
Ben Shahn, *New York*, 1947 (right); second row:
Elie Nadelman, *Dancer*, c. 1920–22 (left), Tiered
Seder Set, 18th–19th century (second from left),
Weegee, *Max is rushing in the bagels to a restaurant
on Second Avenue for the morning trade*, c. 1940
(second from right), Burial Plaque, Venosa (?),
4th–5th century (right); third row: Solomon
Alexander Hart, R.A., *The Feast of the Rejoicing of the
Law at the Synagogue in Leghorn, Italy*, 1850 (left),
Christian Boltanski, *Monument (Odessa)*, 1989–2003
(right); bottom: Ludwig Yehuda Wolpert, Passover
Set, c. 1978 (original design, 1930).

See page 249 for photography credits.

The Jewish Museum
1109 Fifth Avenue
New York, New York 10128
www.thejewishmuseum.org

Yale University Press
P.O. Box 209040
New Haven, Connecticut 06520-9040
www.yalebooks.com

Copyright © 2004 by The Jewish Museum, New
York, and Yale University Press. All rights reserved.
This book may not be reproduced, in whole or in
part, including illustrations, in any form (beyond
that copying permitted by Sections 107 and 108 of
the U.S. Copyright Law and except by reviewers for
the public press), without written permission from
the publishers.

Library of Congress Control Number: 2004101791

A catalogue record for this book is available from
the British Library.

The paper in this book meets the guidelines for
permanence and durability of the Committee on
Production Guidelines for Book Longevity of the
Council on Library Resources.
10 9 8 7 6 5 4 3 2 1

Contents

The Jewish Museum gratefully acknowledges

Jeanette Lerman-Neubauer and Joseph Neubauer

for their generous underwriting of this publication.

The Jewish Museum Board of Trustees

OFFICERS

Susan Lytle Lipton, *Chairman*

John L. Vogelstein, *President*

Leni May, *Vice President*

Leon Black, *Vice Chairman*

Barry J. Alperin,
  Vice Chairman

Jeanette Lerman,
  Vice Chairman

James A. Stern, *Treasurer*

Benjamin Winter,
  Assistant Treasurer

Lynn Tobias, *Secretary*

Phyllis Mack,
  Assistant Secretary

Ann H. Appelbaum, *Assistant*
  Secretary, ex-officio

Joan Rosenbaum,
  Helen Goldsmith Menschel
  Director, ex-officio

MEMBERS

Leslie E. Bains

Corrine Barsky

William H. Berkman

Andrea Bronfman

Charles de Gunzburg

Robert C. Dinerstein

Craig Effron

Susan Feinstein

Nomi P. Ghez

Bernard Goldberg

Rita Goldberg

Leslie Goldstein

Barbara S. Horowitz, *ex-officio*

Robert J. Hurst*

Harry P. Kamen

Robert S. Kaplan

Ilan Kaufthal

Francine Klagsbrun

Seryl B. Kushner

Betty Levin

Hirschell Levine

Ira A. Lipman

Joshua Nash, *ex-officio*

Martin D. Payson

Barbara Perlmutter

Robert A. Pruzan

John A. Ross

Amy Rubenstein

Bernard Spitzer

Bonnie Tisch

Joseph Wilf

Karen B. Winnick

LIFE MEMBERS

E. Robert Goodkind*

Eugene Grant

Fanya Gottesfeld Heller

Dr. Henry Kaufman

Ellen Liman

Morris W. Offit*

Richard Scheuer*

H. Axel Schupf*

Romie Shapiro

Stuart Silver

James L. Weinberg*

Mildred Weissman

HONORARY MEMBERS

Norman E. Alexander

Martin Blumenthal

Harriet Cooper

David Finn*

Sylvia Zenia Wiener

ADVISORS

Rabbi Michael Greenbaum

Sheila Lehman

Dr. Ismar Schorsch

*Chairman Emeritus

Foreword

Joan Rosenbaum
Helen Goldsmith Menschel
Director
The Jewish Museum

This book celebrates the hundredth anniversary of The Jewish Museum—a joyful occasion for an institution that has played a central role in the preservation and study of Jewish culture. Over the last century, the importance of collecting, documenting, and exhibiting artifacts and artworks of the Jewish world has grown. The collection of The Jewish Museum attests to the perseverance of the curators, scholars, collectors, and benefactors who have dedicated themselves to understanding the art and the traditions of a culture that has thrived for centuries.

As you will see in the pages that follow, Jewish culture has produced an amazing variety of artworks and ceremonial objects. The works highlighted here are organized into four sections: Memory and History; Spirituality and Faith; Society and Politics; and Portraiture and Identity. In effect, these sections function as small exhibitions, with works grouped and juxtaposed to suggest common themes. Works of Judaica and art appear together in these sections just as they are displayed side by side in the galleries of the museum. By presenting the collection in this way, we hope to make the abundance and richness of the artworks and objects apparent both to readers of this book and visitors to the installation of the permanent collection.

All museum publications are collaborative, none more so than a book highlighting a wide-ranging collection. Many people contributed their time and skills to *Masterworks of The Jewish Museum*, and I am exceedingly grateful for their involvement and expertise.

Members of the museum's curatorial departments made a preliminary selection of works for possible inclusion in this book. A small committee—Ruth Beesch, Deputy Director for Program; Norman L. Kleeblatt, Susan and Elihu Rose Curator of Fine Arts; and Susan L. Braunstein, Curator of Archaeology and Judaica—made the final selection in consultation with me. Maurice Berger helped shape the book and wrote a wonderful essay as well as the section introductions. The tremendous erudition of Vivian B. Mann, Morris and Eva Feld Chair in Judaica, and Norman L. Kleeblatt is evident in the many entries that they have contributed to this volume. Nineteen current and former staff members (their names appear on the facing page) brought their invaluable knowledge of the museum's collection to the other entries that accompany the selected works.

Michael Sittenfeld, Manager of Curatorial Publications, supervised every aspect of this project, and worked closely with a superb team: editors Sheila Schwartz and Janice Meyerson, project director Mary DelMonico, designer Katy Homans, and the staff of Yale University Press, especially Patricia Fidler, Michelle Komie, and Mary Mayer. Other staff members at The Jewish Museum played important roles, including Ivy Epstein, Barbara Treitel, Stacey Traunfeld, Sari Cohen, and interns Beth Turk and Abigail Deutsch.

I want to express my deep gratitude to Jeanette Lerman-Neubauer and Joseph Neubauer for underwriting *Masterworks of The Jewish Museum*. Their generous gift has made it possible for countless readers to learn about Jewish culture and the museum's collection, which is essential to our mission.

It is with pleasure that I thank The Jewish Museum Board of Trustees for its incomparable generosity and counsel. This book is, in many ways, a tribute to the continued support of the board, which has enabled the museum to assemble a world-class collection and to serve the public with its exhibitions, programs, and publications.

Key to Authors

Maurice Berger	MB
Emily D. Bilski	EDB
Susan L. Braunstein	SLB
Shira Brisman	SNB
Susan Chevlowe	SC
Gabriel de Guzman	GG
Anita Friedman	AF
Leslie Friedman	LF
Johanna Goldfeld	JG
Susan Goodman	SG
Andrew Ingall	AI
Norman L. Kleeblatt	NLK
Mason Klein	MK
Karen Levitov	KL
Joanna Lindenbaum	JL
Vivian B. Mann	VBM
Claudia Nahson	CN
Scott Ruby	SR
Irene Zwerling Schenck	IZS
Valerie von Volz	VV
Fred Wasserman	FW
Aviva Weintraub	AW

New photography of the collection by Richard Goodbody

The Jewish Museum and Its History

Joan Rosenbaum

Context is everything at The Jewish Museum. It is present in the permanent and changing exhibitions, in the publications and education programs, and in decisions about building and shaping the permanent collection. The context of the institution itself has powerful implications. One can visit The Jewish Museum and appreciate many exhibitions solely for the artworks. Yet, seeing a painting by Chagall, Modigliani, Pissarro, or Soutine in a museum dedicated to Jewish culture provides an experience that allows the paintings in these galleries to resonate with historical, ethnic, political, and religious references. This is particularly true when seeing the museum's permanent exhibition, where the emergence of the Jewish artist in the twentieth century is given the context of a four-thousand-year history.

The Jewish Museum began with a gift of twenty-six ceremonial objects. Donated to the Library of the Jewish Theological Seminary of America in 1904 by Judge Mayer Sulzberger (figs. 1–2), these works generated a succession of exhibitions, gifts, and expansions that have contributed to the enormous growth of The Jewish Museum over the last century. It was the first museum of its kind in the United States, and, though the number of Jewish museums has grown tremendously, it remains the largest of its kind in the Western Hemisphere. The collection has grown from twenty-six to over 28,000 works, and the museum's home in the former Warburg mansion on New York's Museum Mile has had two major expansions to accommodate its permanent and changing exhibitions, education programs, and collections. This book, with over 120 highlights of a collection that has been amassed over one hundred years, speaks to the history and dispersion of Jewish people, their enormous diversity, and the complex questions that have been and remain intrinsic to both the subject of Jewish identity and of The Jewish Museum.

How to create collections and exhibitions that best fulfill a museum's mission is a question that pervades the work of all art museums. For The Jewish Museum, the selection of art and artifacts has a dual purpose. Collectively, the goal is to communicate an understanding of Jewish culture, with its various layers of religion, history, memory, and identity. Individually, acquisitions may be appreciated for their intrinsic aesthetic, historical, or narrative content.

The art and artifacts that are in these pages have been designated "masterworks." This means that they are wonderful works of art unto themselves or they have a connection to Jewish culture that is of particular resonance. What one sees in the following pages is a small fraction of our total holdings. Yet the selection of works, both great and small, provides an excellent summary view of the scope, quality, and purpose of the collection. This book presents both a visual cross-section and a representation of influences that have shaped the museum's collection over time: historical events; the donations of major collectors; the emergence, in the last decades of the twentieth century, of art addressing issues of personal identity; and finally, the judgment and expertise of the curatorial staff combined with the advice and oversight of acquisitions committees composed of scholars, collectors, and museum trustees.

The museum's beginning in the first decade of the twentieth century coincided with the establishment of a handful of other Jewish museums in European cities. The context for the emergence of these institutions is one of emancipation, assimilation, and new scholarship. It was a period when the new field of the "scientific" study of Jewish culture began, reflecting and

Fig. 2. Judge Mayer Sulzberger.

Fig. 1. Exhibition of the collection of The Jewish Museum in the Library of the Jewish Theological Seminary of America, 1930s.

Fig. 3. Cyrus Adler.

Fig. 4. Hadji Ephraim
Benguiat.

Fig. 5. Felix Warburg.

reinforcing a cultural self-consciousness that found expression in the idea of a Jewish museum. Such an institution could provide a public venue where the Jewish people might communicate their culture, through the material evidence of their history and religion to the world at large.

The German Jewish immigrants who founded the Jewish Theological Seminary in 1886 and the museum in 1904 believed in the ideals of American life and the importance of maintaining a strong Jewish identity while living fully as citizens in a new country. Cyrus Adler, who became chancellor of the Seminary in the 1920s, epitomized the intellectual idealism of these founders (fig. 3). Formerly curator of the Smithsonian Institution in Washington, D.C., he held that "Judaism, Americanized according to the canons of modern scholarship, could raise the level of knowledge and respect on the part of both Jews and non-Jews for the ancient but still vibrant culture."[1]

The founders of The Jewish Museum were well versed in the origins and uses of ceremonial objects, an expertise that significantly influenced the way in which the collection grew. In 1902, for example, Adler had persuaded the passionate and visionary collector Hadji Ephraim Benguiat (fig. 4) to lend his extraordinary collection of Jewish ceremonial art to the United States National Museum (now the Smithsonian Institution), where it remained for twenty-two years. When Adler joined the Seminary, he arranged for the acquisition of the four-hundred-work collection with the help of Seminary trustee Felix Warburg (fig. 5). This extraordinary body of material is represented in this book by some of the museum's most historically important objects: a case for holding a Torah from Damascus made in 1565/66 (page 99); a sixteenth-century Torah ark from Urbino, Italy (page 97); and a Baroque Hanukkah lamp in the form of a Torah ark (page 122).

Like Benguiat, the collector Benjamin Mintz was a dealer in antiquities (fig. 6). His love of Judiasm and his Zionist beliefs influenced the building of his great collection of fine and folk arts. Because of the strife in Europe, he and his wife remained in New York after bringing their collection of Polish Jewish artifacts to the 1939 World's Fair. For a small sum, Mrs. Mintz

Fig. 6. Rose and
Benjamin Mintz in their
Warsaw home, before
1939.

Fig. 7. *Noisemaker with
Heads of Haman and
Hitler*, Poland, 1933.
Wood: carved and
incised, 7⅞ x 3⅛ in.
(20 x 8 cm). Rose and
Benjamin Mintz
Collection, M 424.

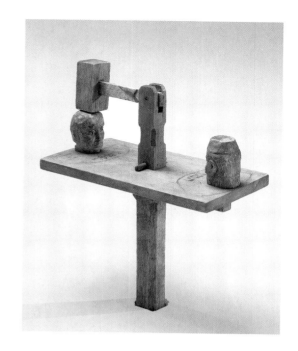

subsequently sold this important body of works to the Seminary and thus to the museum in 1947. Two Mintz Collection works are chilling in their foreshadowing and anticipation of the Holocaust. One is a humble noisemaker used for the holiday of Purim, when Jews celebrate their freedom from oppression in the fifth century B.C.E. During the ceremonial retelling of this story, groggers (noisemakers) are used to mock and deride the vanquished oppressor, Haman. The small, roughly carved wooden grogger (fig. 7) creates a noise by striking the heads of both Hitler and Haman. Made in 1933, it is an astonishing reminder of the events that followed over the next decade. On another scale entirely is an extraordinary painting by one of the earliest known professional Jewish artists, Samuel Hirszenberg, whose *Black Banner* of 1905 (page 177) is an explicit reminder of the pogroms of the early twentieth century.

In the same year that The Jewish Museum in New York was founded, Lesser Gieldzinski, an art collector, connoisseur, and art adviser to Kaiser Wilhelm II, donated his Judaica collection to the Jewish community of Danzig, where it was placed in the museum within the Great Synagogue. In 1939, with the Nazi threat of the community's destruction, the collection was sent to the Seminary for safekeeping, with the stipulation that the objects were to be returned if after fifteen years the Danzig community remained safe. If not, they were to remain in New York "for the education and inspiration of the rest of the world." The works arrived in New York one month before the German army occupied Danzig. It was forty years before this body of work, forming an extraordinary legacy and memorial, was exhibited and then circulated throughout Europe, Israel, and the United States (fig. 8). Two superb objects in this book from the Danzig collection are a Dutch Scroll of Esther from the mid-1600s (page 105), and a Polish tiered seder set created for the Passover holiday (page 38).

A major postwar effort in the rescue of material confiscated from Jewish owners was the Jewish Cultural Reconstruction, managed by a distinguished committee including philosopher Hannah Arendt and art historian Meyer Schapiro. Also among this group was Dr. Guido Schoenberger, who had worked for the Frankfurt Jewish Museum before World War II, and

Fig. 8. Exhibition at the Jewish Theological Seminary of the collection of the Jewish community of Danzig, 1940s.

continued his curatorial work at The Jewish Museum in New York. The works were dispersed to collections in the United States and Israel, and 120 objects entered The Jewish Museum collection. Several are illustrated in this book, including a remarkable Frankfurt spice container dating from about 1550 (page 95). Between 1941 and 1965, six thousand works of fine arts, ceremonial art, and archaeological material came to the museum from the rabbinically trained businessman and philanthropist Harry G. Friedman, an extraordinary collector who sought to rescue works from war-torn Europe and ensure their safety in a public institution (fig. 9). Not surprisingly, a large sampling of works from the Friedman collection are discussed and illustrated in this book, including an exceptionally beautiful portion of a sixteenth-century synagogue wall from Isfahan (page 101), permanently on view in the museum.

A turning point in the museum's history came in 1944, when Frieda Schiff Warburg, wife of financier Felix Warburg and daughter of Jacob Schiff, a trustee of the Seminary for two decades, gave her ornate family mansion to the Jewish Theological Seminary for the expansion of The Jewish Museum (figs. 10–12). With the opening in 1947 of its new home at 92nd Street and Fifth Avenue, just ten blocks from the Metropolitan Museum of Art, the institution was in a more central location in Manhattan and had a new presence in the art world. In 1952, the heirs of Jacob Schiff donated over three hundred turn-of-the-century paintings illustrating the Hebrew Bible by the French artist James Jacques Tissot. Two exquisite images from Tissot's series, *Joseph Dwelleth in Egypt* and *Adam and Eve Driven from Paradise*, are reproduced on page 45.

Fig. 9. Harry G. Friedman.

Fig. 10. Frieda Schiff Warburg.

Fig. 11. Jacob Schiff.

Fig. 12. The etching rooms of the Warburg family mansion, before it became the home of The Jewish Museum in 1947.

Fig. 13. Albert and Vera List (left and second from left), at the opening of the museum's 1966 exhibition *Primary Structures*.

Fig. 14. Visitors to the sculpture court in front of the Albert and Vera List Building of The Jewish Museum, 1960s.

Important acquisitions continued to be made in the postwar years, through the knowledge and generosity of individual collectors and through the vision and expertise of directors and curators, among them most notably Dr. Stephen Kayser. A distinguished collection of coins and medals was assembled and donated between 1935 and 1945 by the late Samuel Friedenberg and his son Daniel (see, for example, page 207). It is a collection that is still growing, containing over 80 percent of all known coins and medals illustrating Jewish history and culture. This collection is also an instructive complement to the museum's archaeological material, acquired in large part through two major acquisitions: a group of six hundred pieces from ancient Israel, obtained in 1973 by a former museum director, Joy Ungerleider-Mayerson; and another collection given by Cleveland collectors Betty and Max Ratner in 1981.

An extensive museum expansion in 1963, made possible by Vera and Albert List, offered opportunities for accommodating more visitors and presenting a program of contemporary art that has been regarded as unprecedented in the country (figs. 13–14). Vera List herself contributed several works to the collection, and she is seen through a portrait of her (about 1965) by Larry Rivers (p. 225). Another key development in the museum's evolution came in 1984, when it launched its National Jewish Archive of Broadcasting, started with funds from the Charles E. Revson Foundation. Today the archive contains over 4,300 recordings of radio and television programs that reflect the way Jewish culture has been represented and seen since the end of World War II.

The last twenty years has been a lively period of acquisition activity for the museum. A major expansion and renovation project, completed in 1993, resulted in a doubling of gallery space and led to the installation of a permanent exhibition, *Culture and Continuity: The Jewish Journey*, which occupies two floors of the museum (fig. 15). This exhibition offered the opportunity to highlight the museum's collection—including many works acquired in the last few years—and a chance to blend the ancient and the modern, and ceremonial objects with the fine arts. In the context of the ceremonial, one sees beautiful and stirring works from an earlier age

Fig. 15. Groundbreaking ceremony in 1990 for the expansion of The Jewish Museum, which was completed in 1993. Left to right: Architect Kevin Roche; Joan Rosenbaum, Director of The Jewish Museum; Morris W. Offit, Chairman of The Jewish Museum Board of Trustees; State Senator Roy Goodman; Congressman Bill Green; City Councilmember Carolyn B. Maloney; Commissioner of Parks and Recreation Betsy Gotbaum; Assemblyman Mark Alan Siegel; Manhattan Borough President Ruth W. Messinger; New York City Comptroller Elizabeth Holtzman; and Assemblyman Daniel Feldman.

as well as contemporary works that use new materials and forms. Moshe Zabari's 1969 Torah crown (page 155), for example, is a poetic blending of modern design and reverence for Jewish law, while Amy Klein Reichert's 1997 *Miriam's Cup* (page 161) represents a contemporary, feminist Jewish ritual adopted for the Passover seder.

During this period, acquisition activity in the museum's Fine Arts Department was marked by several new initiatives. Included was the creation of a separate photography acquisitions program, resulting in a significant body of work, particularly by American and Israeli photographers (see pages 54, 55, 73, 185, 193, 221, 227, and 229). Another step was to focus on the acquisition of works—particularly contemporary art—shown in exhibitions organized by the museum; objects seen in this book were acquired from such exhibitions as *Painting a Place in America: Jewish Artists in New York, 1900–1945* (1991), *Too Jewish?: Challenging Traditional Identities* (1996), and *After Rabin: New Art from Israel* (1998). A third strategy was the commissioning of works that might subsequently be acquired for the collection; notable examples include Eleanor Antin's moody and lyrical *Vilna Nights* of 1993–97 (page 76) and Matthew McCaslin's inventive and charming electrified Hanukkah lamp, *Being the Light*, of 2000 (page 165).

There are humble works in this collection and there are grand works; yet it is the sum of the parts that matters and gives the visitor to the galleries or the reader of this book a sense of Jewish culture in its broadest sense. From ancient objects to contemporary artistic expressions, these works speak not only to the universal need for a cultural identity but to the necessity of individuals to actually create their own identity. For Jews, this creative process has required reinvention and adaptation throughout the centuries, as can be seen in the remarkable assortment of works in these pages. We hope this rich array of art provides an understanding of Jewish culture as well as a touchstone of shared human experience.

1. Quoted in Naomi Cohen, *Encounter with Emancipation: The German Jews in the United States, 1830–1914* (Phila- delphia: Jewish Publication Society of America, 1984), p. 203.

HANUKKAH AMONG THE NATIONS

Museum Without Walls

Maurice Berger

In the introductory gallery of The Jewish Museum's permanent installation, *Culture and Continuity: The Jewish Journey*, the viewer encounters an abstract painting by Michael David, *Warsaw* (1981; fig. 2). The surface of the work, which is in the shape of a Star of David, is built up of brush strokes of unctuous yellow wax. The painting is far from an exercise in formalist abstraction, however, for its golden color as well as its title provokes dark and troubling memories of the Holocaust and of the Warsaw ghetto. *Warsaw* evokes the evil sign system of Nazism, in which basic geometric forms marked innocent human beings for destruction. The work, to a remarkable degree, infuses the cool, pristine geometry of modernist abstraction with historical meaning.

In its ability to summon up a range of memories and ideas through visual form, *Warsaw* is typical of the objects highlighted in *Culture and Continuity*, which bears witness to the complex story of the Jewish people through visual culture in all of its manifestations. The installation contains artifacts from the museum's extensive permanent collection—fine art, ceremonial objects, video and voice recordings, decorative arts, Internet sites, coins, and furniture—that are poised to answer the central question stated in its opening wall label: How has Judaism been able to thrive for thousands of years across the globe, often in difficult and even tragic circumstances? In the ensuing two-story installation, *Culture and Continuity* charts the course of Jewish cultural history through time, a project keenly aware of the shifts and reversals in the fortunes and survival of the Jewish people.

A stroll through this winding and quirky installation yields a range of aesthetic and intellectual experiences: an imposing wall of Hanukkah lamps from places as disparate as India, Iraq, Denmark, Poland, Morocco, the United States, Austria, and Peru (fig. 1); a monumental painting by Solomon Alexander Hart, the first Jewish member of the British Royal Academy, *The Feast of the Rejoicing of the Law at the Synagogue in Leghorn, Italy* (1850); an ornate, late-nineteenth-century pinewood Torah ark from a synagogue in Sioux City, Iowa; a re-creation of an urban café in which viewers are invited to take a seat and listen to excerpts from the texts of famous Jewish writers, such as Sholem Aleichem, Robert Musil, Max Lilienthal, Albert Memmi, and Nathan Alterman; a sculpture of a shackled black man by Aaron J. Goodelman, *The Necklace* (1933), meant to protest the trial of nine African-American men in Scottsboro, Alabama, who were wrongly accused of raping two white women in 1931 (fig. 3); a stark contemporary reinterpretation of the mezuzah by architect Harley Swedler (*Beron Mezuzah*, 1991); excerpts from a half-century of television programs—dramas, situation comedies, variety shows, and documentaries—performed by Jewish entertainers or concerning Jewish issues; and, finally, a gallery of contemporary art about the Jewish experience (fig. 4).

The power of *Culture and Continuity* to move and challenge its audience comes not just from the aesthetic strength of individual objects in the museum's permanent collection but also from their religious, philosophical, or political content. The installation acknowledges that no artifact or work of art is ideologically neutral or free of broader social and cultural meaning. Nor does it make relative qualitative judgments about different forms of culture. The curators have selected the finest examples from the museum's extensive holdings and have allowed TV clips, books, and medals to exist alongside ritual objects, paintings, and sculpture as equal players in

Fig. 1.
"Hanukkah Among the Nations" installation in *Culture and Continuity: The Jewish Journey*.

19

Fig. 2. (top left)
Michael David (American, born 1954). *Warsaw*, 1981. Pigment and wax on Masonite, 63 x 63 in. (160 x 160 cm). Gift of Lenore B. Lippert and Barbara E. Lippert in memory of Michael Myron Lippert, 1986-92.

Fig. 3. (bottom left)
Aaron J. Goodelman (American, born Bessarabia, 1890–1978). *The Necklace*, 1933. Bronze, 22½ x 6½ x 4½ in. (57.2 x 16.5 x 11.4 cm). Purchase: Kristie A. Jayne Fund with the cooperation of the Goodelman family, 1990-158.

Fig. 4. (top right)
Contemporary art in *Culture and Continuity: The Jewish Journey*. George Segal's *The Holocaust* (1982) can be seen in the adjoining gallery.

the exhibition experience. *Culture and Continuity* treats artworks and artifacts as more than self-contained conveyors of aesthetic pleasure and meaning, opting instead for a comparative, almost Talmudic view of culture that places objects in complex and meaningful relationships to one another.

Sometimes these relationships are implicit: the installation ends with George Segal's haunting tableau of a concentration camp (*The Holocaust*, 1982), closing the circle that begins with *Warsaw*. Sometimes they are direct: the gallery devoted to "Interpreting the Torah" juxtaposes a blowup of a page from the Talmud, its various fragments and tangents marked and explained, with Max Weber's painting *The Talmudists* (1934; fig. 5) and an "Interactive Talmud," a computer-based program that enables viewers to experience the Talmudic method of posing questions and debating issues. Sometimes the juxtapositions are oblique but no less thought-provoking: the clips from television programs serve as a compelling backdrop for the contemporary art that follows, much of it also concerned with issues of Jewish identity and self-imagery.

In the end, *Culture and Continuity* captures the diversity and depth of The Jewish Museum's permanent collection. The museum's commitment to a range of artistic disciplines and modes of expression, high and low, as well as its insistence on building powerful social and cultural connections between its myriad artifacts and works of art, helps it to reach, educate, and inspire its audience. The positions that it embraces have not come easily to an institution that has for decades struggled with the question of its mandate and curatorial vision. Yet the collection that has emerged out of these changes has helped to define an unusual and important conception of the museum in an ever-changing world.

Fig. 5.
Max Weber (American, born Russia, 1881–1961). *The Talmudists*, 1934. Oil on canvas, 50 x 34⅛ in. (127 x 86.7 cm). Gift of Mrs. Nathan Miller, JM 51-48.

In the century of its existence, The Jewish Museum has gone through significant transformations. For its first fifty years, the museum's exhibition and acquisition programs concentrated on Jewish ceremonial objects. When the museum moved into the former home of Mr. and Mrs. Felix Warburg on Fifth Avenue in 1947, it was the Warburgs' extensive collection of Judaica that formed the center of its permanent collection.[1] In 1962, however, the museum revised its mandate in an attempt to strike a balance between a commitment to religious artifacts and a newfound attention to secular, mostly abstract contemporary art.

While the museum continued to support its earlier objective of documenting the "continuity of Jewish history and tradition," it also wanted to reach a broader audience and, in the process, contribute "to the aesthetic life of the general community."[2] To meet this aim, it initiated a "program of contemporary art of a general nature," one that would reach out to "the contemporary art scene" and support artists regardless of their religion or ethnicity.[3] Taking up a perceived void left by the Museum of Modern Art, the Guggenheim Museum, and the Whitney Museum in keeping up with the fast-paced changes of contemporary art, The Jewish Museum recast itself as the "foremost showcase for contemporary art among New York's museums."[4]

This shift, in part, reflected the enormous transformation of the art world over the preceding thirty years. The United States, and especially New York City, had become the dominant force in progressive art, replacing Paris as the center of the avant-garde. For the first time, Jewish contributions to the avant-garde were conspicuous, placing a number of Jewish Americans in the forefront of the postwar art world. The dealer Leo Castelli, a Rumanian Jew, became its most powerful tastemaker. The critics Harold Rosenberg, Meyer Schapiro, Clement

Fig. 6.
The Albert and Vera List Building (left) of The Jewish Museum, c. 1967. This 1963 building was enlarged and reconfigured when the museum was expanded in 1993.

Greenberg, Leo Steinberg, Rosalind Krauss, Annette Michelson, Max Kozloff, and Robert Pincus-Witten played a central role in establishing its intellectual tone. And a new generation of Jewish artists—Diane Arbus, Helen Frankenthaler, Adolph Gottlieb, Eva Hesse, Lee Krasner, Sol LeWitt, Morris Louis, Louise Nevelson, Larry Rivers, Barnett Newman, Mark Rothko, George Segal, and Richard Serra—emerged as a dominant force in American visual culture.

The religion and ethnicity of these key figures, however, remained more or less irrelevant to a resolutely secular art world infatuated with geometric abstraction, pop imagery, or a cool, seemingly socially removed conceptualism. This secularism was reflected, as well, in the broader shifts in Jewish-American cultural life that took place throughout much of the twentieth century. As Jews joined the middle class, many "adopted standards of refinement and aesthetics borrowed from the larger culture just as the Jews of Berlin, Vienna, and Paris had done before them."[5] The contemporary art program of The Jewish Museum in the 1960s reflected these changes as it began to see itself as part of a broader shift in the visual arts toward aesthetically and conceptually challenging art, with little or no emphasis on the personal identities of its creators or the social, religious, or political issues that influenced them.[6]

With the 1963 opening of the Albert and Vera List Building, itself a pristine, angular temple to modernism's International Style in direct contrast to the Warburg mansion, the museum's interest in the avant-garde took on an even more public face (fig. 6). In successive appointments—Alan Solomon in 1963 and Sam Hunter in 1965—the museum's board named two modernist critics as directors. Solomon and Hunter placed special emphasis on ground-breaking exhibitions devoted to the avant-garde Minimal, Pop, and Kinetic art movements. In a five-year period, The Jewish Museum organized major one-person exhibitions of (mostly non-Jewish) art-world stars—Robert Rauschenberg (1963), Jasper Johns (1964; fig. 7), Larry Rivers (1965), Philip Guston (1966), and Ad Reinhardt (1967), for example—as well as formative group shows such as *Primary Structures* (1966; fig. 8), the exhibition that some art historians have credited with launching the Minimalist movement.

This ideological shift in The Jewish Museum's mission was short-lived. Hunter resigned in 1967, ostensibly because of the board of directors' decision "to increase the emphasis on Judaica at the expense of contemporary art."[7] The question of assimilation versus separatism—an issue debated by Jews for centuries—came out of the closet as a significant museological problem for both the museum's staff and its board. Some believed that the institution's dedication to secular cutting-edge art, despite its unwavering commitment to Judaica, amounted to a slap in the face of its core constituency—the Jewish community the museum was mandated to serve. The administrators of the Jewish Theological Seminary of America, The Jewish Museum's parent institution, for example, were discomforted by the institution's new direction, wondering how it fit into their program of training rabbis, cantors, and teachers of the Jewish religion.[8] Others felt that the museum's involvement in the avant-garde was both justified and imperative, and that it was the institution's obligation to celebrate the powerful, even catalytic role of Jews in American intellectual and cultural life. But in 1971, the museum's board of directors, after years of internal conflict, voted to discontinue its program of exhibiting and collecting secular contemporary art in favor of work that directly related to Jewish history and culture.

While the board's move at the time seemed regressive and even reactionary to its critics (many of whom continue to see the 1960s as the "heyday" of The Jewish Museum), the institution's new emphasis on culture in its broadest sense, outside of its insistence on identity-based content, eventually motivated acquisitions and exhibition programs as radical, in some respects, as those advocated by Solomon and Hunter. If The Jewish Museum's embrace of the avant-garde in the 1960s represented the culmination of a century of modern artistic and intellectual practices, its revised program allowed it to actively challenge, to an unprecedented degree, the curatorial logic of the modernist era.[9]

The Jewish Museum of the 1960s, though it supported the most aesthetically sophisticated art of its day, reflected institutional hierarchies and sensibilities established more than thirty years earlier by Alfred H. Barr, Jr., the first director of the Museum of Modern Art in New York. Barr believed that analyses of modern art should meet the same scholarly standards as academic studies of the work of earlier epochs. But despite his exposure to debates on the issue

Fig. 7.
Jasper Johns: Retrospective, on view at The Jewish Museum in 1964.

Fig. 8.
Installation of Minimalist sculpture in the 1966 exhibition *Primary Structures*.

of social cause in art (particularly in his travels to Soviet Russia), his exhibitions, collecting priorities, and curatorial essays attended to formal and stylistic concerns above all others. Barr's lack of interest in social context resulted in acquisitions and exhibition programs that retrospectively validated the most apolitical aspects of modern art at the expense of other, more socially oriented expressions—a highly influential point of view that set the tone for nearly all museums of modern and contemporary art.

To a great extent, Barr took his cue from the art that was the subject of his inquiry. Despite the ideological undertow of some modernist art, the mundane details of everyday life were for the most part irrelevant to most abstract painting and sculpture. The starkly rectilinear, whitewashed architecture of the museum and the contemporary art gallery, the ultimate environments for displaying the modern art object, reinvested in this reductive and elitist view of the world. For the modernist art museum, like most modernist objects, aspired to sweep away the messy and incongruous aspects of existence—the vagaries of current events, the contradictions and ambivalence that threaten our sense of moral or ideological certainty, the religious or spiritual belief systems that divide us—that threatened its illusion of aesthetic unity and purity.[10]

Over the past thirty years, The Jewish Museum's reconsideration of this tradition has taken many forms, from its adventurous and wide-ranging exhibition programs to the eccentric installations of many of its shows, designs that depart from the formality and self-imposed rigidity of the modernist grid. The evolution of its collecting habits and priorities during this period—a curatorial vision marked by largesse and open-mindedness—reflects this shift. The museum, committed to Jewish "culture" in its broadest sense, has expanded and enriched its mandate to embrace three broadly defined disciplinary areas: the fine arts (painting, photography, sculpture, drawing, video, and performance art); Judaica (ceremonial objects and artifacts pertaining to Jewish history and culture, such as coins, medals, and archaeological works); and broadcast media (television and radio).

The museum's holdings in the fine arts represent a diverse range of disciplines, conceptual and philosophical concerns, and historical periods. In recent years, the museum's acquisitions program in the visual arts, as *Culture and Continuity* suggests, has succeeded in building a collection that is, for the most part, aesthetically adventurous and sociologically meaningful.[11] El Lissitzky's *Had Gadya Suite* (1919), for example, merges the ideologically charged abstraction of Russian Constructivism with the liturgy of Passover. Paintings by Adolph Gottlieb (*Return of the Mariner*, 1946) and Robert Motherwell (*Tablets of Moses, Jacob's Ladder, and Menorah*, 1951) reveal the complex spiritual and political issues that informed Abstract Expressionism, issues often ignored by the critics of the period. Other works explore the nexus between Jewish and female or gay identity, such as Nancy Spero's *Masha Bruskina* (1995), Ross Bleckner's *Double Portrait (Gay Flag)* (1993), and Hannah Wilke's *Venus Pareve* (1982–84). And a range of works in various media—including Samuel Hirszenberg's *The Black Banner* (1905), Christian Boltanski's *Monument (Odessa)* (1989–2003), William Anastasi's *Untitled (Jew)* (1987), William Kentridge's *Drawings for Projection Series* (1989–91), and James Casebere's *Venice Ghetto* (1991)—examine issues of community, responsibility, antisemitism, and survival in the history of the Jewish people.

The museum's comprehensive holdings of Jewish ceremonial and historical objects remain a strong and important resource for the study of Jewish culture and history. In the period after World War II, the assimilation of American Jews into secular life brought about a decrease in synagogue attendance, the abandonment of synagogue buildings, and a decline in the use of many ceremonial objects for religious observances. Thus ritualistic objects that heretofore had been part of everyday Jewish life were becoming increasingly scarce and unknown in many Jewish homes.[12] The Jewish Museum's mandate to preserve these objects— from an elaborate baroque hanging lamp for Sabbath and festivals by the German silversmith Johann Valentin Schüler (c. 1680–1720) to Ludwig Yehuda Wolpert's sleek Bauhaus Passover service (c. 1978; original design, 1930)—emerges out of multiple curatorial impulses: to preserve them for future generations; to view them as works of art in their own right; and to study their religious, liturgical, or historical implications.

The National Jewish Archive of Broadcasting (NJAB) represents the most recent component of the museum's permanent collection. Established in 1981 with a grant from the Charles H. Revson Foundation, the archive is the largest and most comprehensive repository of radio and television programs relating to the Jewish experience. In addition to collecting and preserving these materials, the museum has produced videos, exhibitions, and public programs based on the archive's holdings. The NJAB, with some 4,300 television and radio programs, represents a unique entity in the museum world. While many cultural institutions are devoted to the fine arts and a number are dedicated to broadcast media, no major American museum has a mandate to acquire both.

The NJAB's holdings constitute an important record of Jewish life and history as they have been represented in the media. The archive also serves to validate and support an art form rarely acknowledged as such in the museum: television. Its curators have searched not just for sociologically significant programs but also for outstanding television. In this regard, the NJAB has acquired some of the most artistically rich television dramas and situation comedies of the past half-century, including *Molly Goldberg, Playhouse 90, The Twilight Zone, All in the Family,*

Fig. 9.
Posters printed in 1898 proclaiming
the innocence or guilt of Captain
Alfred Dreyfus, on view in the 1987
exhibition *The Dreyfus Affair: Art, Truth,
and Justice*.

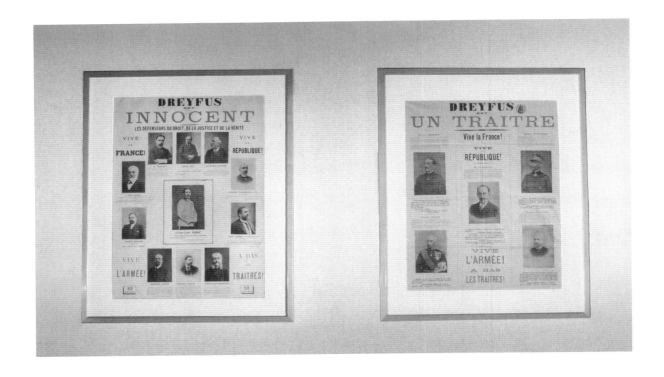

Fig. 9.
Posters printed in 1898 proclaiming
the innocence or guilt of Captain
Alfred Dreyfus, on view in the 1987
exhibition *The Dreyfus Affair: Art, Truth,
and Justice*.

The Mary Tyler Moore Show, thirtysomething, The Simpsons, Brooklyn Bridge, Sex in the City, and
The Sopranos.

In addition to its ambitious acquisition program, The Jewish Museum has organized
temporary exhibitions that reflect the collection's artistic and sociological interests. The museum's
curators have tended to view the stylistic analysis or qualitative evaluation of art not as a goal
unto itself but as part of a holistic and humanistic methodology that places the art object in
its cultural and social context. The shows they have created strike a balance between aesthetic
issues and the sociological and cultural examination of the role of a minority people and their
acceptance and oppression in the society at large.

The Circle of Montparnasse: Jewish Artists in Paris, 1905–1945 (1985), for example, explored
the place of Jewish artists in the formative years of the modernist avant-garde. *The Dreyfus
Affair: Art, Truth, and Justice* (1987; fig. 9) analyzed the war of visual representation around
issues of antisemitism, patriotism, and mortality that gripped *fin-de-siècle* France during one
of its most divisive political scandals. *Painting a Place in America: Jewish Artists in New York,
1900–1945* (1991) documented the role played by Jewish artists in the rise of modernism in the
United States. *Too Jewish?: Challenging Traditional Identities* (1996) examined contemporary art's
engagement of the question of how "Jewishness" is represented in the media and culture at
large. *Voice, Image, Gesture: Selections from The Jewish Museum's Collection, 1945–2000* (2001;
fig. 10) explored the complex and multifarious nature of Jewish identity and history through a
range of artifacts, representing the museum's three major collecting areas—the fine arts, broadcast media, and ceremonial objects. *Mirroring Evil: Nazi Imagery/Recent Art* (2002) radically
departed from traditional cultural approaches to the Holocaust, which concentrate on the victim,
to look at the world of the perpetrator and the nature and complexity of evil itself. And *New York:
Capital of Photography* (2002) analyzed the influence of Jewish artists and of a "Jewish sensibility"
on the photographic vision of a great metropolis.[13]

Fig. 10.
Andy Warhol's *Ten Portraits of Jews of the Twentieth Century* at the entrance to the 2001 exhibition *Voice, Image, Gesture: Selections from The Jewish Museum's Collection, 1945–2000.*

Ironically, the transformation of The Jewish Museum over the past half-century is in many ways consistent with an art world that has radically changed since the heyday of the New York avant-garde. Back then, it was possible to speak of an art-world "mainstream," a white, mostly male bastion of progressive culture. Today, of course, the notion of a traditional "art-world" center no longer holds. Multiple, global, overlapping, and even contradictory interests now compete in the rarefied arena of high culture: the modernist avant-garde, which some interpret as the pinnacle of twentieth-century intellectual ideals and spiritual values, is seen by others as an enigmatic, sometimes hostile hierarchy of exclusion and elitism.[14]

Despite these changes, most museums in the United States still remain marginal to the culture at large: popular music, crafts, film, television, and community, ethnic, or church-based art and theater are far more accessible and come much closer to rank-and-file "mainstream" tastes than most museum exhibitions. In part because of its co-option by academia, in part because of its relationship to the art market, in part because of its fear of change, the art museum remains wedded to highly specialized values, jargon, and cultural hierarchies, sensibilities that are unfamiliar and strange to people outside the world of its elite subculture. "What the configuration of the high culture art world reveals," writes cultural historian Kenneth Ames, "is how peculiar and self-absorbed a specialized part of a larger society can become when it is disconnected from that society."[15]

Fig. 11.
Aaron Siskind (American, 1903–1991). *Wishing Tree*, from *Harlem Document*, 1937. Gelatin-silver print, 11 x 14 in. (27.9 x 35.6 cm). Purchase: Lillian Gordon Bequest, 2000-58.

The modernist museum's self-absorption has encouraged it to erase, ignore, or under-estimate many aspects of the viewer's life and history prior to the exhibition experience. Empha-sizing the primacy of visual experience above all other concerns, it has aspired to a state of aesthetic presentness, in which the spectator encounters self-referential and preeminently optical experiences with little regard for issues outside of the cloistered space of the museum gallery. It is this elitist and abstruse conception of art that The Jewish Museum, an institution devoted principally to the culture of a religious minority that has been persecuted for centuries, has rejected as inappropriate, if not untenable.

Even the most cursory examination of its collection reminds us that art and ideas of the Jewish Diaspora cannot be understood independently of the two forms of expression that the modernist art museum, in its appeal to sensory immediacy, most vehemently rejects: memory and history. Thus, the power of The Jewish Museum's holdings to move, educate, and inspire the viewer depends not just on visual stimulation, but on the voices, objects, and texts that tell the story of a people who "chanted, studied, muttered their prayers, wept, and then were forever silenced."[16]

These stories have allowed the Jewish people—men and women often denied the privi-lege of writing the standard histories of state and culture—to stake their claim to a past that is itself in danger of being lost forever. It is this danger, as the novelist Toni Morrison observes of her own desire as a black woman to give voice to victims of the African diaspora, that motivates oppressed peoples to reclaim history through personal recollection and through the testimony of the souls who lived it:

> My job becomes how to rip that veil drawn over "proceedings too terrible to relate."
> The exercise is critical for any person who is black, or who belongs to any marginalized category, for, historically, we were seldom invited to participate in the discourse even when we were its topic. Moving that veil aside requires, therefore, certain things. First of all, I must trust my own recollections. I must also depend on the recollections of others. Thus memory weighs heavily in what I write, in how I begin, and in what I find to be significant.[17]

Fig. 12. Diane Arbus (American, 1923–1971). *Jewish Giant at Home with His Parents, Bronx, New York,* 1970. Gelatin-silver print, 14½ x 14½ in. (36.8 x 36.8 cm). Purchase: Photography Acquisitions Committee Fund and Horace W. Goldsmith Foundation, 1999-3.

With this imperative in mind, The Jewish Museum, turning away from the esoteric interests of the art market or traditional connoisseurship, views the distinction between "art" and "non-art" as circumspect. Thus it has actively built a collection that is engaging and moving precisely because it allows the multiple voices and cultural expressions—objects, memories, and histories, both personal and collective—to resonate and to flourish.

In addition to the display of objects from the collection in its permanent installations, The Jewish Museum has employed these works in its temporary exhibitions, projects that represent the public face of the museum and its acquisitions program. Just as in *Culture and Continuity,* these objects reverberate with historical meaning and evocative memories. In *Too Jewish?,* excerpts from the National Jewish Archive of Broadcasting—popular television shows such as *Saturday Night Live, Northern Exposure,* and *The Jack Benny Show*—challenge the same stereotypes and clichés as the contemporary art that hangs alongside them. In *New York: Capital of Photography,* a range of evocative images—Diane Arbus's iconic depiction of a Jewish giant at home with his parents in the Bronx (fig. 12), Morris Engel's candid photograph of a shoeshine boy fending off a ticket, Louis Faurer's hazy view of the New York skyline through the window of a Staten Island ferryboat, Aaron Siskind's shot of children playing on a Harlem street (fig. 11)—capture the sensibilities of the world capital of Jewish life and culture. In *Entertaining America: Jews, Movies, and Broadcasting,* viewers look at clips of *Your Show of Shows*

Fig. 13.
Galleries in the 2003 exhibition
*Entertaining America: Jews, Movies,
and Broadcasting.*

and *Seinfeld* or sit on a sofa in a typical 1950s living room and watch Molly Goldberg and her television family play out the trials and triumphs of postwar American immigrant life (fig. 13). In *Voice, Image, Gesture*, a range of artifacts, each afforded equal emphasis and respect—a somber excerpt from Edward R. Murrow's reportage on the first decade of Israeli statehood, artist Elaine Reichek's moving and provocative re-creation of a room from her German Jewish childhood (*A Postcolonial Kinderhood*, 1994), an elaborate seder plate by ceramist Amy Klein Reichert (*Seder Plate*, 1997), footage of Sandy Koufax pitching in the World Series, a hilarious clip of Bette Midler on a United Jewish Appeal telethon—trigger a range of memories and emotions.

These fragments from popular culture, high art, and our collective history reach out to aspects of culture well beyond the limited purview of the modernist museum. In so doing, they create points of emotional "intimacy," to quote the cultural theorist Homi Bhabha, between the viewer and the aesthetic experience.[18] Their appeal to the familiar, to memories and events that to one extent or another belong to every one of us, offers the viewer a powerful way into the issues at the center of complex and often enigmatic artifacts. Thus, they enhance The Jewish Museum's ability to remain consequential at a time when art institutions risk becoming irrelevant in a society dominated by popular culture and the media. One can hope that other museums will take their lead from this institution as they contemplate their future in a culture profoundly different from that of modernism's picture-perfect Golden Age.

1. In addition to exhibitions of Judaica, the museum in this period also occasionally organized shows of contemporary avant-garde art by Jewish artists, such as Adolph Gottlieb (1957) and Helen Frankenthaler (1960).

2. "Objects and Functions of The Jewish Museum, Revised Draft," September 10, 1962, Majorie Wyler Papers, Records of the Jewish Theological Seminary, box 2, folder 12, as quoted by Julie Miller and Richard I. Cohen, "A Collision of Cultures: The Jewish Museum and the Jewish Theological Seminary, 1904–1971," in *Tradition Renewed: A History of the Jewish Theological Seminary*, ed. Jack Wertheimer (New York: Jewish Theological Seminary, 1997), 2:342.

3. Ibid.

4. Ibid., 2:311.

5. Ibid., 2:335.

6. There are many reasons for the preeminence of Jewish Americans in the secular avant-garde of New York in the 1950s and 1960s. For one, the religious proscription against the depiction of "graven images" made abstraction a particularly appealing discipline for Jewish artists. More important, Jewish artists and intellectuals in the United States were becoming increasingly disenchanted with the social activism and Marxist politics that had driven Jewish immigrants in the earlier part of the twentieth century. Thus the engagement of the avant-garde was part of a broader shift away from political specificity and toward ideological centrism and cultural assimilation. The disenchantment with leftist politics—intensified by the espionage trial and execution of Julius and Ethel Rosenberg, a case with great resonance for American Jews—pushed many Jewish intellectuals into moderate or even right-wing politics. In the worlds of art and ideas, America was witnessing a "de-Marxization" of thought, evident in such things as the rise of a new pragmatism in academia and an art world that was replacing the politics of social realism and the Popular Front with the psychoanalysis of Surrealism and the early phases of Abstract Expressionism. If this environment motivated Jewish artists toward the more universal and ahistorical attitudes of postwar abstraction, Jewish intellectuals nevertheless continued to ponder their place in American culture. As late as 1966, the critic Harold Rosenberg stood before an audience at The Jewish Museum and asked a question that was resonating in contemporary Jewish cultural circles: "Is there a Jewish art?"

7. Sam Hunter, as quoted in Milton Esterow, "Director of Jewish Museum Quits in Policy Rift," *New York Times*, October 25, 1967, p. 38.

8. For more on the strained relations between the two institutions, see Miller and Cohen, "A Collision of Cultures," 2:312.

9. For a discussion on the exhibition policies of The Jewish Museum over the past half-century, see Maurice Berger, "Painting Jewish Identity," *Art in America* 80, no. 1 (January 1992): 90–94, 131.

10. Even when nonobjective art carried a political message—for example, Vladimir Tatlin's celebration of political revolution in *Monument to the Third International* (1919–20) or the social utopianism inherent to Kasimir Malevich's Suprematist compositions—it maintained an ambivalent relationship to the corporeal world that was its implicit subject. As the art historian T. J. Clark observes: "Blindness, purposelessness, randomness, blankness; pictures built out of the statistical accumulations of the thrown marks, or touch after touch of pure surfaceness, pure sensation; but equally, pictures clinging to a dream of martyrdom, or peasant leisure, or naked intensity in the woods; and pictures fantasizing themselves the voice—the image, the plan—of a post-human calculus in the making. . . . Modernism is caught interminably between horror and elation at the forces driving it—between 'Less Is More' and 'NO CHAOS DAMN IT.' . . . Modernism's disdain for the world and wish for a truly gratuitous gesture in the face of it are more than just attitudes: they are the true (that is, agonized) form of its so-called purism." See Clark, *Farewell to an Idea: Episodes from a History of Modernism* (New Haven: Yale University Press, 1999), p. 8.

11. The museum's fine arts collection, however, is not without room for growth and improvement. The institution's emphasis on Jewish subject matter, for example, has led to the exclusion of artists whose religious identity is overshadowed by the secular nature of their work. The absence of these art-historically significant figures in the collection—a diverse list that includes Mel Bochner, Claude Cahun, Anish Kapoor, Barbara Kruger, Sherrie Levine, Laslo Moholy-Nagy, and Carolee Schneemann—suggests the need for an important, albeit subtle, shift in the museum's acquisitions policies.

12. For more on this subject, see Emily D. Bilski, "Seeing the Future Through the Light of the Past: The Art of The Jewish Museum," in Vivian B. Mann, *The Jewish Museum, New York* (London: Scala, 1993), pp. 9–12.

13. For the catalogues of these exhibitions, important scholarly publications in their own right, see Kenneth E. Silver and Romy Golan, *The Circle of Montparnasse: Jewish Artists in Paris, 1905–1945* (New York: Universe Books, 1985); Norman L. Kleeblatt, ed., *The Dreyfus Affair: Art, Truth, and Justice* (New York: The Jewish Museum; Berkeley: University of California Press, 1987); Norman L. Kleeblatt and Susan Chevlowe, eds., *Painting a Place in America: Jewish Artists in New York, 1900–1945* (New York: The Jewish Museum; Bloomington: Indiana University Press, 1991); Norman L. Kleeblatt, ed., *Too Jewish?: Challenging Traditional Identities* (New York: The Jewish Museum; New Brunswick, N.J.: Rutgers University Press, 1996); Norman L. Kleeblatt, ed., *Mirroring Evil: Nazi Imagery/Recent Art* (New York: The Jewish Museum; New Brunswick, N.J.: Rutgers University Press, 2001); and Max Kozloff, *New York: Capital of Photography* (New York: The Jewish Museum; New Haven: Yale University Press, 2002).

14. In this regard, identity-based art histories are unearthing and validating the work of ethnic and racial minorities, women, and gay men and lesbians long excluded from the mainstream, and such foundational concepts as art-historical periods and movements, quality, and standards have come into question.

15. Kenneth L. Ames, "Outside Outsider Art," in *The Artist Outsider: Creativity and the Boundaries of Culture*, ed. Michael D. Hall and Eugene W. Metcalf, Jr. (Washington, D.C.: Smithsonian Institution, 1994), pp. 258–59.

16. Stephen Greenblatt, "Resonance and Wonder," in *Exhibiting Cultures: The Poetics and Politics of Museum Display*, ed. Steven D. Lavine and Ivan Karp (Washington, D.C.: Smithsonian Institution, 1991), p. 47.

17. Toni Morrison, "The Site of Memory," in *Out There: Marginalization and Contemporary Cultures*, ed. Russell Ferguson et al. (Cambridge: MIT Press, 1990), p. 302.

18. Homi K. Bhabha, *The Location of Culture* (New York and London: Routledge, 1994), p. 13.

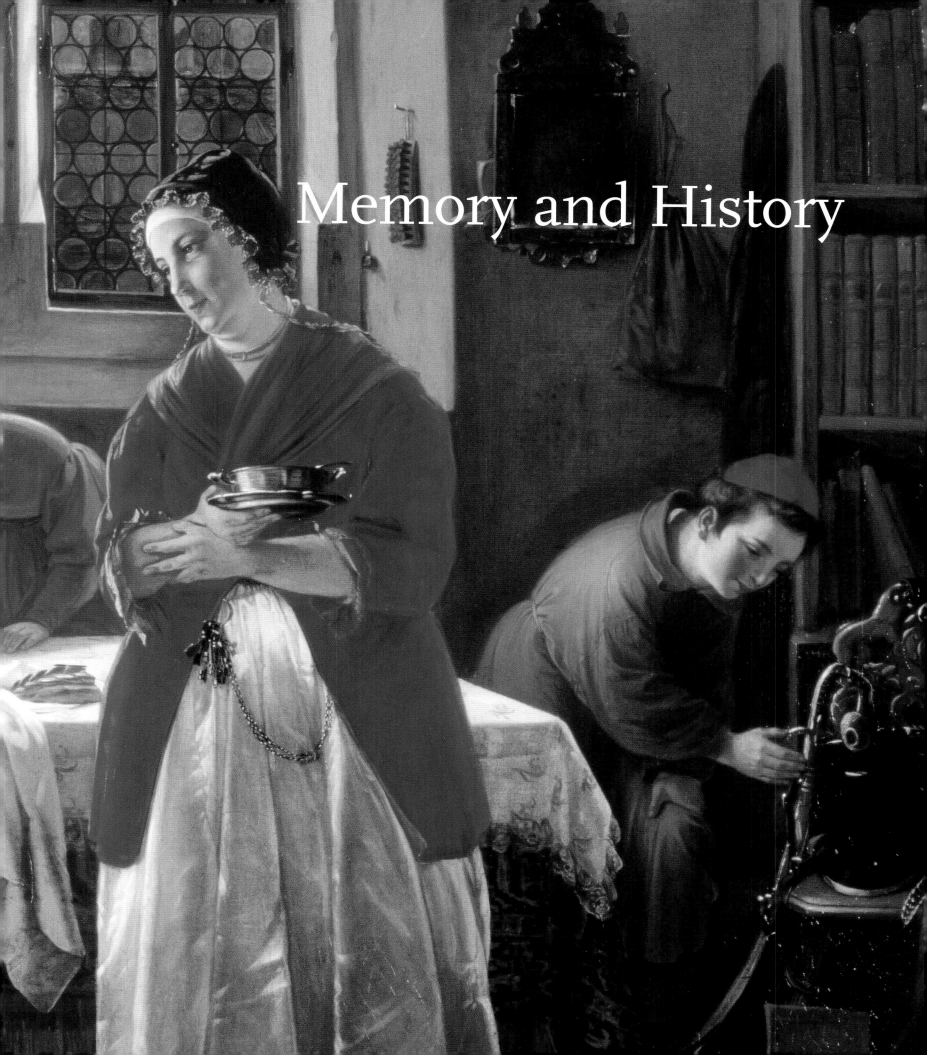

Memory and History

Memory and History

For centuries, the official histories of nations, culture, and war have usually concentrated on the lives of the famous, the wealthy, the dominant, and the powerful. The rise of twentieth-century movements devoted to the rights of workers, the poor, people of color, ethnic minorities, women, and gay men and lesbians has contributed to a significant reevaluation of the meaning of history. In recent years, historians have asked themselves fundamental questions about the content, methodology, and role of their discipline: Who owns history? Who does history serve and for whom is it written? Who has been left out of history and whose voices should be heard?

The Jewish Museum's permanent collection reflects this desire to expand the meaning of history and to recover the voices and events all too often erased from it. Because the museum is devoted to the complex story of an oppressed and persecuted people, its holdings reflect three areas of historical significance: collective history, personal memory, and the memorial. The collection brings together more traditional depictions of Jewish history (James Tissot, *Joseph Dwelleth in Egypt*, c. 1896–1902) with objects and images that have been informed by personal experiences and recollection (Louis Faurer, *Staten Island Ferry*, 1946) or that represent private manifestations of historical Jewish life (*The Grand Costume*, Rabat, late nineteenth century).

The German painter Moritz Daniel Oppenheim's *The Return of the Jewish Volunteer* (1833–34), for example, represents the first time a Jewish artist painted a specifically Jewish historical subject—a wounded Jewish soldier who has just returned to his family after serving in the German army in the war against Napoleon. The Abstract Expressionist painter Adolph Gottlieb, in *Return of the Mariner* (1946), turns to a more conceptual lexicon of premodern, tribal, and mythological symbols to represent our shared primeval past. The museum's National Jewish Archive of Broadcasting contains many extraordinary radio and television programs devoted to the documentation of the recent history of the Jewish people. These shows, which record history in the making, cover a range of significant events, such as journalist Edward R. Murrow's brave and aggressive reporting on the tactics of Senator Joseph McCarthy and the blacklist, which affected many Jews in the entertainment industry (*See It Now*, 1954), the birth and survival of the State of Israel ("Into the Future," from the series *Heritage: Civilization and the Jews*, 1984), and the trial of SS officer Adolf Eichmann (*Verdict for Tomorrow*, 1961).

Many works in the collection exemplify the intersection between collective history and personal memory, objects that represent historical events and periods through the artifacts and stories of everyday life. Alfred Stieglitz's iconic photograph *The Steerage* (1907) is a poignant image of the lower-class passengers of a ship, dispirited refugees returning to Europe after being rejected by United States immigration officials. Ben Shahn captures Jewish life on

New York's Lower East Side in a vivid, realistic painting, *New York* (1947), based on images culled from both memory and direct observation. And an ornate tiered seder plate from eighteenth- or nineteenth-century Poland stands as a fragment of Jewish culture tragically lost to a nation all too willing to persecute its Jewish population.

In recent years, the issue of how to memorialize and commemorate important historical events through art—who should be heard, seen, and remembered and how they should be represented—has also come into sharp focus, a debate spurred, in part, by controversial projects such as the Vietnam War Memorial in Washington, D.C., the Berlin Holocaust Memorial, and memorials to the victims of terrorist attacks on the Oklahoma City Federal Building and the World Trade Center. The Jewish Museum's permanent collection contains a number of works dedicated to memorializing significant episodes and periods in the history of the Jewish people. Commensurate with these recent debates about the nature of the memorial, these works contemplate tragedy and loss through different and sometimes divergent approaches.

Anni Albers's *Six Prayers* (1965–66), for example, commissioned by The Jewish Museum in 1965 to memorialize the victims of the Holocaust, consists of six vertical tapestries. Rather than a direct representation of violence, death, and loss, Albers's tapestries are abstract, solemn, and intimate; they offer a space for personal contemplation about overwhelming historical events. George Segal's haunting installation *The Holocaust* (1982) is a stark, hyperrealistic tableau of plaster casts of models depicted as dead or dying. And *Masha Bruskina* (1995), a painting by the American artist Nancy Spero, allegorizes the dual disenfranchisement of Jews and women in the twentieth century through the tragic story of a real person: a young volunteer nurse and leader of the Minsk resistance movement who was publicly hanged by the Nazis in 1941.
M B

Funerary Inscription in Gold Glass

Probably Rome, 4th century C.E.

Glass: blown; gold leaf
4½ in. diam. (12.1 cm)

Purchase: Estate of Anna D. Ternbach Fund; gift of Dr. Harry G. Friedman, by exchange, 1999-73

Greek inscription: Here lies Anastasia, mother, and Esther, daughter, in peace may their sleep be. Amen

Hebrew inscription: Peace

The glassmakers of antiquity perfected a technique of decorating their vessels by sandwiching gold-leaf imagery between two layers of glass. In the third and fourth centuries C.E., this method became popular in the Roman Empire for the production of portrait medallions and vessels with ornamented bottoms. The latter, referred to as "gold glass," often contained inscriptions relating to drinking and wishes for long life, as well as pagan, Christian, or Jewish religious imagery. These vessels appear to have been given as gifts at the Roman new year festival, and at birthdays and weddings as well. A peculiarity of these gold glass vessels is that only the ornamented bases have been found, often with the edges of the vessel deliberately chipped away. In addition, those that have been found *in situ* come almost exclusively from underground burial complexes, where they were embedded in the wall next to a burial niche. This has led to the speculation that the gold glass vessels were used during the lifetime of the deceased and then placed next to the niche so that the survivors could identify the burial from among the multitude of others interred in the catacomb.

Of the hundreds of gold glass pieces that exist, only thirteen have been identified as Jewish. All bear elements of what came to represent the quintessential visual statement of Jewish identity after the destruction of the Jerusalem Temple in 70 C.E. This includes the Torah ark, often guarded by lions, and the implements that were once used in the ancient Temple of Jerusalem: the seven-branch menorah, the palm frond bundle and etrog employed in the celebration of Sukkot, and the shofar (ram's horn). These were sometimes accompanied by inscriptions that were similar to those on non-Jewish gold glass.

The gold glass in The Jewish Museum collection is unique in several ways. The decorative scheme is dominated by the inscription, while the Temple implements are rendered inconspicuously. A small shofar is situated at the end of the third line, and a menorah at the bottom. More important, this is the only example that contains an explicitly funerary inscription, and was therefore not used during the lifetime of the deceased. The phraseology is quite similar to that found on the hundreds of marble burial plaques placed as grave markers in the Roman-period Jewish catacombs, as is the incorporation of the Temple implements and the Hebrew word for peace (see p. 92). Finally, the technique in which this piece was made differs from other examples of Jewish gold glass in that it is not true sandwich glass. The gold inscription was placed on a glass vessel base, but the second layer of glass was never added over the surface. A large crack in the piece suggests that perhaps it broke before completion and was thus left in this unfinished state. One can only wonder at the tragic circumstances that led to the death of a mother and her daughter and that occasioned the commission of this memorial inscription.

SLB

REFERENCES
Rutgers, *The Jews in Late Ancient Rome*; Schwabe and Reifenberg, "Ein jüdisches Goldglas," pp. 341–46.

Tiered Seder Set

Poland, 18th–19th century

Brass: cast, cutout, engraved; wood: painted and stained; ink on paper; silk: brocade; linen; cotton

13½ in. high x 14 in. diam. (35 x 35.6 cm)

Gift of the Danzig Jewish Community, D 115

Jews all over the world hold a home service called a "seder" on the first night of Passover, and those outside the Land of Israel repeat the seder on the second night. All tell the story of the Exodus and eat symbolic foods that recall the bitterness of bondage and the haste with which the ancient Israelites began their flight to freedom. This unique seder set combines wooden trays for matzah, the unleavened bread, with wooden holders for the other symbolic foods and a pedestal for the wine cup that is always filled for the prophet Elijah, herald of the messiah.

Although there are other nineteenth-century examples of tiered seder sets, none are similar to this one. Most are refined silver works made in Germany or Austria by trained silversmiths or are imitations in base metals. They lack the robust energy that is conveyed by this piece, with its rampant lions that stand, mouths agape, holding cartouches bearing the blessings recited over the symbolic foods. The curvature of the lions' bodies and their notched paws are echoed in the shapes

of the grillwork surrounding the wooden trays. Similar brasswork appears on Eastern European Hanukkah lamps of the eighteenth and nineteenth centuries. Rampant lions often decorate the back-plates of these lamps, while decorative grillwork sometimes forms an apron panel in front of the lights and on the sides. The maker of the Danzig seder set was familiar with the artistic traditions of the Hanukkah lamp. In this work, he wed familiar forms to new materials, creating a dynamic composition that rises from the dark wooden base, through the open pattern on the middle zone, to the triumphant lions; the whole is crowned by the base for Elijah's cup, which would have added a further vertical accent.

VBM

REFERENCES

Katalog der alten jüdischen Kultusgegenstände Gieldzinski-Stiftung in der neuen Synagoge zu Danzig, no. 81; Kayser and Schoenberger, *Jewish Ceremonial Art*, no. 109; Kleeblatt and Mann, *Treasures of the Jewish Museum*, pp. 122–23; Mann and Gutmann, *Danzig 1939*, no. 51; Roth, *Jewish Art*, pl. 25; *Sammlung jüdischer Kunstgegenstände der Synagogen-Gemeinde zu Danzig*, no. 115.

El-keswa el-kbira (The Grand Costume)

Rabat, late 19th century

Skirt: silk velvet with gold metallic ribbon and passementerie; lining: polished cotton; bodice: silk velvet with gilt metallic embroidery, leather; sleeves: transparent silk chiffon with gold brocade

Skirt: 118⅛ x 39⅜ in. (300 x 100 cm)
Waistcoat: 23⅝ x 24¾ in. (60 x 62.9 cm)

Purchase: Judaica Acquisitions Committee Fund, 1993-195a-e

This nearly complete Grand Costume consists of a floor-length wraparound skirt (*zeltita*) of silk velvet embroidered with gold metallic threads, a *plastron*, or bodice, and a *gombaz*, or waistcoat, of the same materials and similarly embroidered. The diaphanous, billowing sleeves (*kmam*), which are separate from the costume, are made of striped silk embroidered with gold threads. The Grand Costume was worn by brides during the henna ceremony, when patterns in henna were applied to the bride to bring good luck before the actual marriage, and was later worn on festive occasions. This ensemble was made for Mas'uda, the bride of David Ohaion of Marrakech, in the late nineteenth century, and was worn by her descendants into the twentieth century.

For a number of reasons, the *keswa el-kbira* is thought to have been brought to Morocco by Jews who left Spain. The character of the Grand Costume, usually made of a rich, dark velvet adorned with gold ribbon and embroidery, and having separate sleeves, is reminiscent of late medieval Spanish garb, while the elaborate ceremony for dressing the bride before the henna ceremony is accompanied by songs and poems in Spanish. Further, this type of wedding dress is limited to Moroccan cities settled by Jews from Spain after the persecutions of 1391 and the Expulsion of 1492.

The impressive appearance of the *keswa el-kbira* made it a favorite subject for European writers and painters who came to Morocco. Delacroix, who visited in the 1820s, is but one example of an artist who depicted it several times.

VBM

REFERENCE
Mann, *Morocco*, no. 146.

Decoration for the Eastern Wall (Mizraḥ)

Israel Dov Rosenbaum

Podkamen, Ukraine, 1877

Paint, ink, and pencil on cutout paper
30¼ x 20¾ in. (76.8 x 52.7 cm)

Gift of Helen W. Finkel in memory of
Israel Dov Rosenbaum, Bessie
Rosenbaum Finkel, and Sidney Finkel,
1987-136

Despite the destruction of the Second Temple in 70 C.E. and the dispersion of most Jews, the Land of Israel has remained a primary focus of Jewish identity. A commonly felt, deeply rooted bond to the Land of Israel and the hope of all Jews to return eventually to it have been important unifying factors. One expression of this intense bond is found in the practice of facing toward Jerusalem during prayer. For Jews in the West, this direction is east, and the custom developed of placing a decorative plaque on the eastern walls of homes and synagogues to indicate the direction of worship. Such a sign came to be known as a *mizraḥ*, Hebrew for "east." *Mizraḥ* is also an acronym composed of the initial letters for the Hebrew phrase "from this side the spirit of life." This inscription appears in the four corners of the central panel of this papercut, indicating that it functions as a *mizraḥ*.

In Eastern Europe, *mizraḥ* plaques were often made out of cut paper, resembling the carved wood Torah arks of Polish synagogues in the intricacy of their design. As is common in many other extant examples, the composition in this papercut is symmetrical, designed on one half of a sheet of paper, folded vertically, and cut out through both halves, thus creating a mirror image revealed upon unfolding the sheet. Papercuts were usually mounted on a plain or colored paper background to provide a contrasting effect, as seen here. Although architectural features such as columns and arcades often balance the composition of papercuts, the use of an imposing building as the central element, as seen in this example, is rare. Whether the building was based on an existing or imaginary one, Israel Dov Rosenbaum, the creator of this extraordinary papercut, made sure to include a clock at its dome, possibly a hint at his profession as clockmaker to the local count in the small town of Podkamen, Ukraine. A Jewish community existed in Podkamen at least since the seventeenth century, and by the late nineteenth century, the town was home to more than a thousand Jews.

The elaborate design and the repeated use of thin connecting lines make this *mizraḥ* an exquisite example of its kind. The creatures, both mythical and real, as well as the vegetal motifs and *horror vacuii* of this composition, are typical of Eastern European art. Included here are lions, deer, eagles, and what appears to be a pair of small leopards atop the dome of the central building. These four animals usually appear in Jewish papercuts to illustrate the saying "Be bold as a leopard, light as an eagle, swift as a deer, and strong as a lion, to do the will of your Father who is in Heaven" (*Ethics of the Fathers* 5:23). The doubled-headed eagle is often interpreted as a political symbol associated with the Russian Empire. Several Eastern European artifacts in The Jewish Museum collection feature the double-headed eagle, including Torah shields and Hanukkah lamps as well as a mold for pastries baked for the holiday of Purim.

Among the mythical beasts featured in this papercut are the leviathan (portrayed as a curled fish) and the wild ox—the legendary food of the righteous in the world to come (Leviticus Rabbah 13:3, 22:10)—depicted in the lower register, and the unicorn, seen in the outer frame. The interiors of wooden synagogues were often filled with elaborate animal and plant designs, many having symbolic meaning. Animals are also found in carved Jewish tombstones in Eastern Europe. Likely more portable or readily available sources were printed books such as Hebrew primers featuring a depiction of an animal for each letter of the Hebrew alphabet or illustrated copies of the *Meshal ha-Kadmoni*, a collection of animal fables written in 1281 by the Spanish Hebrew author Isaac ibn Sahula. First printed in Brescia, about 1491, the work soon gained popularity and was reprinted many times, including nine known Yiddish editions. Many of the extant copies are embellished with illustrations, mostly portraying the disputing animals, who "converse" in biblical Hebrew and are all well versed in Jewish learning: the rooster is a Bible scholar, and the deer an expert in the Talmud. Two pairs of roosters appear on the upper margin of the *mizraḥ*, flanked by a pair of birds. In one of the illustrations for the *Meshal ha-Kadmoni*, the rooster and a similar quail-like bird (though referred to as a hawk) are paired in "conversation."

CN

REFERENCES
Shadur and Shadur, *Jewish Papercuts: A History and Guide*; idem, *Traditional Jewish Papercuts: An Inner World of Art and Symbol*, pp. 44–45, pl. 2.36.

Moritz Daniel Oppenheim

(German, 1800–1882)

The Return of the Jewish Volunteer from the Wars of Liberation to His Family Still Living in Accordance with Old Customs (Die Heimkehr des Freiwilligen aus den Befreiungskriegen zu den nach alter Sitte lebenden Seinen), 1833–34

Oil on canvas
34 x 36 in. (86.4 x 91.4 cm)
Gift of Richard and Beatrice Levy, 1984-61

The Enlightenment of the eighteenth century and its Jewish counterpart, the Haskalah, resulted in the emancipation of Jews and their subsequent entry into professional fields previously closed to them. No account of this emancipation in Western Europe is complete without a discussion of the painter Moritz Daniel Oppenheim, born in Hanau, near Frankfurt am Main. Through the lifting of restrictions, Oppenheim, an observant Jew, was able to acquire proper academic training and become a highly successful artist.

The Return of the Jewish Volunteer, Oppenheim's undeniable masterpiece, is a signal work in the history of the artistic contribution of the Jews. It is generally considered the first effort of a known Jewish artist to confront a specifically Jewish subject. Like many works from the Romantic School, and more specifically that of Biedermeier painting in Germanic countries, the picture falls into the category of historical genre. Oppenheim represents a wounded Jewish soldier in a Hussar's uniform who has just returned to his family after helping to defend Germany against the Napoleonic armies. In his haste to be reunited with his family, the young man has, contrary to Jewish law, traveled on the Sabbath.

Love of detail and the petit-bourgeois concerns of the Biedermeier period are evident in this comfortable domestic setting. Ritual objects and food, carefully depicted, indicate the richness and grace of Jewish culture. A portrait of Frederick the Great, emperor of Prussia, adds a politically expedient note of German patriotism. The soldier's mother and siblings appear in various states of concern and delight as they fawn over their just-returned relative and simultaneously express admiration for his uniform and other military accoutrements. The father's rapt gaze at his son's Iron Cross, a military decoration that is also a Christian symbol, exposes a struggle to resolve his conflicted emotions of pride and anxiety.

The Return of the Jewish Volunteer was painted when Jewish civil rights were again in a tenuous state. In the wake of political unrest following the 1830 revolutions in France and their reverberations in Germany, many German states reimposed repressive legislation that affected rights recently won by Jews. This painting has been interpreted as a reminder to Germans of the significant role played by Jews in the Wars of Liberation, and its political overtones are unusual in the generally apolitical nature of Biedermeier art.

Popular in early-nineteenth-century art, images of departing and returning volunteers served as sources for Oppenheim's work. He must have followed the career of his fellow Hanauer Johann Peter Krafft, whose paintings *The Departure of the Militiaman* (1813) and *The Return of the Militiaman* (1820) were bought by the Hapsburg emperor. Additional sources include François Rude's Paris monument *The Departure of the Volunteers*, also begun in 1833, along with numerous genre representations of departures and returns executed around the time of the French Revolution. The conception of *The Return of the Sons* (c. 1800), by the eminent German artist Phillip Otto Runge (1777–1810), is strikingly similar to Oppenheim's. Both Runge's and Oppenheim's characterizations depend thematically and compositionally on popular eighteenth-century interpretations of the *Return of the Prodigal Son*.

Oppenheim's privileged life and artistic career are charmingly chronicled in his autobiography, *Erinnerungen* (Remembrances). The part recording his stay in Rome is particularly poignant, describing the conflicts of an observant Jew, united with his fellow artists in creative sensibility but separated from them in his religious beliefs and practices. This tension—between country and religion, modernity and tradition—plays a central role in Oppenheim's life and in many of the subjects he explored during his sixty-five-year career.

NLK

REFERENCES
Berman, *Cultural Studies of Modern Germany*; Cohen, *Moritz Oppenheim*; Goodman, *The Emergence of Jewish Artists in Nineteenth-Century Europe*; Heuberger and Merk, *Moritz Daniel Oppenheim*.

James Jacques Joseph Tissot

(French, 1836–1902)

Joseph Dwelleth in Egypt,
c. 1896–1902

Adam and Eve Driven from Paradise, c. 1896–1902

Gouache on board,
9¹⁄₁₆ x 10⅞ in. (23 x 27.6 cm);
5¹⁵⁄₁₆ x 8⅛ in. (15.1 x 20.6 cm)

Gift of the heirs of Jacob Schiff,
X1952-141 and X1952-71

Few reputations have benefited as much from the late twentieth century's appreciation of the wide range of late-nineteenth-century art as James Tissot's. While most of the reawakened admiration for his work focuses on his depictions of the fashionable society of Paris and London, he also produced two large bodies of paintings devoted to the Hebrew Bible and the New Testament. During the final two decades of his career, one might say that he was consumed with painting the Bible.

Tissot's idea for illustrating the life of Jesus came first. This enormous project prompted his travels to Palestine and the Near East in 1886. His purpose was to observe the landscape where biblical narrative originated, to research archaeological sites, and to study ethnological details. His focus on the material reality of the present, inevitably built on colonial attitudes and Orientalist imaginings, naively presumed these aspects unchanged for nearly two millennia. His goal, a historically accurate visual recreation of biblical passages, resulted in nearly four hundred drawings. These met with enormous public success and were subsequently published.

Tissot made an additional trip to Palestine in 1896 to gather material for another series of drawings illustrating the Hebrew Bible. This project occupied much of the artist's time until his death in 1902. More than half the works in this series were completed posthumously by several other artists. Published in 1904, the Hebrew Bible suite toured the United States for several years. Curiously, Tissot's biblical paintings were the very works that turn-of-the-century audiences most closely associated with his name.

Tissot's obsession with a frame-by-frame narrative for his immense biblical suites may be seen to foreshadow the invention of film in 1895, and in his later years he may have been directly influenced by this new phenomenon of moving images. While the artist's stab at historical veracity can easily be faulted by contemporary standards, he nevertheless created rich, romantic, and accessible images. These, in turn, have provided sources for the biblical visions of twentieth-century filmmakers, from D. W. Griffith to Steven Spielberg.

In the "imaginative" truth of his reconstructions, the artist fell prey not only to biased, inaccurate research, but also to personal penchants evident in his earlier works. For example, he used the head-dress of a recently excavated Greek bust as a model for the coiffures of his biblical heroines. This prop served his predilection for archaeological sources and his love of complex, well-designed costumes so apparent in his society painting. Tissot's observation of the brightly colored camelback traveling compartment, which he assumed to be an ethnographic variation on a much earlier prototype, provided him with as much local color as did the vibrant banners on his earlier masterpiece *The Ball on Shipboard*. Totally undocumented pastiches are evident in *Joseph Dwelleth in Egypt*. Here motifs found on Egyptian jewelry have become imaginary standards, through which he transformed stylized animal and vegetal motifs into cinematic pageantry. Finally, Tissot had no compunction about rendering Joseph with the same youthful face throughout the series of works that record his long life span.

Tissot's companion, Kathleen Newton, whose premature death at the age of twenty-eight helped turn the society artist into biblical chronicler, served frequently as the inspiration for his matriarchs and heroines. Devastated by her demise in 1882, Tissot attended séances in an effort to contact her spirit. As the artist recalls her oval face, widely spaced eyes, bow lips, and prominent chin as Eve in *Adam and Eve Driven from Paradise*, he may have been thinking of his lost love and his seeming exile from Eden. Even in his biblical paintings, he remained— as one recent critic cleverly remarked—"the painter of modern love."

NLK

REFERENCES
Marshall and Warner, *James Tissot*; Schiff, "Tissot's Illustrations for the Hebrew Bible."

Quilt

Russia and the United States, c. 1899

Velvet embroidered with wool, silk, and metallic threads; glass beads
81½ x 65 in. (207 x 165.1 cm)

Purchase: Judaica Acquisitions Committee Fund, 1986-119

This colorful patchwork quilt bearing Eastern European and American imagery is a wonderful testimony to the acculturation process undergone by new Jewish immigrants as they arrived in the United States. Originally owned by a Russian Jewish family believed to have immigrated to the United States, the quilt incorporates several panels embroidered in the cross-stitch technique often used in late-nineteenth-century Jewish ceremonial textiles from Eastern Europe. A black velvet panel above center featuring a floral design embroidered with metallic threads appears to be older than the other textiles forming the quilt. Reminiscent of the work found in Torah ark curtains and mantles from Ashkenazic lands, this panel was replicated in the lower half, center. It is likely, therefore, that the quilt was done in America, incorporating Russian textiles and motifs.

Although the maker of the quilt seems to have organized the individual panels in rows, the overall arrangement of the multicolor triangular panels creates a visual effect reminiscent of crazy quilts. This form of quilting, by assembling together pieces of fabric of various shapes and sizes, became highly popular in the late nineteenth and early twentieth centuries. Of particular interest in this quilt are four panels featuring figures dressed in Russian costumes: a woman raising the side of her skirt, a common gesture in folk dancing; a dancing man; and a seated musician playing the balalaika. The source for these three figures can be traced to Russian folk art, where they are found as a group in a design known as the "Russian border." This design became popular in the late nineteenth century in printed textiles marketed among peasants. A printed calico from the 1870s in the State History Museum in Moscow features the so-called Russian border with the motif of a dancing couple and musician in a repeat pattern.

Four panels feature roosters, a motif also found in late-nineteenth-century Jewish textiles from Eastern Europe. The roosters in this quilt all face left, probably embroidered after a set pattern. In the 1880s and 1890s, however, the rooster was being used in America as a symbol for the Democratic Party. A political crazy quilt dated 1885, incorporating political ribbons and other memorabilia from the Cleveland-Hendricks presidential campaign, features a strutting rooster facing left. Another crazy quilt made in 1885–90, and today in the collection of the American Folk Art Museum (1985.23.3), also features the Democratic rooster. Its appearance there has been interpreted as possibly reflecting the maker's aspiration for the women's vote, implemented only in 1920. It is difficult to ascertain, however, whether the rooster has a political significance in The Jewish Museum quilt.

The decoration in the border relates mainly to life in America. Symbols of patriotism such as the American flag are combined with the Star of David, a symbol of Jewish heritage. Two crossed American flags are flanked by depictions of Admiral Dewey and of a typical Russian woman dancing, representing the Old and the New Worlds. The popularity of Admiral George Dewey (1837–1917) was at its peak in the United States in the late nineteenth and early twentieth centuries. The hero of the Spanish-American War, Dewey had returned to New York to lead a victory parade in 1899, briefly running for president in 1900. Dewey's victory prompted the manufacturing of a wide array of products bearing his image. In a letter to Dewey, his colleague Thomas O. Selfridge writes: "They are selling Dewey hats, Dewey cigarettes, Dewey canes. There are Dewey spoons, Dewey candlesticks, Dewey paper weights." Since Dewey was not promoted to the rank of admiral until March 1899, the quilt could only have been completed after this date, although the central panel bears an 1898 date.

Several motifs in the border are connected to various sports that became popular in America beginning in the late nineteenth or early twentieth century, including tennis and hot-air ballooning. The Davis Cup tennis tournament was inaugurated in 1900, and the first international hot-air balloon competition was launched in Paris in 1906 and won by an American, who popularized the sport in the United States. A crazy quilt in the Herbert Offen Collection features tennis racquets in combination with butterflies, as seen in this example. The inclusion of these motifs reflects a vivid interest in pastimes that were a novelty to Jewish immigrants coming from Eastern Europe, where life, especially for Jews, was filled with harshness.

CN

REFERENCES

Bacon, *American Patchwork Quilts*, p. 116, pl. 33; Cavigga, *American Antique Quilts*, pp. 86–87, pl. 79; Hilton, *Russian Folk Art*, pp. 221–22, fig. 15.4; Spector, *Admiral of the New Empire*, pp. 64–67.

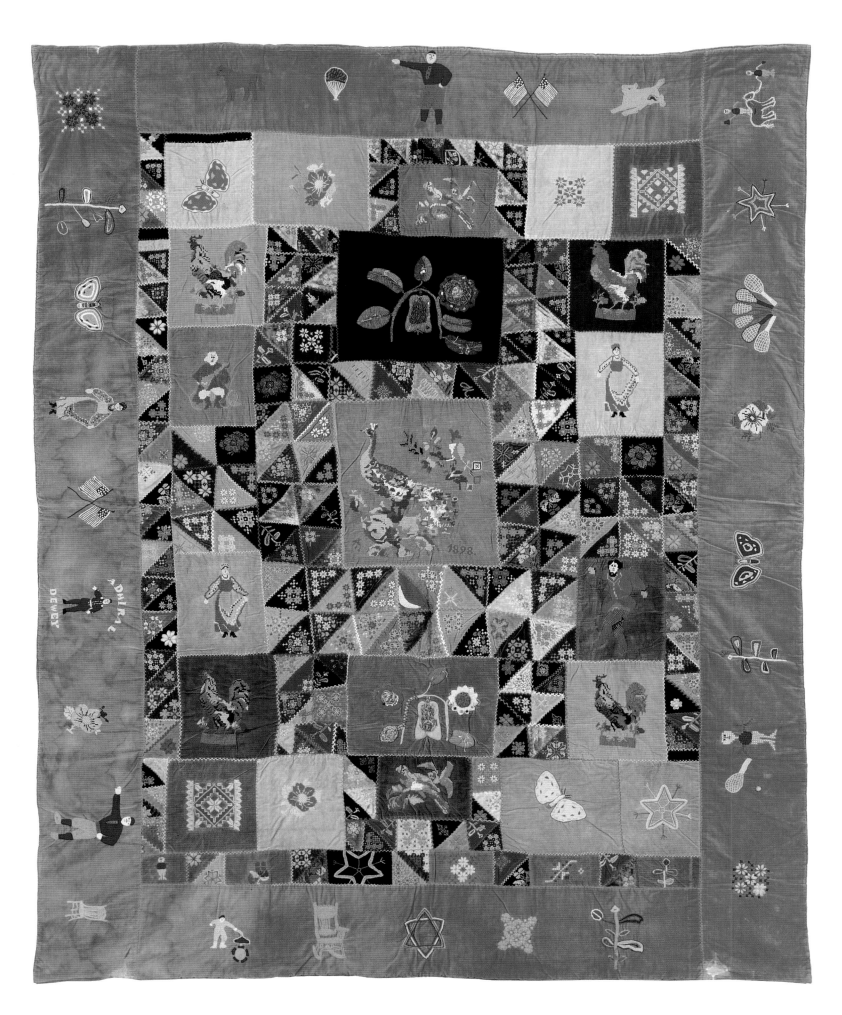

Alfred Stieglitz

(American, 1864–1946)

The Steerage, 1907

Photogravure
13⁷⁄₁₆ x 10⅛ in. (34.1 x 25.7 cm)

Purchase: Mr. and Mrs. George Jaffin
Fund, 2000-6

Alfred Stieglitz's Little Galleries of the Photo-Secession, founded with Edward Steichen in 1905 and better known as 291, for its Fifth Avenue location, was the first in the United States to show the work of European modernist artists including Matisse, Cézanne, and Picasso, predating the famous Armory Show of 1913 by five years. Stieglitz also championed photography as a fine art—his own as well as that of others—long before it gained such recognition in America. His iconic photograph *The Steerage* provoked extensive discussion, both for its striking composition and for the questions its class-oriented subject matter raises.

Born in Hoboken, New Jersey, to German Jewish immigrant parents, Stieglitz and his family moved to Berlin in 1881, as his father believed Germany would provide a better education for his children. Stieglitz, who was in his second year at City College in New York City, enrolled in the mechanical engineering program in Berlin, where he also began to experiment with photography, becoming adept at its technical processes. Returning to New York in 1890, Stieglitz began photographing his changing urban environment, focusing on the people, buildings, and industry that had yet to be accepted as subjects of artistic photography. In the United States in the late nineteenth century, suitable subject matter included landscapes and people photographed in a romantic, impressionistic style. In his early work, Stieglitz favored the blurred, impressionistic style of pictorialist photography but advocated modern, urban subject matter.

Stieglitz formed the Camera Club of New York in 1886 and, in 1902, founded the Photo-Secession, a group of pictorialist photographers modeled on the English Linked Ring and European Secessionist groups. While his own style changed from pictorial to straight photography, he continued to support and exhibit modern pictorialist photographers. In 1903, he inaugurated the journal *Camera Work*, which published technical articles, essays on aesthetics, literature, criticism, and theories of modern art. Through 291 and *Camera Work*, Stieglitz supported the work of American modernists such as Arthur Dove, Marsden Hartley, Elie Nadelman, Max Weber, Paul Strand, Charles Demuth, and Georgia O'Keeffe, whom he eventually married.

The Steerage epitomizes Stieglitz's urban, straight style of photography, which emphasized clarity of detail and photography's ability to capture reality. Taken on a large ship bound for Paris, the photograph is evenly divided between the upper, or first-class, and lower, or steerage, decks of the ship, separated by the sharp diagonal of the suspended walkway. Both decks are crowded with people: Stieglitz was traveling on the top deck, which consisted of well-off leisure travelers; the steerage level below held lower-class immigrants returning to Europe. The question remains as to whether the immigrants are being forcibly returned to Europe by the United States government—as many were for reasons of disease, "poor moral health," or lack of financial support in the States—or if they returning of their own accord, disillusioned with the country they had believed would change their fate.

Furthermore, does Stieglitz's photograph express class consciousness or is it simply an observation of his surroundings, focusing as much on the shapes formed by the picture's elements as much as its subject? Although Stieglitz stated that he felt displeasure with the nouveaux riches of the upper deck and an affinity with those on the lower deck, by this point his family was well established in the States and he was entrenched in the privileges of his stature. This photograph typifies Stieglitz's dual interests in urban modernity and formal harmony, in this case played out through the saga of American immigration.

KL

REFERENCES

Abrahams, *The Lyrical Left*; Greenough, *Modern Art and America*; Greenough and Hamilton, *Alfred Stieglitz: Photography and Writings*; Homer, *Alfred Stieglitz and the American Avant-Garde*; Kozloff, *New York: Capital of Photography*.

Reuven Rubin

(Israeli, born Rumania, 1893–1974)

Goldfish Vendor, 1928

Oil on canvas
29½ x 24 in. (74.9 x 61 cm)

Gift of Kitty and Harold J. Ruttenberg,
1985-227

By 1920, many young artists in Israel had reacted against the classical Western orientation of Jerusalem's Bezalel Academy (see entry on a Bezalel rug in this volume, p. 179). They became disenchanted with the use of Oriental motifs and local landscape in the service of biblical subjects. Instead, these painters and sculptors—who knew contemporary European artistic developments firsthand—sought to incorporate everyday visions of the Near East into a modernist vocabulary. Thus, influenced by the newly adopted use of the modern Hebrew language, they defined their goals for a "Hebrew" rather than a "Jewish" art.

Reuven Rubin was one of the most important of these young pioneers, and his new land was a constant source of inspiration for him. The lyricism of his *Goldfish Vendor* (also known as *Arab Fisherman*) is typical of Rubin's colorful and self-consciously naive vision of the Land of Israel. The painting also exemplifies a theme recurrent in Israeli art of that decade—the portrayal of the Arab. The appeal of the physical vitality of these people becomes almost stereotypical in the literature and art of the 1920s. According to Nahum Gutman, Rubin's colleague, the Arab who maintained a continuing tie with the land constitutes the antithesis of the Diaspora Jew. His sense of belonging and his instinctual assets are exaggerated, even monumentalized.

Rubin's paintings of that period have been stylistically linked to the earlier French *naïfs* such as Henri Rousseau and André Bauchant. Also evident is the debt owed to the Jewish members of the School of Paris, particularly Modigliani, whose monumental figures seem to press the edges of the canvas and could easily have served to trigger Rubin's powerful figure. Yet Rubin's subject matter and purposefully innocent style must also be viewed in light of other Israeli paintings of the decade; their pervasive aesthetic combined the tenets of modernism with a confident depiction of the land, creating a style appropriate for the infancy of Israel's national rebirth.

NLK

REFERENCES
The Jewish Museum, *Artists of Israel: 1920–1980*, p. 118; Ofrat, *One Hundred Years of Art in Israel*, chap. 3; Rubin, *My Life, My Art*; Rubin, *Rubin: Retrospective Exhibition*.

Marc Chagall

(French, born Russia, 1887–1985)

Untitled (Old Man with Beard), c. 1931

Gouache and watercolor over charcoal
or graphite on paper
24¼ x 19 in. (61.6 x 48.3 cm)

Gift of Frances Gershwin Godowsky
and family in memory of
George Gershwin, 1999-77

Although Chagall never created a school of his own, he managed to invent images that have captured the imagination of Western society, becoming part of our visual language. His first major public recognition as an avant-garde painter occurred in Paris, where his art continued to explore images and themes from his life as a Russian Jew. Absorbing Fauvist color and Cubist faceting and blending them with his own folk style, Chagall gave the grim life of Hasidic Jews in Vitebsk the romantic overtones of a charmed world. Combining aspects of modernism with his unique artistic language, he caught the attention of European critics, collectors, and an art-loving public.

Old Man with Beard depicts the outsize figure of a Jew standing alone in a snowy landscape before the backdrop of a Russian village. No one else can be seen, and there is not even a human footprint on the ground. The head is framed in the center of the canvas by the houses of the village. Wearing a Russian visored cap and dark caftan, the figure projects an aura of meditation. The depiction of a religious Jew derives from Chagall's store of images of Russian shtetl life. But the image is generalized and timeless without iconographic specificity and is rendered with a modernist vocabulary fused with folkloric elements and an odd disjunction of figure and houses behind. The remarkable dominance of the figure in the space, the tilt of the head, the hand gesture, and the houses that frame the head suggest that the artist continued to make use of various stylistic devices that he had employed previously.

From Chagall's early years in Paris, his fantasy world was occupied with the ordinary figures of Vitebsk. The old man with the beard in The Jewish Museum painting is a subject derived from one of the poor Jews whom he saw in Russia and used as models for his cycle of Old Jews. As Chagall states in *My Life*, his models were old beggars or itinerant Hasidic rabbis. From chance encounters with beggars, peddlers, and itinerant Jewish preachers, Chagall conjures up the eternal figure of the migrant rabbis and Jewish miracle workers so prevalent in Eastern European Jewish communities. Often they were wandering Jews, filled with holy inspiration, proclaiming the word of God, and they seemed to resonate with a spiritual radiance. In *Old Man with Beard*, we are aware that the figure is not employed merely as an actor in a scene. Rather, the singular nature of the figure allows us to experience his profound humanity.

Vitebsk, where Chagall was born and bred, remained an emotional and intellectual source that existed in later years solely in memory and imagination. The artist continuously transformed his vision, whether he lived in the Soviet Union or in faraway Paris or New York. Vitebsk was always with him, sustaining him for the rest of his life.

S G

REFERENCES

Baal-Teshuva, *Chagall: A Retrospective*; Chagall, *My Life*; Compton, *Marc Chagall: My Life, My Dream*; Goodman, *Marc Chagall*; Guggenheim Museum, *Marc Chagall and the Jewish Theater*; Meyer, *Marc Chagall*; Vitali, *Marc Chagall*.

Tim Gidal

(Israeli, born Germany, 1909–1996)

Night of the Cabbalist,
1935

Gelatin-silver print
12 x 11¼ in. (30.5 x 28.6 cm)

Purchase: Gruss Family Fund in honor
of Regina Gruss, 1994-598

Many photographers of Tim Gidal's generation, such as André Kertész and Henri Cartier-Bresson, depicted aspects of daily life and banal events, planning the composition and all the formal elements in the frame in order to create a visual harmony. Gidal, on the contrary, believed more in intuition and stated, "I leave it to the object to express itself with the assistance of my camera."

Tim Gidal's photographic career spanned the greater part of the twentieth century, and he was one of the innovative photographers whose work helped guide the development of modern photojournalism from the late 1920s. His photo reportages, transmitted in his direct, photographic style, are invaluable historical and social documents.

The 1930s witnessed a massive immigration of photographers from Europe to the Land of Israel. At the beginning of his career, Gidal was not under the influence of other photographers, nor did he know any of the leading figures in the field. Nonetheless, in his accomplished modernist photographs taken in the 1930s, he was clearly aware of prevailing artistic attitudes as he experimented with composition, viewing angle, and other aspects of photographic language.

Born Ignatz Nachum Gidalewitsch in Munich in 1909, he began his photographic reporting in 1929, with images that appeared throughout Europe. In 1932 and again in 1935, Gidal spent several months in Palestine. He immigrated there in 1936 but continued to travel and work as a photographer for magazines around the world.

In the photograph *Night of the Cabbalist*, which also has been called *Night at Meron* or *Lag B'Omer on the Tomb of Rabbi Shimon Bar Yohai*, the man sleeps atop the building, waiting for the night to pass and the moon to wane. In this near-Surrealist depiction, time seems to stand still, and yet it marks Lag B'Omer, the thirty-third day of the counting of the omer, which begins on the second day of Passover and continues until Shavuot. The photograph documents the major celebration held in Meron, in Upper Galilee, believed to be the spot where Bar Yohai, the second-century rabbinic scholar whom kabbalists consider to be the author of the Zohar, is buried. The man on top of the roof is one of thousands of Hasidim and kabbalists who gather to celebrate, sing, and dance. It is not unusual for Jewish pilgrims to travel to Meron and other burial sites to prostrate themselves on the tombs of holy people, where they beseech the deceased to intercede with God on their behalf.

This work signifies Gidal's ability to recognize and record special moments, and the incident captured in *Night of the Cabbalist* is the result of careful observation and sympathetic concern for human situations. Gidal often made photographs in series comprising a journalistic essay that conveyed the subject, the event, and the atmosphere. In the series of photos taken in Meron during the same period as *Night of the Cabbalist*, Gidal conveyed the impact of the festival of Lag B'Omer.

In this work, Gidal sympathetically captures the man propped on the roof while acknowledging the ceremony being marked. He merely documents what he saw and experienced. He has no mission or agenda, and stated: "The viewer can take what he sees, if he sees, or leave it."

SG

REFERENCE
Gidal, *Jerusalem in 3000 Years*; Gidal, *My Way*.

Louis Faurer

(American, 1916–2001)

Staten Island Ferry, also called *I Once Dreamed about the Most Beautiful City in the World, Staten Island Ferry*, 1946

Gelatin-silver print
8 x 8 in. (20.3 x 20.3 cm)

Purchase: Judith and Jack Stern Fund,
2000-57

Louis Faurer's quiet and melancholy images capture individuals at their most contemplative moments, even amid the tumult of the big city. In the presence of his photographs, the viewer feels privy to the secret world of their subjects.

Faurer grew up in a Polish Jewish immigrant family in Philadelphia. Before attending the School of Commercial Art and Lettering in 1937, he earned money by drawing caricatures in Atlantic City, New Jersey, and in his spare time took photographs on the boardwalk there. In 1946, he began commuting to New York, where he took freelance fashion photographs for publications including *Harper's Bazaar* and became friendly with the photographer Robert Frank, who allowed him to use his Manhattan loft and darkroom. For the next thirty years, Faurer continued to do fashion photography, which sated his aesthetic sensibility and perfectionist inclinations, for publications such as *Flair*, *Vogue*, and *Seventeen*. He also developed his own photographic techniques. Although he did not actively promote his own work, advocates such as the actress Viva, with whom he had been romantically involved in the 1960s, curator Walter Hopps, and dealer Deborah Bell have played integral roles in preserving his work and bringing it to the fore.

Faurer often used reflections and double exposures to create stunning visual juxtapositions and compositions. In *Staten Island Ferry*, Faurer captured the ghostly panorama of New York obscured by the window of the ferry. He provided clues that there is a man seated on a bench in front of the window by showing a segment of a suited shoulder and a silhouette of a head. We can only assume that the figure on the right is the photographer, but who is the man that his shadow makes visible? And can he see the majestic cityscape that the photographer is showing us? Without seeing their faces, we perceive the men as entrenched in the skyline before them and thoroughly isolated from each other.
JG

REFERENCES
Kozloff, *New York: Capital of Photography*; Livingston, *The New York School: Photographs, 1936–1963*; Tucker, *Louis Faurer*.

Adolph Gottlieb

(American, 1903–1974)

Return of the Mariner, 1946

Oil on canvas
24 x 20 in. (61 x 50.8 cm)

Partial and promised gift of an
anonymous donor, 2002-54

In 1943, Adolph Gottlieb and Mark Rothko became the first artists to articulate the tenets of the movement that would become known as Abstract Expressionism. In a letter to the *New York Times*, they wrote: "There is no such thing as good painting about nothing. We assert that the subject is crucial and only that subject matter is *valid which is tragic and timeless.* This is why we profess spiritual kinship with primitive and archaic art." Gottlieb was at the center of this diverse group of artists that included Jackson Pollock, Willem de Kooning, Barnett Newman, and Mark Rothko. Along with writers and musicians, these Abstract Expressionist painters and sculptors transformed New York into the new intellectual and artistic center, replacing Paris as the avant-garde mecca. These artists were aware of the European modernists because of their recent arrival to New York, in exile during World War II. However, seeking independent identities, the Abstract Expressionists strove to create a distinctly American idiom. Fourteen years after their declaration of artistic ideals, The Jewish Museum mounted a solo exhibition of Adolph Gottlieb's work. This inaugurated the focus on avant-garde art that became seminal to The Jewish Museum's mission during the 1960s and provided New York with its first major museum exhibition of the work of an Abstract Expressionist artist.

Return of the Mariner is an example of Gottlieb's aesthetic and conceptual innovation that he called the "pictograph." He began by dividing his canvases into a grid, which was a process that refers not only to Mondrian's rational modernist compositions, but to the partitioned panels of Renaissance narrative altarpieces. He then used free association, a Freudian method formerly used by the Surrealists, to fill the compartments with symbols. He invented these from a lexicon of premodern, tribal, and mythological sources that he had seen during his travels. Through his concentration on Carl Jung's theories of archetypes and the collective unconscious, Gottlieb began to understand how to synthesize these various sources. His paintings were also, for the artist, vehicles for addressing the brutality and destruction of World War II.

Gottlieb was one of the more reserved and intellectual of the Abstract Expressionists, spending time at his home in Brooklyn Heights instead of in the raucous Cedar Tavern in Manhattan, where his cohorts gathered regularly. For most of his life, he kept a small boat at a dock in Brooklyn and sometimes raced regattas in New England. The title *Return of the Mariner* refers to the voyages of Theseus and Odysseus, as well as to Gottlieb's own recollections of his time on the sea. The artist's conflation of the heroic and intimate, the powerful and serene, accounts for some of the mysterious force that imbues his paintings with a transcendent aura. JG

REFERENCES
Alloway and MacNaughton, *Adolph Gottlieb: A Retrospective*; Hirsch, *Adolph Gottlieb: A Survey Exhibition*; Hirsch, *The Pictographs of Adolph Gottlieb*; Kleeblatt and Chevlowe, *Painting a Place in America: Jewish Artists in New York, 1900–1945*; Polcari, *Abstract Expressionism and the Modern Experience*; Sandler, *The New York School: The Painters and Sculptors of the Fifties*.

Ben Shahn

(American, born Lithuania, 1898–1969)

New York, 1947

Tempera on paper mounted on panel
36 x 48 in. (91.4 x 121.9 cm)

Purchase: Oscar and Regina Gruss
Charitable and Educational Foundation,
1996-23

Ben Shahn is acclaimed for his social realist works from the 1930s, including a series on the French military officer Alfred Dreyfus, a Jew convicted of treason in 1894 and later acquitted; and a cycle exposing the xenophobia and prejudice surrounding the trial and execution of the anarchist Italian émigrés Nicola Sacco and Bartolomeo Vanzetti in Dedham, Massachusetts, from 1921 to 1927. An immigrant himself, Shahn traced his hatred of injustice to the religious education he received during his early childhood in Lithuania and his own rebellion against tradition. He arrived in the United States prior to World War I, at the age of eight. Shahn's memories of his emigration experience and adjustment to life in America came flooding back to him as an adult, inevitably reshaped by the trauma of World War II and the Holocaust, which his own family had avoided but which no doubt served as traumatic reminders of earlier European pogroms and refugees. Shahn's connection to the European past, the blurring and layered personal and topical allusions to specific Old World milieus, and the longing and nostalgia evidenced in his paintings are characteristic of later émigré artists of the modern Diaspora, such as R. B. Kitaj and Ben Katchor.

Shahn's reflections on his boyhood are evident in such works as *Portrait of Myself When Young*, 1943 (Museum of Modern Art, New York), *Spring*, 1947 (Albright-Knox Gallery, Buffalo), and *New York*, 1947. Ostensibly related to a "small boy's emblematic impressions of a fish market," the last painting's nostalgic and dreamlike composition recontextualizes a visual pastiche of images culled from memory and reality, from present and past. Shahn based the composition of his painting on two photographs he had taken on the Lower East Side, to create a haunting and disjunctive scene. From one image, a photograph he took in 1936 outside Gelbwachs fish market, Shahn borrowed the image of a bearded traditional Jew—a fish peddler—at right, and a scale, at left, but replaced the carp painted on the shop's window in the photograph with a pike. The absence in the painting of the glass-plated storefront visible in the original photograph results in the fish floating surrealistically in the air at the center of the composition. In the foreground of the painting, a young boy wearing swimming trunks lies prone, apparently in the street. This figure has been taken from the second source photograph

(about 1932–35), which also included windowed apartment and factory buildings surrounding a park. Such a sparsely landscaped city park would have had great significance for Shahn, who as an adult remembered his childhood yearning for the countryside of his native Vilkomir, and as a boy in Brooklyn searched desperately for whatever small patches of green might be found in his new urban milieu. The young boy in the painting, one of two in the original photograph, perhaps alludes to Shahn's younger brother, Hymie, who drowned at the age of seventeen near the artist's home in Truro, on Cape Cod, in 1926, an event that resulted in the abrupt end of the artist's relationship with his mother and the severing of other connections to his past.

In 1967, the artist observed: "For imagination is images, traces of experience, the residue of impacts made upon us by all sorts of forces both from outside and inside ourselves. It is such images retained, and the power to re-invoke them, the power to re-group them and out of them to create new images according to our uses and intentions." In *New York*, using a limited array of personally resonant symbols from his photographs of the 1930s, Shahn was able to communicate a powerful visual impression of a particular immigrant Jewish experience—one haunted by an irredeemable sense of loss, yet recognizable to those who shared a similar journey or to others who may seek their own roots through a connection to the collective experience of an imagined past.

S C

REFERENCES

Benison and Otter, *Interviews with Ben Shahn*; Chevlowe, *Common Man, Mythic Vision*, pp. 6–7, plate 13; Greenfield, *Ben Shahn: An Artist's Life*; Kao, Katzman, and Webster, *Ben Shahn's New York*, pp. 34–35, 243, 250; Rodman, *Portrait of the Artist as an American*, pp. 163–64; Shahn, "Imagination and Intention," pp. 187–88, 197–200.

Hanukkah Lamp

Otto Natzler
(American, born Austria, 1908)

Simi Valley, California, 1956

Ceramic, gray-green lava glaze
21 x 5½ x 42 in. (53.3 x 14 x 106.7 cm)

Purchase: Judaica Acquisitions Committee Fund and funds provided by Mimi R. T., Ruth I., and Lewis D. Surrey gift, in honor of Albert W. Surrey, 1988-30

Gertrud and Otto Natzler's fascination with ceramics began in 1930s Vienna, where they met, formed a relationship, and launched their careers as ceramists. Their training was largely a self-taught experience fraught with trial and error, which Otto later characterized as a "series of accidents." It often consisted of tireless experiments that gradually revealed to them how they could achieve a specific shape or glaze effect. For example, Otto conducted more than 2,500 glaze experiments and kept copious records of the results, giving him a repertoire of surfaces and finishes that would later bring them much acclaim and success. Gertrud devoted herself to the creation of the vessels, and her uncanny sense for shape and line was described by Otto as a kind of innate "feeling for form" (*Formgefühl*): "At times I had the feeling in observing her turning or throwing that literally one millimeter change in one dimension meant the difference between day and night to her." As a team, the Natzlers created strikingly beautiful forms with remarkable surface finishes.

The Natzlers focused on ceramics as a sculptural and artistic medium, rather than as a vehicle for functional objects, which may explain why ceremonial objects were never a high priority for them. However, in 1956 Shlomo Bardin, founder and director of the Brandeis Institute (now the Brandeis-Bardin Institute) in California, encouraged them to explore Judaica. From 1956 until 1960, the Natzlers served as artists-in-residence and instructors at Brandeis Camp Institute, which offered intensive studies in Jewish-related subjects and the arts for college-age students. Bardin persuaded the Natzlers to create *Yahrzeit* (memorial) lamps for the Brandeis collection. Each lamp that the couple created was inscribed with the Hebrew text that translates as "Man comes from dust and returns to dust."

During their years at Brandeis, Otto Natzler also began making slab-constructed Hanukkah lamps, such as The Jewish Museum's example. Unlike Gertrud's sinuous, wheel-thrown forms, Otto's work was slab-built and architectural in feeling. The Jewish Museum's lamp, which dates to 1956, is coated with a gray-green glaze that Otto first developed in 1940 and called "lava." It was precisely the type of surface treatment for which the Natzlers were known, and capitalizes on what some people would view as glaze defects—craters and rough surface texture. Otto purposely cultivated these glazes to evoke "what has been done by nature in the process of earth's creation." The verdigris color and encrusted surface also have associations with the antique and may recall the ancient story of Hanukkah.

The Natzlers' body of Judaica is small and rarely seen, yet the pieces are informed by a spiritual quality and evince a mood of quiet contemplation. S R

REFERENCES
Brown, *American Studio Ceramics, 1920–1950*, pp. 37–45; Clark and the Everson Museum of Art, *A Century of Ceramics in the United States, 1878–1978*, p. 311; Conroy, "Earth, Fire and Love"; Gilbert, "Earth and Spirit: Otto Natzler at 80"; The Jewish Museum, *Ceramics: An Exhibit, Gertrud and Otto Natzler*; Kardon, *Gertrud and Otto Natzler*; Levin, *The History of American Ceramics*; Los Angeles County Museum of Art, *Today: Contemporary Ceramists and Their Work*.

Mordecai Ardon

(Israeli, born Poland, 1896–1992)

Landscape with Black Sun,
1961

Oil on canvas
31 x 39½ in. (78.7 x 100.3 cm)

Purchase: Beren Foundation Fund,
1998-59

Most of the German Jewish artists who emigrated to Eretz Yisrael in the early 1930s settled in Jerusalem. A number of them became involved with the Bezalel School of Arts and Crafts, which was founded there in 1906. It was forced to close in 1929 as a result of financial and organizational problems, as well as harsh criticism of its rejection of modernism. When the school was reopened in 1935, its teachers were mostly of German Jewish origin. Mordecai Ardon was an important member of this artistic group, along with Jakob Steinhardt, Anna Ticho, and Leopold Krakauer. Regardless of their stylistic differences, these German artists had a great deal in common, and their culture and point of view were completely different from those of the Jewish expressionists in Paris. They were opposed to aestheticism for its own sake and believed that artists had a moral mission and that their work should have social meaning.

Born Mordecai Eliezer Bronstein in Tuchow, Poland, Ardon moved to Germany in 1919. His studies at the Bauhaus in Weimar from 1921 until its closing in 1924 brought him into close contact with Paul Klee, Wassily Kandinsky, and Lionel Feininger. From 1930 to 1933, he taught painting at Johannes Itten's school in Berlin. When compelled to flee Germany in 1933, he decided to immigrate to Palestine, although he was a Communist, not a Zionist. Once settled in Jerusalem, he joined the New Bezalel School of Arts and Crafts, becoming its director in 1940.

Until the 1940s, most of Ardon's paintings showed the panorama of the Judaean hills, with their mysterious light. In 1946, however, the artist turned to subjects related to the Holocaust. In the 1950s, Ardon's work developed in the direction that is reflected in *Landscape with Black Sun*.

This painting, a paradigmatic work by Ardon, attempts to address solemn tradition and historical events, couching their meaning in symbolic and ancient mystical signs and allegorical visions. While the artist does not refer explicitly to the Holocaust, the black sun and intense hues have been interpreted as a tragic vision of those events. Although the landscape symbolizes rather than narrates, the fiery red patterns that spread across the surface of the painting suggest a universe suffused with blood. Even the sun has turned black, suggesting a form of cosmic eclipse. This symbolic landscape hovers between nature and abstraction, creating a dynamic interaction between earth and sky, a space that brims with emotional energy. The lower portion of the painting reveals a black ground with yellow and red flat planes or color scattered in an irregular pattern. This layered painting, with rich textures, incisions, and broad brush strokes creates a mottled, tactile surface.

Using animated brush strokes for this and other landscapes as well as portraits, Ardon began in the early 1950s to condense full volumes into flat planes and compress figurative details into linear and geometric designs. Within a short time, his compositions developed into a poignant inner visual language divorced from external reality, formed by pictograms and abstract shapes that emerged in earthly, celestial, and apocalyptic backgrounds.

S G

REFERENCE
Vishny, *Mordecai Ardon*.

Anni Albers

(American, born Germany,
1899–1994)

Six Prayers, 1965–66

Beige, black, white cotton, linen, bast,
and silver Lurex
Overall dimensions: 73¼ x 117 in.
(186.1 x 297.2 cm)

Gift of the Albert A. List Family,
JM 149-72.1-6

To capture the unconscionability of historical fact and suggest the intimacy of details—the individual lives, stories, and dreams that were lost—is a unique challenge for memorializing the Holocaust in the visual arts. For some artists, representations of the specific—possessions, faces, names—serve as synecdoche, parts of the larger, missing whole. These images provide a channel for our compassion, which, having rested on the apprehension of individual souls, unleashes the imagination to conjure the absent millions. For other artists, the denial of figuration itself evokes the vastness of the destruction. The abstract image, in its refusal to tell, calls attention to the inadequacy of language. Yet whether crafted in the vernacular of the representational or the idiom of the abstract, the work must affect viewers, perhaps more compellingly than other art, with unmediated immediacy.

In 1965, The Jewish Museum approached Anni Albers with a commission to memorialize the victims of the Holocaust. An artist, designer, writer, and teacher, Albers elevated textiles from utilitarian product to a medium of powerful aesthetic statement. Born into an assimilated Jewish family in Berlin, Albers studied weaving before immigrating to America with her husband, Josef, a painter and instructor at the Bauhaus School. As a student at the Bauhaus, Anni learned from Paul Klee the expressive liberties of the formal grid, and in the fabrics of ancient Andean cultures she recognized a powerful visual language. Albers developed her own style of "pictorial weavings," which she mounted on linen bases and framed—elevating textile to a pure aesthetic. Her Holocaust memorial, *Six Prayers*, achieves both universality and intimacy and gently, though powerfully, provokes the viewer into private contemplation.

Albers's elegy is composed of six vertical tapestries woven of beige, black, white, and silver. While the use of so limited and somber a palette might call attention to the problem of differentiation in response to mass murder, Albers varies the weave, allowing one of these colors to dominate in each of the six panels, thereby giving each segment a unique tone. Against the structural grid of warp and weft, Albers sets meandering threads of black and white whose spontaneous irregularity is suggestive of an individual will—or individual wills—charting some personal terrain across an imposed order of overlapping verticals and horizontals. Poised within the restrained quiet of abstraction, these ambling filaments are texts that spread across the scroll-like tapestries, transcending the limited utterances of verbal language for a more universal elegy. Words are at once evoked and denied by the appearance and disappearance of these threads. Though the six commemorative stelae are solemn in their monumentality, there is an intimacy to the tapestries. Weaving—which consists of the intertwining of disparate threads—symbolically suggests the process of *tikkun*, or social repair.

Wilhelm Worringer, a theorist whom Albers much admired in her Bauhaus days, wrote in *Abstraction and Empathy* that beauty in representational art derives from our sense of being able to identify with an object, which reflects our confidence in the world as it is. Abstract art, by contrast, is the result of our insecurity and alienation from a world in which we can no longer comfortably envision ourselves or empathize with others. When conceiving of her Holocaust memorial, Albers may have meant to evoke something of Worringer's sense of anxiety and loss. Yet Albers, who devoted her life to developing the language of abstraction, believed in the potential of nonobjective art to reach beyond the communicative capacities of the representational. In mediating between abstraction and the suggestion of script, and between the assertiveness of art that is framed and hung on the wall and the intimacy of entwining threads, Albers creates a place of rest, something in between the world of things and the transcendental unknown. Her woven textiles not only elicit thought and hope; they are themselves six prayers.

SNB

REFERENCES

Albers, *Selected Writings on Design*; Albers, *The Woven and Graphic Art of Anni Albers*; The Jewish Museum, *Fabric of Jewish Life*; Weber, *Anni Albers*; Worringer, *Abstraction and Empathy*.

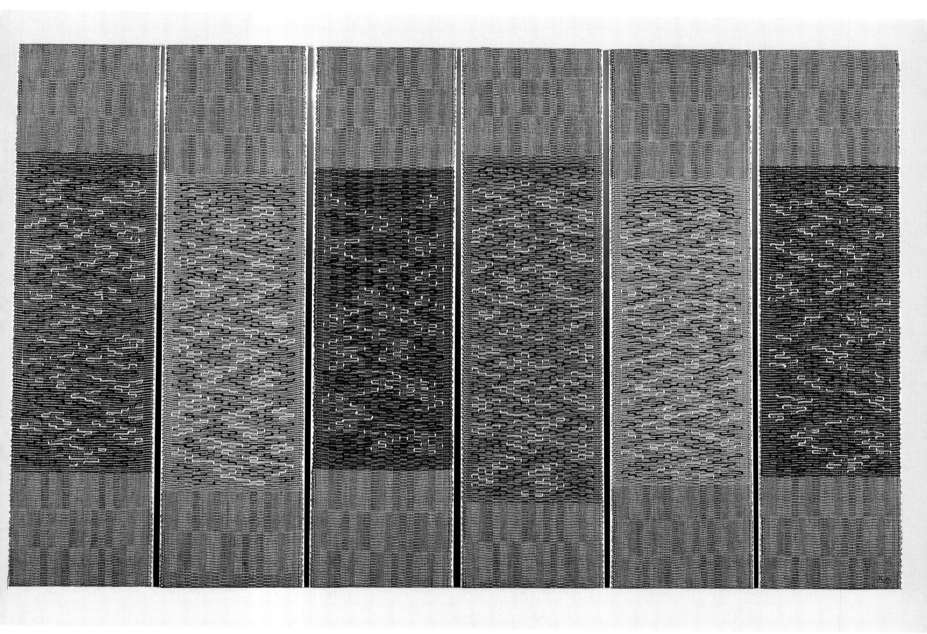

Fabio Mauri

(Italian, born 1926)

Small Closet with Shirt,
from *Ebrea (Jewish)*
installation, 1971

Mixed media, hair
Dimensions variable

Purchase: Dr. Jack Allen and
Shirley Kapland Fund, 2000-18a-e

A young woman, Ebrea, walks into the area, approaches the mirror, and removes her clothes. With haunting deliberateness, she repeats her ritual: standing naked in front of the medicine cabinet and mirror, the young woman slowly cuts her hair with a small pair of scissors and, rolling it into threads with glue, attaches the pieces to the mirror. Her actions gradually form a Star of David. The cutting of the hair, the prominent star, and the shirt, reminiscent of a concentration-camp uniform, remind the viewer of the indignities suffered by Jews during the Holocaust. *Small Closet with Shirt* is the focal point of *Ebrea,* Fabio Mauri's large installation and his most famous performance work, which was first staged in Venice in 1971 and revived at the 1993 Venice Biennale.

For the non-Jewish Mauri, who came of age in post–World War II Italy, the specter of the Holocaust has determined his core artistic vision. This moral imperative has been inflected by the minimalist aesthetics and theatricality of the Arte Povera movement from which Mauri's work emerged. Arte Povera was a politically motivated effort to break down the barrier between art and life, the equivalent of the neo-Dadaist and Fluxus happenings in the 1960s in the United States. The lack of preciousness of *Small Closet with Shirt,* for example, is consistent with other components of *Ebrea,* whose commonness, yet dramatic isolation, underscores the political opposition of Arte Povera to the elitism of the fine arts.

Another part of *Ebrea* is the *Western Wall,* with its iconic construction of old leather suitcases. Referring directly to the Wailing Wall in Jerusalem, the vestiges of Solomon's Temple, this part of *Ebrea* also alludes to the ideals and faith of a people, here symbolized by the remnants of individuals who were uprooted, incinerated, but who remain. Around the wall are placed simulated artifacts of the kind that constituted the economy of the death camps— human by-products: skin, hair, leather, soap—each bearing a label onto which the word "Jewish" is written next to the name of the object in question.

In light of such historical identification and the feeling, as he puts it, of "unconsummated lament," twentieth-century Europe's scourge of anti-Semitism has served as Mauri's paradigm for all kinds of ethnic, religious, and sexual oppression that persist in the world. It was the artist's sense that his country had begun to demonstrate an increasing ambivalence toward history and a will to forget its fascist past that impelled him to create *Ebrea* initially, and to revive it in 1993 in the wake of the civil war and genocide in former Yugoslavia. Beyond the need to reenact the horror of the past, what informs and pervades Mauri's work as a whole is the continuing presence of ethnic intolerance throughout the world and the universally alarming tendency to forget how easily such behavior can become endemic.
M K

REFERENCES
Carboni, "Fabio Mauri"; Codognato, "Fabio Mauri"; Dubow, *Imagining the Unimaginable,* pp. 30–33; Vetrocq, "Minimalia: A Matter of the Mind."

Wallace Berman

(American, 1926–1976)

Untitled, 1972

Stones, wood, paint, Plexiglas,
and screws
9¾ x 13½ x 6½ in. (24.8 x 34.3 x 16.5 cm)

Purchase: Joshua Lowenfish Bequest,
1987-109a-vvv

Within a simple wooden box in Wallace Berman's *Untitled*, an assortment of round stones, some hand-painted with Hebrew letters, rests against a Plexiglas window, settled in what appears to be a random pile. The Hebrew letters inscribed on the stones do not form actual words but call attention to Berman's interest in Jewish mysticism, specifically the kabbalah, a text that itself requires a scholarly and creative deciphering of arcane signs and symbols. Such a remove from linguistic function immediately restores to these letters the source of mystery and contemplation they possess in the kabbalah, in that God is believed to have created the universe by means of the Hebrew alphabet. But the letters' wondrous, inchoate meaning also assumes the ordinariness of objecthood, reflecting Berman's fascination with the shapes of the letters themselves.

Like other members of the Beat movement and the poets of his generation, Berman pursued an interest in the commonplace and a belief in the transformative potential of the everyday, blending a neo-Dadaist/Surrealist sensibility and a spirituality founded in mystical kabbalistic beliefs. Berman personified the Beat Generation, especially its interdisciplinary concerns and its strong association with literature. After moving from New York to California in the early 1950s, he founded *Semina* (seed), a handmade magazine of art and poetry that was also a folio or assemblage scrapbook, which he published and sent to friends. As its editor, Berman exercised little discrimination, concentrating instead

on shaping the context so that each folio issue would possess an overall collage-like aspect. Such an openly interpretive positioning of meaning, to be completed by the observer/reader, was integral to the poetics of neo-Dadaism, which was spelled out in the first *Semina* packet in a poem by Hermann Hesse: "Wherever the seeds of light, the magnificent, falls / Comes change."

In the 1968 film *Easy Rider*, director Dennis Hopper, a collector of Berman's work, gave the artist a bit part, consisting of sowing seeds in the arid soil of a desert commune. A modest homage to this prominent member of the West Coast Beat Generation whose cross-cultural pursuits, in addition to his art, included photography, poetry, music, and film, the role symbolized not only Berman's broad cultural influence but also his distance from the East Coast art establishment. In the 1950s, Berman, along with other California artists such as Bruce Conner, George Herms, and Edward Kienholz, produced his own version of Pop Art, employing a process of accumulation to produce a style that has come to be known as California Assemblage. Citing this historical, albeit peripheral, movement as "completely autonomous, full of rich narrative and the closest development to a true surrealist root in the American vernacular," artist/critic John Coplans went on to credit its distinct character to Berman's influence.

In addition to its more obvious metaphor of dissemination, Berman's incidental movie role of propagation is also symbolic of the repetition and the chance effects that characterize his work. In his collages and assemblages, an almost cinematic recurrence structures the poetic flow of imagery, allowing the varying number of individual units, often loosely organized according to a grid, to interconnect or function independently. Language provides the principal undergirding to the associative potential of the works' poetic images, an unpredictable chemistry whose power is echoed in the random arrangement of Hebrew letters. For Berman, it is the fundamental, inexhaustible assemblage of language—rather than its restrictive codes—that is primary.

MK

REFERENCES

Glicksman, *Wallace Berman Retrospective*; Lipschutz-Villa, *Wallace Berman: Support the Revolution*; Tuchman, *Art in Los Angeles*.

Moshe Kupferman

(Israeli, born Poland, 1926–2003)

Untitled, 1974

Oil on canvas
51 x 62⅛ in. (129.5 x 157.8 cm)
Gift of Mrs. Nitza Etra, 1984-57

Largely self-taught and working on a kibbutz in deliberate isolation, Kupferman pursued a personal vision and a style unaffected by other directions and trends in the art world. He invented an abstract visual language of great subtlety. The color of *Untitled*, as in many other of his paintings, relies upon a palette of purple (for which he is celebrated), green, and gray, in addition to black and white. In this work, the purple suggests a deep mauve to an earthy gray, and the limited number of colors heightens the abstraction of the image. Within a gridlike structure, there is a mechanical reiteration of parallel and intersecting lines in the painting. His expressive gestural lines enhance or negate one another, through what the artist terms "activities." Each activity is a response, and each response results in another; thus, the work is constructed tier by tier. These spiritual landscapes are created through the addition and removal of layers and lines of paint and the interaction between the revealed (overt) and the concealed. The result is a superstructure of painterly activities that the artist has hidden. The final image in *Untitled* appears to fall between a work of severe Minimalism and one of a more aggressive Expressionism.

Kupferman's hidden past figures strongly in his work, although the artist declined to discuss the connection between his European childhood and adolescence and his later life as a kibbutz member in Israel. Born in eastern Poland, Kupferman was raised in a traditional Jewish family. With the outbreak of World War II, his childhood and formal schooling ended abruptly. Escaping the Nazis, his family fled east to the Soviet Union, where they were interned in work camps in Siberia and central Asia. The only surviving member of his family, Kupferman immigrated to Israel in 1949. A year later, he joined other refugees in the western Galilee, founding a kibbutz (Lohamei Ha-Gettaot) where he lived and worked for over forty years. It has been suggested that the lines in his paintings are a metaphor for the kibbutz fields, or perhaps the scaffolding of those houses in whose construction he took part. Others suggest that his grid is an image that recalls the barbed-wire fences that surrounded concentration camps. Attempts to interpret Kupferman's painting are based on the assumption that the reality is one of personal and historical memory and based on associations, both hidden and overt.

S G

REFERENCES
Coffey, *Moshe Kupferman: Between Oblivion and Remembrance*; Harshav, *Moshe Kupferman: The Rift in Time*.

Joshua Neustein

(Israeli, born Germany, 1940)

Weimar Series II, 1981

Paper and acrylic construction
74 x 58³⁄₁₆ in. (188 x 147.8 cm)

Gift of Stanley and Selma Batkin,
1981-241

Art critic Robert Pincus-Witten coined the term "epistemic abstraction" for the art movement that began simultaneously in New York and Jerusalem around 1968. The term refers to art pertaining to the nature of knowledge—hence how a viewer understands basic physical truths. The New York epistemologists Mel Bochner and Dorothea Rockburne are concerned with the visual examination of the Pythagorean theorem and the golden-mean ratio, respectively. Israeli artist Neustein's work concentrates on a comprehension of the fold, the tear, and the cut. In his use of these methods for the manipulation of paper, Neustein makes the viewer retrace the artist's process—imagining a restraightening, realigning, and mending. The beholder is also forced to contemplate what is hidden under and behind the visible surfaces.

Neustein's constructions during the formative years of epistemic abstraction (1968–72) were leaden gray, devoid of color. It was only in 1978, with the beginning of the *Weimar* series, that he began to add color. Named for the failed German republic during which an acid palette and eerie subject matter of late German Expressionism and the New Objectivity (*Neue Schlichkeit*) conveyed artists' frustrations, Neustein's homage to Nolde, Kirschner, Schad, and others is best expressed in his own words, as an "attempt to paint portraits of paintings in their own debris." The adjectives "fragile," "torn," and "impermanent" are frequently used to describe Neustein's constructions and apply as well to the work of other Israeli members of this movement—notably, Pincas Cohen Gan, Benni Efrat, Moshe Gershuni, and Micha Ullman. These Israeli artists opt for destructive physical processes such as tearing, erasing, and scratching, or, as with Efrat, optical negation of the physical surface through light. The contrast between their nihilistic expressions and the constructive and more mathematically analytical techniques of their American counterparts conveys different national concerns. The Israeli artists' vandalization of their own material echoes the country's precarious war-torn plight in the aftermath of the Six Day War and the 1973 war. The contrast between Israel's political manipulation of epistemic abstraction's philosophical tenets and New York's sheltered analytical approach may appear subtle on the surface; nevertheless, their differences—political, philosophical, and aesthetic—cannot be underestimated.

NLK

REFERENCES
Barzel, *Art in Israel*, chap. 4; Kotik, *With Paper, About Paper*, pp. 21–24, 54–55; Pincus-Witten, "The Neustein Papers," pp. 102–15.

George Segal

(American, born 1924)

The Holocaust, 1982

Plaster, wood, and wire
10 x 20 x 20 ft. (3 x 6.1 x 6.1 m)

Purchase: Dorot Foundation gift,
1985-176a-l

Monuments to the Holocaust and art that memorializes its victims have of necessity been approached with caution in the nearly sixty years since those tragic events. Questions about whether this subject should be conceived abstractly or realistically have vied with the quandary about whether it is even fitting to attempt a tangible monument to these victims. Many of these works have proved provocative; others have been hotly debated. When it was first installed, George Segal's *The Holocaust* sparked impassioned discussions over what some called its hyperrealistic representation of Holocaust victims. However, the work—despite its unusual combination of visual challenge and emotional pathos—has quickly evolved into an icon.

Determined to establish such a memorial, the city of San Francisco organized a competition for the commission in 1981. Segal was asked to submit an entry, and he used his hallmark technique of casting living persons directly in plaster for the original model. His proposal was selected as the winning entry and was installed in 1984. Cast in bronze with white patination, it is now prominently sited in Lincoln Park, near San Francisco's Palace of Legion of Honor. The original plaster models constitute the work in The Jewish Museum's collection.

In his haunting representational manner, creating plaster casts of actual individuals and using real props, Segal has condensed many of the horrific images of the devastation into one. A pile of corpses lies behind an actual barbed-wire fence; the figure of a solitary survivor stands mute in the foreground, clutching the sharp metal. As sources, Segal used infamous images taken shortly after the Allied liberation of the camps by such venerable photographers as Margaret Bourke-White and Lee Miller. Similar photographs of disordered mounds of cadavers had already served Picasso for his well-known painting *The Charnel House* (1944–45). Segal reacted strongly to the obscene disarray of bodies that he was forced to confront in these visual documents. He was shocked by the notorious disregard for the usual sacred rituals of death.

As noted by Sam Hunter, Segal purposely organized the composition to neutralize chaos and inject human meaning into this sculptural transposition from journalistic photography. The indistinct modeling of the ten bodies and the presence of a lone survivor relieve the harrowing reality, permitting the viewer enough remove to engage in Segal's tragic poetry.

The ordered composition functions on a number of levels relating to artistic and literary sources, to Segal's personal iconography, and to his earlier works. The stack of corpses is a realization of Segal's earlier concept for the FDR Memorial (which opened in Washington, D.C., in 1997), the discomforting motif that he had also considered for *The Execution* of 1967. The star-shaped arrangement of the bodies in *The Holocaust* includes the figure of a woman holding a half-eaten apple, an allusion to Eve; a figure with outstretched arms, symbolic of Jesus and suffering; and an older man lying near a young boy, referring to Segal's earlier, controversial *Abraham and Isaac* (1978), which he originally created to memorialize the students killed at Kent State University in Vietnam War protests in 1970. The man poised by the fence is based on a Bourke-White photograph and was modeled from a friend of Segal's, an Israeli survivor of the camps. This living presence emphasizes hope and survival. The figure's physical isolation and psychic pain—exaggerated by an unconscious clutching at the sharp edge of the actual barbed wire—are perhaps best described in words of another survivor and eloquent witness of these atrocities, Elie Wiesel: "How can one repress the memory of indifference one had felt toward the corpses? Will you ever know what it is like to wake up under a frozen sky, on a journey toward the unknown, and record without surprise that the man in front of you is dead, as is the one before him and the one behind you? Suddenly a thought crosses one's mind: What if I too am already dead and do not know it?"
NLK

REFERENCES
Baigell, "Segal's Holocaust Memorial"; Hunter and Hawthorne, *George Segal*, pp. 132–34; Livingstone, *George Segal Retrospective*; Tuchman, *George Segal*, pp. 58–107; Wiesel, *A Jew Today*, p. 188; Young, *The Art of Memory*.

James Casebere

(American, born 1953)

Venice Ghetto, 1991

Gelatin-silver print
37½ x 25⅛ in. (95.3 x 63.8 cm)

Purchase: Max Rees Shulman Fund,
Eileen and Michael Cohen Fund, and
the Morris Fox Bequest, 1993-102

James Casebere builds and then photographs architectural models, transforming them into large-scale two-dimensional images. His table-sized models, created from simple materials such as foam core, cardboard, and plaster, are often based on the artist's studies of actual buildings, such as prisons, Old West corrals, and suburban homes. Eschewing color and detail in favor of dramatic lighting and a low camera angle that distorts the scale of the buildings, Casebere examines cultural structures through architectural models that enact both fiction and reality.

In the photograph *Venice Ghetto*, stark white tenement buildings draped with clotheslines stand out from a black sky and the dark waters of the Venetian canals at night. Lights in only a few of the windows and two small boats docked against the buildings emphasize the emptiness of the nighttime scene. While the scene of Venice's stone buildings and canals may evoke nostalgia for the charm of Old Europe, the photograph's title alludes to the city's darker past. The Venice ghetto was established in 1516, when a Jewish settlement was set aside, shutting its occupants off from the rest of the city. Although no longer a restricted area, the Venice ghetto evokes historical Jewish subjugation and is a reminder of the Venetian origin of the word "ghetto." In Casebere's photograph, the eerie shadows enveloping the buildings hint at this area's somber history.

Casebere's architectural models serve as frameworks for cultural representations. His fictional spaces, structured by societal paradigms of living and working, most often allude to a conformity of living mandated by the standardization of built environments. His subjects of prisons, ghettos, interior courtyards, hospitals, tenements, and tunnels are places of confinement and control. Casebere's prison series stems from French philosopher Michel Foucault's ideas on the Panopticon system of control through surveillance. In this system, the architecture of the prison allows a prison guard to observe, and therefore wield power, from an all-seeing vantage point. Making connections to a seemingly unrelated structure, Casebere's suburban backyards similarly appear as places of regulation, uniformity, and restriction. In other words, Casebere positions architecture as society's means of imposing order through physical systems of control. Yet it is not just his subject that is one

of control; it is his working method as well. By miniaturizing his subject in meticulously built models, the artist imposes control over reality through its diminutive scale, reconstruction, and eventual representation. Casebere's models, which are often based on photographs of buildings, are several times removed from their archetype, and the photographs themselves, which carry with them the false imprimatur of reality, are carefully constructed fictions.

Scenes in Casebere's more recent work appear more realistic through sophisticated models and the use of subtle color, but his black-and-white photographs of the 1980s and early 1990s, including *Venice Ghetto*, have a self-consciously fabricated appearance. The initial perception of the image's reality dissolves upon closer inspection of the monolithic surfaces of the buildings, boats, and clothes hung out to dry. Yet the constant play between fiction and truth produces something mysterious in the scene. Devoid of human occupants, the photographed tableau appears as a deserted stage set, film still, or a moment of stopped time, leaving the viewer to contemplate a possible narrative that the scene might suggest. In Casebere's world, a diminutive, fictional architecture becomes an overwhelming presence where shadowy emptiness suggests isolation within the social sphere.
K L

REFERENCES
Berger and Grundberg, *James Casebere*; Galassi, *Pleasures and Terrors of Domestic Comfort*; Köhler, *Constructed Realities*; Vidler, *The Architectural Unconscious*; Vidler, Chang, and Eugenides, *James Casebere*.

Shimon Attie

(American, born 1957)

Joachim-Ecke Auguststrasse: Slide Projection of Former Jewish Resident, Berlin, 1991, 1991

Chromogenic color print
20 x 24 in. (50.8 x 61 cm)

Gift of David Kluger, by exchange, 1993-174

Like many of the more provocative artists of the last two decades, Los Angeles–born Shimon Attie works in a range of disciplines and media. Archivist, historian, political scientist, and pedagogue are but some of the roles he fills—all crucial to the themes explored and meanings produced in his ambitious projects. Aesthetically rich, Attie's art embodies a well-orchestrated amalgam of conceptual thinking and sculptural handling in which he collapses performance with site specificity, photography with light projection. His synthetic work can be linked to the playful "curatorial" interventions of the 1960s Belgian conceptualist Marcel Broodthaers and to the politically engaged institutional critique of his African-American contemporary Fred Wilson.

Attie also is an artist-anthropologist, a practitioner who digs into historical archives and then reconfigures his nonartistic material into prodigious works of public sculpture. His well-known projections are at once ephemeral and monumental. Yet the photographs that Attie creates to record these intensively staged projections go well beyond their original documentary purposes. Brilliantly colored, perfectly composed, and dramatically lit, they are beautifully crafted objects that play out in a more intimate scale the artist's investigation of the fragile negotiations between history and memory.

Berlin was the stage for Attie's breakthrough work of 1991–93, *The Writing on the Wall,* which emerged from his reaction to Germany's resuscitated capital. In the early wake of the unification of the bustling and formerly bifurcated city, a dark, brooding, and broken Berlin made a striking contrast with Attie's dizzying trajectory of pasts, both remembered and buried. As an American Jew, Attie became particularly interested in Berlin's Jewish past, but not in the Jewish past of its politically, socially, or economically prominent citizens. Those legendary heroes and heroines, with names like Mendelssohn, Benjamin, and Rathenau, had already become a cherished part of Berlin's and Germany's official history.

Instead, *The Writing on the Wall* concentrated on images of working-class Jewish life in Berlin's Scheunenviertel, the old ethnic neighborhood where the city's immigrant Eastern European Jews lived from the nineteenth century until World War II. Here Attie projected large-scale images of modest black-and-white historical photographs onto the dark and deteriorated architecture that surrounded the settings where domestic, religious, and entrepreneurial life once thrived. One of the best-known pieces in the series—perhaps the most formally sophisticated and politically loaded—is *Joachim-Ecke Auguststrasse,* a view of old Berlin apartment buildings in which we see, projected onto a bricked-over window, a Star of David that appears above the head of a praying man. This work shows how knowingly Attie transforms the images of his projections into photographs. Attie's worm's-eye view artificially creates crosslike forms from the transoms and mullions in the windows of the splay of looming buildings on the right. The subtle implication of the Christian religious symbol thus evokes the age-old conflict between the socially dominant Christian culture and a Jewish microcosm, while playing off a fleeting projection of memory and an enduring architectural reality.

NLK

REFERENCES
Attie, *Sites Unseen*; Kleeblatt, "Persistence of Memory"; Young, *At Memory's Edge,* pp. 62–89.

Eleanor Antin

(American, born 1935)

Vilna Nights, 1993–97

Mixed media installation

Gift through the Estate of Francis A. Jennings in memory of his wife, Gertrude Feder Jennings, and an anonymous donor, 1997-130

Infused with a deep sense of loss and sadness, Eleanor Antin's *Vilna Nights* creates an environment of a place and a time that are long lost. Commissioned by The Jewish Museum for the 1993 *From the Inside Out: Eight Contemporary Artists* exhibition to inaugurate the museum's new exhibition space, the mixed media installation appears as a ruined shtetl with a bombed-out courtyard. Through a demolished wall, the viewer can peer in on three vignettes of life-size projections onto windows.

Each of the vignettes is a fragment of shtetl life in a private interior. One scene depicts a woman sitting by a furnace and weeping, the fire illuminating her face. She reads from a bundle of letters tied in a ribbon. As she reads each letter, possibly from a dead or lost lover, she becomes increasingly distressed until she throws the letters, one by one, into the furnace to be burned. In another window, the viewer peeks in on an old Jewish tailor working by candlelight at his sewing machine. A sadness pervades the scene as the old man sews articles of clothing and then carefully folds them. This melancholy reaches its height as the tailor finds a yarmulke that prompts him to begin crying, and then the candlelight flickers out. The third scene captures a young boy and girl, presumably brother and sister, appearing cold and hungry as they share a small piece of bread. Magically, a lit menorah appears in midair, and following it chairs and a table set with food and drink. The youngsters are ecstatic as they sit down to enjoy this unexpected meal. However, just as they are about to begin eating, the magical objects disappear, one by one, leaving the children alone and hungry as they first began.

Recalling Antin's 1991 feature-length film *The Man Without a World*, this mixed media installation allows the viewer a glimpse of a vanished world and life that no longer exist. Vilna, the capital of Lithuania, was the major European center of Jewish culture and learning and home to the largest Eastern Europe Jewish population in the eighteenth and nineteenth centuries. However, the Holocaust exterminated that Jewish population and life; this fact, while never directly named, suffuses the entire installation. Each of the three filmic vignettes recalls Yiddish cinema and the fantastical qualities of early film and film editing, again underscoring the fact that this genre abruptly stopped thriving at the onset of the Holocaust. The theme of a fire or flame

that is extinguished and its association with sorrow in each of the narratives mirror the life and culture in Vilna that were extinguished.

Along with the architecture and images in *Vilna Nights*, a soundtrack of shtetl life saturates the environment. One can hear the wind howling, a train passing by, a dog barking, and church bells ringing. The sound begins at a low level and increases throughout the soundtrack, adding drama to the scenes in each window. The combination of the architecture, the images, and the ambient noise creates a nearly realistic environment, underscoring that this world is no longer a reality. The installation emphasizes constructed experience of memory, especially the memory of events that one has not personally witnessed, leaving visitors with the sense that they are merely voyeurs into these private, lost, fabricated lives.

J L

REFERENCES

Antin and Sayre, *Ghosts*; Fox, *Eleanor Antin*; Goodman, *From the Inside Out*.

Nancy Spero

(American, born 1926)

Masha Bruskina, 1995

Acrylic on linen
122¼ x 146½ in. (310.5 x 372.1 cm)

Purchase: Fine Arts Acquisitions
Committee Fund, Blanche and Romie
Shapiro Fund, Kristie A. Jayne Fund,
Sara Schlesinger Bequest,
and Miki Denhof Bequest, 2002-12a-c

Nancy Spero played an integral role in the feminist art movement of the late 1960s and early 1970s, joining a group called Women Artists in Revolution and developing manifestos and staging protests that demanded inclusion of women in museums and galleries. In 1972, along with five other artists, she created AIR (Artists In Residence, Inc.), the first women's gallery in New York, which paved the way for the recognition of female artists today.

Spero's art addresses how women are represented and often overlooked in history and in the art world. This painting is about Masha Bruskina, a volunteer nurse and leader of the Minsk resistance movement, who is a frequent subject of Spero's work. As the text printed on the canvas explains, Bruskina was a seventeen-year-old Communist partisan who, under the guise of a Gentile, helped wounded Soviet prisoners escape. She was eventually arrested by the German authorities; imprisoned and tortured, she never surrendered the names of other members of her group. She was publicly hanged in 1941, and the Nazis meticulously documented her execution. Many years later, scholarly research revealed her name and Jewish identity, but because of antisemitic sentiment, her Jewishness is still disputed in her home country of Belarus.

Enticing the viewer to decipher the words and digest the images taken from many decades and sources simultaneously, Spero intersperses and overlaps image and text from Masha Bruskina's story. In the background, she prints images of Bruskina's march through the streets to her death and of her execution. The layers of text begin with a newspaper from October 26, 1941, describing the hanging of an anonymous girl by the Gestapo and seamlessly flow into a segment of an article from twenty-five years later, revealing the discovery of this victim's Jewish identity. Spero adds a faint red scrawl to the top of the canvas that refers to Bill Keller, a *New York Times* reporter who covered the Soviet Union during the cold war, alluding to the way we process the many layers of information delivered by the media.

The three-part, monumental, unstretched canvas with frayed edges is attached to the wall by pushpins. Spero's use of ragged and quotidian materials makes the painting look more like a political banner or wall drawing than a precious, framed icon, and exemplifies the nonelitist principles that pervade the artist's work.

J G

REFERENCES
Bird, Isaak, and Lotringer, *Nancy Spero*; Broude and Gerrard, *The Power of Feminist Art*; Ulmer Museum, *Nancy Spero: Woman Breathing*.

ECHO OF '41

WAS THE PARTISAN A JEW?

MINSK, U.S.S.R.

Oct. 26, 1941: Impassive SS men lead a teen-age girl, a boy and a man through the streets of Minsk and hang them side by side at the gates of a yeast factory...

...the girl remains officially, resolutely "nyeizvestnaya"— "unknown."

But a trove of evidence...

backed by the testimony of survivors... supports the claim that the girl is MASHA BRUSKINA, a Jew Minsk ghetto who was active in the Partisan resistance.

The girl in the photograph is widely believed to have been the first person publicly executed during the Nazi occupation of

the Nazi occupation of Soviet territory. The two companions hanged alongside her— Kirill Trus and Volodya Shcherbatsevich. Partisans of Byelorussian stock—were identified... and posthumously from the decorated... During the occupation witnesses recounted, Masha Bruskina smuggled civilian clothes and false documents to escaping Soviet officers (prisoners). She was in league with Partisan groups...

She lightened her hair and used her mother's name which was not distinctively Jewish. She reportedly refused to inform under torture, and walked to her execution with her head erect. She was 17 years old.

Sol LeWitt

(American, born 1928)

Wall Drawing #926 Loopy (yellow and purple), 1999

Acrylic paint
102½ in. wide (260.4 cm)

Gift of an anonymous donor, 2000-28

Wall Drawing #927 Loopy (green and blue), 1999

Acrylic paint
176½ x 133 in. (484.4 x 337.8 cm)

Gift of an anonymous donor, 2000-29

Born in Hartford to Russian Jewish immigrant parents, Sol LeWitt pioneered the Conceptual Art movement at a time when art was reacting against the subjectiveness of 1950s Abstract Expressionism. LeWitt's objective methodology employs grids, serials, and sets of instructions, enabling one idea to generate multiple works. His typical strategy—finding and representing all combinations of a particular set of simple elements, such as lines, colors, or three-dimensional forms—creates finite series, the number of permutations predetermined by a preset number. By declaring the rules by which an image is created, LeWitt makes the image itself somewhat redundant, or even negligible.

To LeWitt, who seldom veers from these self-imposed rules, the most important principle is that the idea is central and the execution is secondary. While the idea itself, simple and logical, often ends up being perceptually illogical, perception is subjective and the artist is unable to perceive the work until it is complete. To eliminate what LeWitt calls "caprice, taste, and other whimsies," the idea must be predetermined. Having worked for I. M. Pei, LeWitt takes inspiration from the architectural process. Drawn first by him on paper, wall drawings are later executed by a team of studio assistants. As in architecture, the artist is separated from the actual construction of the art.

Breaking with the tradition of putting paint to canvas and canvas to wall, wall drawings, more than nine hundred of which exist today, are considered LeWitt's most innovative artistic achievement. His early wall drawings, first done in 1968, were simply transferred from drawings on paper, having no relationship to their environment. A major turning point occurred in 1970, when LeWitt created his first site-specific wall drawing. In the 1990s, LeWitt began using acrylics, a traditional painting medium that radically changed the aesthetic of the wall drawings. His exuberant designs of the 1990s feature intense hues, geometric arcs, and waves that push the boundaries of their architectural confines. The vibrancy of these works allows the wall drawings to stand up to their architectural surroundings, while LeWitt's most recent wall drawings engage their surroundings, using architectural elements as foils or as integral components. Throughout their development, LeWitt's wall drawings have retained their internal logic and serial sensibility while increasingly playing with geometry, sensuality, and color.

In 1999, LeWitt designed these two wall drawings for two bays of the west wall of The Jewish Museum's second-floor galleries, a space that still retains architectural details of the French Gothic-style Warburg mansion, which houses the museum. One wall drawing has a yellow background with purple arabesques. The other exhibits a complementary color scheme of a green background with blue. LeWitt chose the site for this wall drawing, a decision befitting his recent interest in installing his abstract, decidedly modernist designs in spaces with historical references, a radical departure from his earlier, gridlike works that were meant to be installed in the "white cube" spaces of galleries and museums. The idea remains central to LeWitt's work, as do strategies that refute the primacy of the artist and the notion of permanence in art.
LF

REFERENCES
Garrels, *Sol LeWitt*; LeWitt, "Paragraphs on Conceptual Art"; Miller-Keller, *Sol LeWitt*; Singer, *Sol LeWitt*; Wadsworth Atheneum Museum, *Noncomposition*.

Christian Boltanski

(French, born 1944)

Monument (Odessa),
1989–2003

Six gelatin-silver prints, three tin
biscuit boxes, lights, wire
Installation approximately 80 x 72 in.
(203.2 x 182.9 cm)

Purchase: Melva Bucksbaum
Contemporary Art Fund, 2003-11

Christian Boltanski's *Monuments* series explores the themes of loss and death perceived through the prism of memory. These installations memorialize unknown persons at the same time that they raise questions about the veracity of the photographic medium. Using appropriated images and mundane objects, Boltanski follows the tradition initiated in Paris in 1913 by the iconoclast Marcel Duchamp, who abandoned the conventional tools of art by using a bicycle wheel for his first ready-made sculpture. Challenges to orthodox media and exhibition venues continued in the 1960s with the international Fluxus group, which sponsored mail art, concerts with audience participation, and improvised performances by Joseph Beuys and others. Breaking down the barrier between life and art culminated with Andy Warhol, the Pop Art master who transformed journalistic photographs of movie stars as well as anonymous accident victims into cool but dazzling silk screens. Boltanski situates his practice between the irony of Pop Art and Fluxus and the pathos that Beuys reinscribed into his manipulated found objects.

In 1985, Boltanski began his *Monuments* installations, currently grouped under the title *Lessons of Darkness*, focusing on vernacular photographs of children as the means to convey the transience of life and awaken a collective consciousness of the dead. Here, childhood assumes a *vanitas* role, representing temporality and an irrevocable loss reclaimed only by memory. Characteristically shown in semidarkness in museums and churches, these poignant works effect a haunting atmosphere and quasi-religious tone with their altarlike design and incandescent lightbulbs substituting for votive candles. Although the subjects are anonymous, the children in *Monument (Odessa)* have all been identified from a group snapshot as Jewish students celebrating Purim in France in 1939. The artist customarily reshot and manipulated the original photograph with croppings, facial enlargements, and dramatic variations in shading to create a less personal, iconic image. Knowing the religion of these children and the year in which they were photographed inevitably links them to the Holocaust and evokes thoughts about their unknown fate. Now the lights illuminating their images beg another interpretation, namely, *Yahrzeit* candles, to honor and remember the dead. The empty, rusted tin biscuit boxes, a fixture in Boltanski's works, hold more than childhood treasures and memories—they hold unwritten histories of unrealized lives.

Born in Paris, of Catholic and Jewish heritage—*Odessa* refers to his grandfather's place of origin—the artist has said, "My work is about the fact of dying, but it's not about the Holocaust itself." However, for Boltanski, having grown up in postwar France with the knowledge of his father hiding in fear during the occupation, the reality of genocide was never far nor forgotten. Certainly, the six children in Boltanski's altar offer a silent elegy for the six million they suggest.

IZS

REFERENCES

Gumpert, *Christian Boltanski*; Gumpert and Jacob, *Christian Boltanski: Lessons of Darkness*; Marmer, "Boltanski: The Uses of Contradiction," pp. 169–81, 233–35; Semin, Garb, and Kuspit, *Christian Boltanski*; Solomon-Godeau, "Mourning or Melancholia."

Israel and the Television Documentary: Voices and Images of Conflict

Modern Israel and television developed concurrently in separate and distinct contexts but have a surprising common history. Both emerged after World War II as means for radical change: one as a national movement demanding the right for its people to return home; the other as an electronic revolution that disseminated information, ideas, commerce, and entertainment with unprecedented speed and scope. In the past fifty years, television has shaped varied portrayals of Israel, positive and negative: a vulnerable democracy; a military powerhouse; deserts and swamps transformed into an agricultural paradise; a high-tech, industrialized nation; and religious fanaticism and secular cosmopolitanism. But above all, the dominant image of Israel is a land in conflict with its Arab residents and neighbors.

Originally aired in 1984 and rebroadcast in 2001, the nine-hour series *Heritage: Civilization and the Jews* qualifies as a public television "event" for its ambitious and unparalleled research, scope, and expense. *Heritage* presented a sweeping survey of Jewish history from biblical times to the late twentieth century, using interviews, archival photographs and film, extensive original footage, and art—including works from The Jewish Museum's collection.

Produced by WNET/ Thirteen, *Heritage* reached an audience of fifty-one million and garnered Emmy and Peabody Awards for generating public discussion about Israel, the Diaspora, and the resonance of Judaism in world culture.

"Into the Future," the final episode of *Heritage*, includes an overview of Israeli history from independence in 1948 through the late twentieth century: the ingathering of Holocaust survivors and other immigrants, the ethnic diversity of its citizens, the kibbutz movement, and the struggle for peace. *Heritage* notes that the future of Israel is bound to its conflict with the Palestinians, a divisive and controversial subject that consumes Jews and non-Jews around the world. Additionally, *Heritage* acknowledges that for the first time in millennia, Jews—once powerless—are coming to terms with the exercise of state power and the limitations of military force.

The television documentary series, a genre revived by *Heritage*, has its roots in *See It Now* (1951–58), produced by Fred W. Friendly and the esteemed journalist Edward R. Murrow. *See It Now* devoted several reports to the Middle East conflict in the decade following Israel's independence. In an effort to provide a balanced presentation of the Middle East conflict, the

Edward R. Murrow
interviewing Prime Minister
David Ben-Gurion in Israel
for *See It Now*, 1956.

See It Now broadcast "Jerusalem: Both Cities" of 1953 features interviews with two opposing border guards in the Old City, one representing the Arab Legion Army and the other from the Israeli Defense Forces. *See It Now* humanizes the conflict by documenting the homes and families of these two Jerusalem natives. In 1956, *See It Now* returned to the Middle East for the broadcast "Egypt-Israel." Over a period of several weeks, Murrow and his colleague Howard K. Smith met with citizens and political leaders in cities and rural communities. Again, using a comparative approach, the "Egypt-Israel" broadcast selects subjects such as government, the military, agriculture, land settlement, and the arts for perspectives on two cultures and two countries.

In the Emmy Award–winning *Promises* (2001), filmmakers B. Z. Goldberg, Justine Shapiro, and Carlos Bolado emulate Murrow's courageous spirit and desire to offer the diverse opinions of Israelis and Arabs. But *Promises* diverges from previous documentaries in its highly personal approach. Shot between 1997 and 2000 (a period of relative calm), the film follows the journey of B. Z. Goldberg, an Israeli-American journalist, and seven Israeli and Palestinian children between the ages of nine and thirteen. Daniel and Yarko, secular Israeli twins, agree to meet some Palestinian children living in the Deheishe Refugee Camp. Warming up to one another quickly, the children share a meal, play soccer, and dance. They also wrestle seriously with discussion topics such as checkpoints, terrorism, the peace process, and

human rights. At the end of the visit, Faraj, a handsome Palestinian boy with a broad smile, starts to cry: "This afternoon I started thinking that B. Z. will leave soon. And now we've become friends with Daniel and Yarko. And they will forget our friendship as soon as B. Z. leaves. And all our effort will be in vain." Faraj's prediction about his relationship with the twins was regrettably true. But the meeting at Deheishe was not entirely in vain. *Promises* renewed hope in the Middle East peace process during its airing on the PBS documentary series *P.O.V.*

Robert Gardner, the internationally renowned ethnographic filmmaker, also aspires to a nonpartisan approach in *Arab and Jew: Wounded Spirits in a Promised Land* (1989/2002), a film based on David K. Shipler's Pulitzer Prize–winning book. Gardner and Shipler (who served as principal writer, executive producer, and narrator) devote the latter half of the film to education and children. They include interviews with Interns for Peace, a thirteen-year-old Jewish poet grappling with the murder of other young settlers in the West Bank, and angry Palestinian youths who describe their motivation to participate in the Intifada.

A I

REFERENCES
Curtin, *Redeeming the Wasteland*; Wolfsfeld, *Media and Political Conflict.*

left: Abba Eban, narrator of *Heritage: Civilization and the Jews*, at the Western Wall in Jerusalem.

above: Two boys talking in the Deheishe Refugee Camp in the documentary *Promises*.

"Are You Now or Have You Ever Been . . .": The Blacklist

See It Now, "Challenge to Senator Joseph McCarthy," March 9, 1954, CBS, T1090

See It Now, "Senator McCarthy's Answer," April 6, 1954, CBS, T1091

The Defenders, "Blacklist," January 18, 1964, CBS, T1179

Television played an important role in covering and influencing the events collectively known as McCarthyism, which implicated many American Jews in its maniacal drive to identify Communist sympathizers. The National Jewish Archive of Broadcasting's holdings include historic *See It Now* coverage of the events as well as a fascinating drama program that aired ten years later.

See It Now (1951–58) is regarded as one of the most courageous news/documentary series in broadcast history. Host Edward R. Murrow and producer Fred W. Friendly helped to define television's ideal role in news coverage and analysis. Unlike other news programs that used newsreel companies to record events, *See It Now* maintained its own camera crews to coordinate filming on location, using 35 mm cameras to record the most striking images. Murrow and Friendly also deviated from standard practice by mandating that interviews not be rehearsed and that no background music accompany the visuals.

After broadcasting several reports related to the Communist "witch hunt" in the United States, *See It Now* exposed the architect of the paranoia himself in "Challenge to Senator Joseph McCarthy." Interspersing footage of McCarthy and his supporters with comments and questions, Murrow refuted Senator McCarthy's half-truths and accusations. In his dramatic concluding remarks, he urged the American people to act: "We will not walk in fear. . . . This is no time for men who oppose Senator McCarthy's methods to keep silent, or for those who approve."

Toward the beginning of the program, Murrow offered the senator the opportunity to respond. McCarthy did so, in a prerecorded film segment that aired a month later. In this episode, "Senator McCarthy's Answer," McCarthy delineated his version of history and in particular the Communist threat, using maps and charts. He also launched attacks on Murrow and his beliefs.

McCarthy's bullying behavior and remarks (including a reference to Murrow as "the leader and cleverest of the jackal pack") shifted public opinion and contributed to the downfall of the senator's career.

The Defenders (1961–65) was one of the most socially conscious and politically liberal shows in television history. E. G. Marshall and Robert Reed starred as Lawrence and Kenneth Preston, a father-and-son team of defense attorneys. In the "Blacklist" episode, Jack Klugman plays a blacklisted actor who finally receives a serious role after ten years, only to be harassed by vehement anti-Communists.

Interestingly, Klugman's character remained steadfast in his belief that he did no wrong by joining certain organizations, such as anti-Franco committees during the Spanish Civil War, which were later accused of being Communist fronts. The episode exposed the paranoia of the local anti-Communist crusader. "It's poison," he said of Communism, "and it spreads by contagion. There are only two sides—you're either for them or against them." In Klugman's speech to his son, he alluded to the "culture of fear" that allows such paranoia to grow and fester. Scriptwriter Ernest Kinoy and actor Klugman both won Emmy Awards for this episode.
AW

REFERENCES
Hoberman and Shandler, *Entertaining America*, pp. 67–70; MacDonald, *Television and the Red Menace*.

left: Senator Joseph McCarthy and chief counsel Roy Cohn conducting anti-Communist hearings, as seen on *See It Now*.

right: Robert Reed and E. G. Marshall in *The Defenders*.

The Eichmann Trial

The Trial of Adolf Eichmann, videotape footage, 1961, Capital Cities Broadcasting Corporation, E1-178

NBC News Special Report, "The Trial of Adolf Eichmann," April 23, 1961, NBC, T28

Verdict for Tomorrow, 1961, Capital Cities Broadcasting Corporation, ABC, T382

Witnesses to the Holocaust: The Trial of Adolf Eichmann, December 2, 1987, T848

The Jewish Museum's National Jewish Archive of Broadcasting is one of three repositories of the extant videotaped record of the trial of SS Officer Adolf Eichmann (the other two are the Steven Spielberg Jewish Film Archive at the Hebrew University of Jerusalem and the United States Holocaust Memorial Museum in Washington, D.C.). Eichmann was tried in the Jerusalem District Court from April to December 1961 and found guilty of all crimes charged: crimes against the Jewish people; crimes against humanity; war crimes; and membership in a criminal organization, as established by a judgment of the International Military Tribunal at Nuremberg. For these crimes, Eichmann was sentenced to death.

The videotaped record of the Eichmann trial was produced as a nonprofit venture for the State of Israel by the Capital Cities Broadcasting Corporation. (Approximately a third of the trial no longer exists on video.) Twice daily, proceedings of the trial were viewed by network reporters in Jerusalem, who distilled what they saw as the most important moments into half-hour or one-hour segments. In this pre-satellite age, the videotapes were usually driven from Jerusalem to Israel's Lod airport, then flown to various American and European destinations. In most cases, these tapes aired on American television one day after the proceedings in Jerusalem.

The broadcast of the Eichmann trial is historic for several reasons. According to Jeffrey Shandler, "Scholars and critics have long recognized the Eichmann case as a threshold event in America's Holocaust memory culture in the United States; they often identify the trial as marking the end of a period of 'silence' on the subject. . . . These broad-casts constitute a major landmark in the chronicle of American Holocaust television. It was the first time that the Holocaust received extended television coverage, in the form of news reports, public affairs programs, documentaries, and dramas aired over a period of months. The Eichmann case provided the first opportunity for television networks to deal with the Holocaust in the context of reporting a major news story. In fact, American television audiences are most likely to have first heard the word *Holocaust* used to describe the Nazi persecution of European Jewry during broadcasts of the trial."

At the time of the trial, NBC News aired a special report, "The Trial of Adolf Eichmann," in which Frank McGee discussed the educational role of the trial with Bergen-Belsen survivor Josef Rosensaft, as well as with the head of a kibbutz founded by Holocaust survivors and with German, Japanese, and British journalists. In *Verdict for Tomorrow*, which also aired in 1961, Lowell Thomas narrated a documentary account of the Eichmann trial, which included excerpts from the videotaped trial in Jerusalem and archival footage.

In March–May 1986, The Jewish Museum presented an exhibition entitled *Justice in Jerusalem: The Eichmann Trial Twenty-Five Years Later*, which featured continuous screenings of the Eichmann trial sessions, as well as a series of public programs. The museum also coproduced a one-hour documentary, narrated by Joel Grey, *Witnesses to the Holocaust: The Trial of Adolf Eichmann*, in 1987.
AW

REFERENCES
Hausner, *Justice in Jerusalem*; Shandler, *While America Watches*, pp. 81–83.

left: Adolf Eichmann during his trial in Jerusalem.

right: Producers and technicians watching the proceedings of the Eichmann trial.

Spirituality and Faith

Spirituality and Faith

The museum's collection is rich in items relating to Jewish religious practices and faith. In the twentieth century, the assimilation of many Jewish people into cultures throughout the world resulted in the decline of observant Judaism and the attendant need for traditional ceremonial or sacred objects. Religious ceremonial objects became irrelevant to many people. Synagogues fell into disuse or disrepair. And assimilated Jews, seeing themselves as part of mainstream society, drifted away from Jewish religious and cultural education. The museum's mandate to preserve religious artifacts and document their cultural, art historical, aesthetic, and theological significance dates back to its founding a century ago—an imperative that has resulted in a collection of Judaica that is unparalleled in the United States.

Many of the museum's holdings were created for use in Jewish religious rites, such as on the Sabbath and the festivals of the Jewish year. Two silver spice containers—one by Zelig Segal (1986), a fine example of Bezalel Academy metalwork, the other from Germany (c. 1550) —attest to the historical continuity of the tradition of havdalah, the ceremony that marks the conclusion of the Sabbath and holy days. Ludwig Yehuda Wolpert's sleek *Passover Set* (1930) of silver, ebony, and glass and Amy Klein Reichert's hammered silver *Miriam's Cup* (1997) are ceremonial objects for the seder table, artifacts from two distinct stylistic sensibilities: the Bauhaus and contemporary Judaica.

A range of Hanukkah lamps from various periods and countries—Frankfurt (1706–32), northern Morocco (late nineteenth–early twentieth century), Poland (1787), and a contemporary piece by the American artist Joel Otterson (*Unorthodox Menorah II*, 1993)—testifies to the dissemination of Jewish religious practices throughout the world. Other works speak to religious rituals in everyday life—from mezuzahs (mezuzah cover of Mess'ud el-Carif, Morocco, twentieth century, and Harley Swedler, *Beron Mezuzah*, 1991) to items associated with the various stages of the life cycle (marriage canopy, Ottoman Empire, 1867–68; three burial plaques, Venosa and Rome, third–fifth century; and a casket with zodiac signs and other motifs, Germany, fifteenth–sixteenth century).

The Jewish reverence for the Torah—the first five books of the Hebrew Bible—has inspired the creation of many beautiful objects designed to adorn it, safeguard its sanctity, and protect it from damage. The collection contains a broad range of Torah-related articles: mantles and arks (Torah ark, Urbino, c. 1500; Torah ark from Adath Yeshurun Synagogue, Sioux City, Iowa, 1899), finials (finials for the Torah case, Cochin, India, eighteenth–ninteenth century; Heinrich Wilhelm Kompff, Torah finials, Kassel, 1797–99; Moshe Zabari, Torah crown, New York, 1969), cloth binders (Rikah Polacco, Torah binder, Florence, 1662–63), and curtains (curtain for the Torah ark, Venice, 1680–81; curtain and valance for the Torah ark, 1772–73; and Adolph Gottlieb, Torah curtain, 1950–51).

The collection also includes important paintings and sculptures that celebrate Jewish religious ritual, ceremony, and faith. Solomon Alexander Hart, the first Jewish member of the British Royal Academy, captures the exotic dress of the nineteenth-century Sephardic congregants and the ornate decoration of the interior of an eighteenth-century Italian synagogue in *The Feast of Rejoicing of the Law at the Synagogue in Leghorn, Italy* (1850). *Sabbath* (1919), one of Max Weber's earliest religious paintings, melds the modernist visual vocabulary of Cubism with traditional Jewish subject matter. The Austrian painter Isidor Kaufmann, in *Friday Evening* (c. 1920), depicts an Orthodox, upper-middle-class housewife initiating the Sabbath with the lighting of the candles. Jacques Lipchitz's bronze sculpture, *The Sacrifice* (1949–57), is both a Cubist representation of the slaughtering of the sacrificial lamb and an allegory about the peaceful coexistence between Christians and Jews at the time of Israel's founding. Leonard Baskin's *The Altar* (1977), one of the sculptor's most important carvings in wood, represents a modernist interpretation of the biblical tale of Abraham's attempt to sacrifice Isaac.

M B

Three Burial Plaques

Left: Venosa (?), 4th–5th century

Marble: incised
9½ x 11 x 1 in. (24.1 x 27.9 x 2.54 cm)

Gift of Samuel Friedenberg, JM 3-50

Inscription: *Here lies Flaes the Jew; peace*

Right: Rome, 3rd–4th century

Marble: carved and painted
11½ x 10⅜ x 1⅛ in. (29.2 x 26.4 x 2.9 cm)

Gift of Henry L. Moses in memory of
Mr. and Mrs. Henry P. Goldschmidt,
JM 5-50

Below: Rome, 3rd–4th century

Marble: incised
9½ x 9¹⁵⁄₁₆ x ⅞ in. (24.1 x 25.2 x 2.2 cm)

Gift of Dr. Harry G. Friedman, F 4714

Inscription: *Ael[ia] Alexandria set up [this
stone] to Ael[ia] Septima, her dearest
mother, in grateful memory.*

Jews settled in Rome in the second or first century B.C.E. Their ranks swelled with the coming of diplomats, merchants, and captives taken after the Roman invasion of Judaea in 63 B.C.E. Some Latin authors who mention the Jews living in their midst confused them with early Christians, since the groups shared many practices. One of these practices was the burial of the dead, a sharp contrast to the earlier pagan custom of cremation. Jews and Christians both owned cemeteries outside Rome, which were a series of subterranean chambers that were extended as needed. Christian examples of these burial grounds, called catacombs, are widely known. There are also six Jewish sites in Rome and another in Venosa, near Naples.

In Jewish catacombs, as in Christian, the dead were buried in niches dug into the walls of underground chambers that were sealed with plaster. A tombstone, inserted in the plaster, identified the deceased. Tombstones were generally written in Greek or Latin, with an occasional Hebrew word added, which was sometimes misspelled, as in the example to the left made for Flaes the Jew. Like the majority of Christian tombstones of the period, most ancient Jewish grave markers from Italy were decorated only with rudely executed symbols. However, while the Christian symbols represent faith in personal salvation, the symbols used on Jewish tombstones express belief in national redemption. Implements of the destroyed Temple— the menorah (left and right), the shofar, incense shovel, and amphora (right)—signify the hope that the Temple will be rebuilt, as do the palm frond and citron (lulav and etrog), which are used on Tabernacles, once a major Temple festival. The tombstone below made for Aelia Septima, features symbols that probably represent offerings brought to the Temple: the pomegranate for first fruits and the ram for animal sacrifice. The same symbols appear on other works made for Jews during the Roman period: gold glasses, stone reliefs, mosaics, and the frescoes that decorated the catacomb walls. VBM

REFERENCES
Ackerman and Braunstein, *Israel in Antiquity*, cat. nos. 127, 128, and 130, pp. 126–27; Kleeblatt and Mann, *Treasures of The Jewish Museum*, pp. 26–27; Mann, *Gardens and Ghettos*, pp. 76–78.

Sabbath and Festival Lamp

Germany, 14th century

Bronze: cast and engraved
6⅝ x 7 in. diam. (16.8 x 17.8 cm)

Gift of Mr. and Mrs. Albert A. List,
JM 200-67

During the Middle Ages, star-shaped hanging lamps illuminated rooms in houses and castles throughout Europe. Each lamp consisted of a shaft from which was suspended a star-shaped container for oil and wicks, and a catch basin for overflow fuel (missing on this example). In Jewish communities, such lamps were also used for rituals—the kindling of lights in the home to inaugurate Sabbaths and festivals, and for havdalah. Havdalah—literally, "separation"—is the ceremony that marks the conclusion of Sabbath and holy days, that is, their separation from the workday week. By the sixteenth century, the star-shaped lamp had fallen into disuse among Gentiles, but it retained its form and function in Jewish homes. In fact, the type had become so closely associated with Jewish ritual that it was known as a *Judenstern*, or Jewish star.

The faceted form of this lamp is characteristic of fourteenth-century Gothic metalwork, such as the set of five nested beakers, dated before 1330, that belonged to a Jew in Kutna Hora. Like the lamp, the beakers are decorated with ridged moldings that run horizontally. On the lamp, however, the moldings are interpreted as architecture—they become part of the cupola that serves as the lamp shaft. In this sense, The Jewish Museum's lamp follows an established practice of the time, for miniature architectural forms were incorporated into a wide variety of medieval metalwork, including reliquaries, monstrances, and censers, as well as lamps.

According to the records of the first known owner of The Jewish Museum lamp, Siegfried Strauss, it was excavated in the Jewish quarter of Deutz, a city across the Rhine from Cologne. There is a Star of David incised on the underside of the star-shaped section, but its use in the fourteenth century does not necessarily indicate Jewish ownership.

VBM

REFERENCES
Kleeblatt and Mann, *Treasures of the Jewish Museum*, pp. 34–35; Mann, "'New' Examples of Jewish Ceremonial Art from Medieval Ashkenaz," pp. 13–24; Oklahoma Museum of Art, *Songs of Glory: Medieval Art 900–1500*, no. 54; Schoenberger, "A Silver Sabbath Lamp from Frankfurt-on-the-Main," p. 196, no. 23.

Spice Container

Frankfurt(?), c. 1550; repairs and
additions, 1651

Silver: cast, engraved, and gilt
9⁵⁄₁₆ x 2¹⁵⁄₁₆ x 2⅞ in. (23.6 x 7.5 x 7.3 cm)

Jewish Cultural Reconstruction,
JM 23-52

Since antiquity, the ceremony known as havdalah has marked the conclusion of Jewish Sabbaths and holy days. As early as the first centuries of this era, the smelling of aromatic spices was part of this ritual. Nevertheless, the first literary mention of a container for havdalah spices appears only in a twelfth-century source, and the earliest known example is this work, dated to the mid-sixteenth century.

The spice container is shaped like a four-story Gothic tower whose masonry is pierced by various openings: two rose windows; pairs of lancets with an oculus above, surrounded by an ogival arch; and rectangular fenestrations. A pinnacle with four surrounding turrets caps the tower. The silversmith created an appealing balance between the lightness provided by the openings and the heaviness of the articulated masonry, between the verticality of the

tower form and the horizontality of the moldings and the balustrade separating the stories.

Comparison with a similar German table decoration suggests that The Jewish Museum's example dates from about 1550. Many parts of the work, including the balustrade, were repaired later. A second flat base was riveted to the original, and there are silver patches on the turrets. A Hebrew inscription on the back apparently dates these changes:

רעכלה בת / אליעזר / דין תי׳א לפק

*Rekhlah daughter of Eliezer Dayan [5]411
[= 1650/51]*

That the earliest spice containers are shaped like towers is not surprising, given the widespread use of architectural forms in medieval metalwork, including censers for church ceremonies. It is very likely that the similarity in function between censers and spice containers (to give off aromatic odors) led to the adoption of the tower shape for havdalah containers. Among the objects made for Jews that are recorded in the sixteenth-century register of the Frankfurt Goldsmiths Guild is a *Hedes oder Rauchfass. Hedes* is a transliteration of the Hebrew for "myrtle" and was the term used for a spice container in the Middle Ages; the Frankfurt records equate it with *Rauchfass*, the German word for "censer."

VBM

REFERENCES

The Israel Museum, *Towers of Spice: The Tower Shape Tradition in Havdalah Spice Boxes*, no. vi; Kayser and Schoenberg, *Jewish Ceremonial Art*, no. 84; Mann, "The Golden Age of Jewish Ceremonial Art in Frankfurt"; Mann, " 'New' Examples of Jewish Ceremonial Art from Medieval Ashkenaz," pp. 13–24; Mann, *A Tale of Two Cities*, no. 74; Kleeblatt and Mann, *Treasures of The Jewish Museum*, pp. 34–35; Oklahoma Museum of Art, *Songs of Glory: Medieval Art from 900–1500*, no. 72.

Torah Ark

Urbino, c. 1500/renovated 1623

Wood: carved, gilt, stained, painted
94 x 110 x 34 in. (238.8 x 279.4 x 86.4 cm)

Gift of H. Ephraim and Mordecai
Benguiat Family Collection, S 1431

Many of the Torah arks used in Italy during the Middle Ages and later were of wood and similar in form to large-scale furniture found in church sacristies and homes. As a result of their lightweight material and their independence of the architectural structure of the synagogue, they could be removed. Historical records indicate that congregations forced to flee a particular Italian state took their arks and incorporated them into the house of worship of their new towns and cities.

This ark was made for the Jewish community of Urbino around 1500, just after Baccio Pontelli had finished carving two wooden *studioli*, or *Kunstkammern*, rooms for the display of collections, for the duke's palaces in Gubbio and Urbino. Today, the earlier Gubbio *studiolo*—completed in 1482—is in the Metropolitan Museum of Art, New York. It has the following features in common with The Jewish Museum's ark: classical fluted pilasters with pseudo-Corinthian columns that divide the upper surface into separate units; gilt details on stained wood; and monumental inscriptions in both friezes. This original Hebrew inscription was revealed in the course of conserving the ark and may be seen on the left side:

בצדקה תכונני

You shall be established through righteousness
(Isaiah 54:14)

The Gubbio *studiolo* is composed of a series of trompe l'oeil "open" cabinets above a series of workbenches. In the ark, the cabinets all open for the storage of Torah scrolls and prayer books.

In 1624, the duke of Urbino favored the Jewish community of his duchy by reaffirming their privileges and issuing an edict designed to protect them from harm. These positive developments seem to have inspired the renovation of the ark, which was painted a teal blue and inscribed with a new dedicatory poem beseeching the Almighty to bless the people of Urbino, an expression of gratitude to Duke Francesco Maria II. Unfortunately for the Jewish community, the duke abdicated in 1627, and the duchy passed to the Papal States, whose treatment of its Jewish residents was far more oppressive.

V B M

REFERENCE
Mann, "The Recovery of a Known Work," pp. 269–78; see nn. 1 and 3 for the older literature.

Samaritan Torah Case (Tik)

Master Matar Ishmael ha-Ramḥi
(active mid-16th century–beginning
17th century)

Damascus, 1565/66

Copper: inlaid with silver
25¼ in. high x 8 in. diam.
(64.1 x 20.3 cm)

Gift of H. Ephraim and Mordecai
Benguiat Family Collection, S 21

In antiquity, cloth mantles or bags (*tikim*) were used to protect the Torah scroll, the most sacred object in Judaism. By the eleventh century, rigid cases, also called *tikim*, were made from wood, copper, and silver, according to an inventory of 1059 from the Jerusalemite Synagogue that was found in the Cairo Genizah, a repository for old and worn Hebrew texts dated from the eighth to the thirteenth century. This case belongs to the earliest group of Torah cases to have survived; all five were made for the Samaritan community in the Near East during the sixteenth century. Three are still in use in the community today, while the fourth is at the University of Michigan.

Shortly before the fabrication of the *tik* in 1565/66, political power in the region had passed from the Mameluke Dynasty to the Ottomans. Nevertheless, the style and forms of Mameluke art continued to be used as on this case, where the silver inlays form circular fields with pointed terminals. Arabesques fill the fields, forming an area of dense ornament, which is repeated in the corners of the surrounding rectangular frames. Except for inscriptions, the remainder of the field is blank, forming an effective contrast with the ornamented areas. The same system of decoration was used on Mameluke and Ottoman book covers made in the sixteenth century.

When enclosed in a *tik*, the Torah is set in a vertical position and rolled by means of its staves. The manner of its use is the opposite of that of a Torah protected by a mantle. In that case, the textile mantle is removed, and the Torah scroll is laid flat for reading during the service.

Before the modern period, Torah cases were used in Spain and the Spanish diaspora, in North Africa, and in Near Eastern communities. The large-scale emigration of Jews from Arab lands after the founding of the State of Israel in 1948 brought many *tikim* to the West, leading to their adoption by traditional Ashkenazic communities.

VBM

REFERENCES
Kayser and Schoenberger, *Jewish Ceremonial Art*, no. 4; Mann,
"Gospels Covers, the *Tik* and the Koran Box."

Portion of a Synagogue Wall

Isfahan, 16th century

Faience tile mosaic
8 ft. 8 in. x 15 ft. 6 in. (264.2 x 472.4 cm)

Gift of Adele and Harry G. Friedman,
Lucy and Henry Moses, Miriam Schaar
Schloessinger, Florence Sutro
Anspacher, Lucille and Samuel Lemberg,
John S. Lawrence, Louis A. Oresman,
and Khalil Rabenou, F 5000

The Jews of Oriental communities generally house their Torah scrolls in a rigid cylindrical container known as a *tik*. When not in use, the *tik* may be placed in a conventional ark or in a niche that is part of a synagogue wall, a usage that can be traced back to the period of the early synagogues. On some holy days of the Jewish year, three sections of the Torah are read, for which congregations may use separate scrolls, resulting in the need for three niches. This mosaic once decorated the face of a wall housing niches for the Torah scrolls in an Isfahani synagogue.

The mosaic is composed of monochromatic sections of faience tile that were cut, after firing, to form the design. Arabesques, flowers, and leaves create a dense background pattern from which the light blue borders and gold letters appear to project. Hebrew letters form two sentences from Psalms. On the second line is a quotation found on many Torah curtains and reader's desk covers from Islamic countries: "This is the gateway to the Lord, the righteous shall enter through it" (Psalms 118:20). The second quotation is "But I through Your abundant love, I enter Your house; I bow down in awe at Your Holy Temple" (Psalms 5:8). The word *heikhal* in this quotation, which generally translates as "Holy Temple," is also used by Jews of Sephardic and Oriental origin to refer to the place in which the Torah is stored in the synagogue. The inclusion of these verses from Psalms on the mosaic wall identifies the purpose of the structure, much as Koranic quotations were incorporated into Muslim houses of worship to articulate their function.

The ancient Persians used glazed tiles as architectural decoration as early as the third century B.C.E. The technique was revived in the twelfth century and had evolved by the fifteenth century into the complex multicolored mosaic seen here. From then on, mosaic tiles were used on various Persian buildings as both interior and exterior decoration. The closest stylistic comparisons suggest a date in the sixteenth century for The Jewish Museum wall.

The size of the wall indicates that it stems from a fairly large synagogue, which implies that the building was erected by a community of some prominence. Several factors point to Isfahan as its probable location. The Jewish community of Isfahan reached a height of prosperity in the sixteenth century, when the wall was created, though it later declined because of persecution in the seventeenth century. The city was a center for this type of tile work, and similar decoration is found there on many public buildings. Furthermore, according to the records of the dealer who was instrumental in The Jewish Museum's acquisition of the wall, it was acquired in Isfahan. This synagogue wall represents a blend of a Muslim Persian tradition of architectural decoration with Jewish patronage and function.

VBM

REFERENCES

Freudenheim, "A Persian Faience Mosaic Wall in the Jewish Museum, New York"; Kleeblatt and Mann, *Treasures of the Jewish Museum*, pp. 38–39; Mann, *The Jewish Museum*, no. 30.

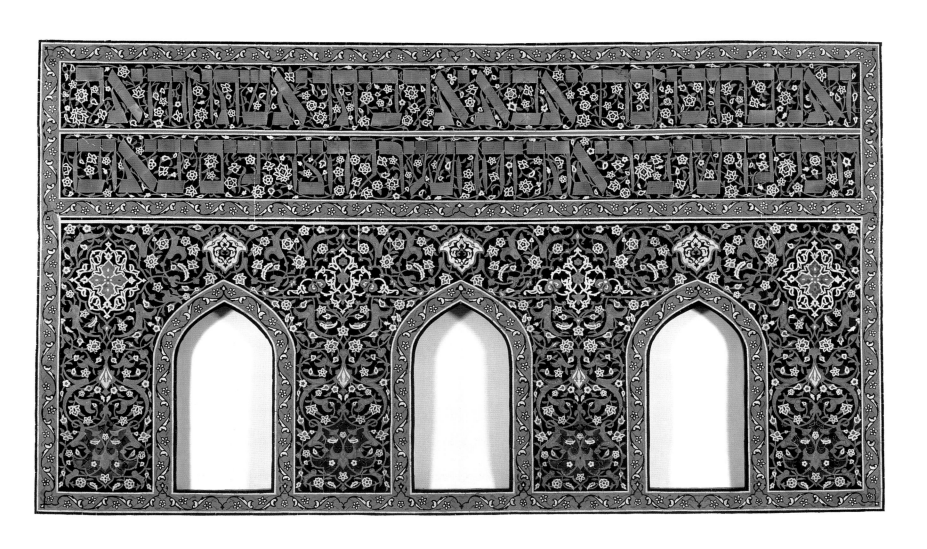

Casket with Zodiac Signs and Other Motifs

Germany, 15th–16th century,
later additions 1737–38

Fruitwood: carved and painted
9½ x 2³⁄₁₆ x 1¾ in. (24.1 x 5.2 x 4 cm)

Gift of Mr. and Mrs. Norman Zeiler in
memory of Mrs. Nan Zeiler, JM 35-66

The entire surface of this small wooden casket is covered with carved decoration. Zodiac signs in roundels surrounded by decorative motifs range along the front and back. There are single birds carved on the end panels, and four of the five cover panels are filled with vine scrolls inhabited by human and animal figures. The fifth panel bears a mnemonic Hebrew inscription that signifies the blessing over circumcision, and the date, [5]498 (= 1737/38). This inscription, as well as the evidence of structural alteration, together with the present contents of the box, shows that the casket was transformed into a container for circumcision implements during the eighteenth century. The remaining reliefs indicate that the box had another, prior use.

In shape and decoration, this work belongs to a group of late medieval caskets called *Minnekästchen* or *Briefladen*, which were given as love gifts, wedding presents, or New Year's gifts. Guilds and fraternal societies used similar boxes to hold important documents. The size, form, and decoration of The Jewish Museum box are closest to a painted *Minnekästchen* dated about 1300. However, the style of the carving of The Jewish Museum casket suggests a later date, about 1550.

The zodiac signs are the key to understanding the original purpose of the casket. When viewed from the front, the sequence starts with Libra, the sign for Tishri, the first month of the Jewish year. Further, the cycle reads from right to left, the way Hebrew is read, and nearly all the signs shown in profile are oriented from right to left. This consistency of orientation suggests that the zodiac reliefs were based on the illuminations of a Hebrew manuscript.

Zodiac cycles appear in two types of medieval Hebrew manuscripts: *maḥzorim* (festival prayer books) and *haggadot* (service books for Passover). In the *maḥzorim*, the cycle is illustrated alongside prayers for dew, and has the meaning of an orderly passage of time through the year, during which God ensures the fertility of the soil. Several later printed books with zodiac cycles contain commentaries to the illustrations, indicating that the cycle expresses the wish for a good year. By beginning the zodiac series with the sign for the first month of the Jewish year, the carver of this casket created a pictorial equivalent to the messages on other *Minnekästchen* wishing the owner a happy new year.
VBM

REFERENCES
Kleeblatt and Mann, *Treasures of the Jewish Museum*, pp. 32–33; Mann, "A Carved Mohel's Box of the Eighteenth Century and Its Antecedents," pp. 45–49; Mann, "A Sixteenth-Century Box in the New York Jewish Museum and Its Transformation," pp. 54–60; Mann, *A Tale of Two Cities*, no. 36; Oklahoma Museum of Art, *Songs of Glory: Medieval Art from 900 to 500*, no. 171.

Torah Binder

Rikah Polacco

Florence (?), 1662–63

Linen: embroidered with silk and metallic threads; modern lining
110¾ x 6½ in. (281.3 x 16.5 cm)

Gift of Cora Ginsburg, 1988-21

A binder for the Torah scroll, a long strip of cloth, is a means of holding the staves together when the Torah is not in use, thereby preventing damage to the parchment. The sacredness ascribed to the Torah scroll in Judaism necessitates its protection.

This petit-point binder is divided horizontally into two bands of decoration: above, series of naturalistically rendered flowers such as tulips and roses; and below, an inscription that reads:

לכבוד האל ותורתו מעשה ידי מרת ריקה מב'ת אשת
המפואר כמר חיים בר יוסף פולאקו ס'גל יצ'ו בשנת
הת'כג' לפ'ה

In honor of God and His Torah, the work of
Signora Rikah . . . wife of Ḥayyim, the son
of Joseph Polacco, the Levite . . . in the year 5423
a[ccording to the] l[arge counting].

The making of a Torah binder by a woman who dedicates it to a male member of her family was a common custom among Italian Jews.

This work is the key to the authorship of a large needlepoint Torah curtain now in the Victoria and Albert Museum, London (511–1877), which was made in 1675–76. According to its inscription, Joseph, son of Ḥayyim Polacco, restored this needlepoint curtain in 1702–3. The Victoria and Albert curtain has many features similar to the binder made by Rikah Polacco. The inclusion of numerous flowers, their style, and the original date of the curtain's fabrication suggest that it was made by Rikah Polacco, the wife of Ḥayyim and mother of Joseph. Two related, but undated, needlepoint curtains, one in The Jewish Museum, New York (F 3432), and the other in the Jewish Museum, Florence, were probably made in the 1670s as well.

VBM

REFERENCES
Mann, *Gardens and Ghettos*, no. 128; Mann, *The Jewish Museum*, no. 58.

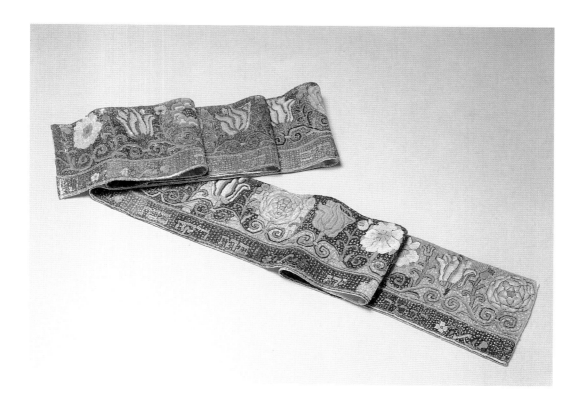

Scroll of Esther

Engraver: Salom Italia, Amsterdam
(1619–after 1655)

Amsterdam, after 1641

Parchment: engraved and manuscript
7¹⁵⁄₁₆ x 98⅝ in. (20.2 x 250.5 cm)

Gift of the Danzig Jewish Community,
D 76

The Book of Esther, read on the festival of Purim, recounts the escape of the Jews of Persia from annihilation during the reign of King Ahasuerus (probably Xerxes I, ruled 485–464 B.C.E.). Haman, the king's vizier, plotted to kill all the Jews in the kingdom and cast lots (*purim*) to determine the day of their destruction. His plan was stymied through the intervention of Esther, Ahasuerus's beautiful Jewish queen, who, guided by her uncle Mordecai, persuaded the king to save the Jews and execute the evil Haman in their place. Having triumphed over their enemies, the Jews of Persia engaged in "days of feasting and joy," and it is this spirit of merrymaking that characterizes the celebration of Purim to this day when the Scroll of Esther is read in the synagogue. Congregants may follow the text in their own scrolls, which may be lavishly decorated.

The elaborate engraved borders of this scroll are the work of the Jewish artist Salom Italia, born into a family of printers in Mantua. When the Austrians invaded Mantua in 1630, Jews were forced from the city, and Salom Italia probably went to the Venetian States before settling in Amsterdam in 1641. There he found a prospering community of Jews with the means as well as the inclination to commission and collect the works of a young printmaker.

This scroll was printed from one engraving plate consisting of four arches, which was repeated five times to produce a large arcade as a frame for the text; above, each arch is crowned by a broken pediment surmounted by lions. Below are Dutch cityscapes that reflect the influence of Italia's new home. Figures from the Purim story stand flanking the arches: King Ahasuerus facing Queen Esther, and Mordecai facing Haman. Below each figure is a scene from the story, each printed from a separate plate, forming a narrative cycle of nineteen images. The only exception to this composition is the first panel, which consists of naturalistically rendered peacocks and other birds, and an empty cartouche intended to frame the blessings recited before reading the scroll. On the lip of the vase of flowers on the right, Salom Italia signed his name in Hebrew. The squirrel to the right is an element from the insignia used in Mantua by his family.

Salom Italia's great innovation and contribution to the design of Esther scrolls was setting the text within portals derived from triumphal arches. The practice of conducting triumphal processions through arches dates back to ancient Rome, and the building of temporary arches to honor rulers as they entered a city continued in Europe until the nineteenth century. By the sixteenth century, the triumphal entries of monarchs were commemorated by the publication of their iconographic programs, complete with woodcuts or engravings of the temporary arches and decorations specially created for these events.

In 1642, shortly after Italia's arrival in Amsterdam, the city mounted a magnificent triumphal entry for the stadtholder Frederik Hendrik and his in-laws, the English royal family. Italia may also have been influenced by designs for the 1638 entry of Marie de' Medici into Amsterdam (published in 1639)—for example, an arch surmounted by lions with columns similar to the ones on this scroll. Italia's figures flanking the arches stand beneath festoons of fruit suspended from masks, which appeared in the decorations for a triumphal entry into Lisbon in 1619 (published in Madrid, 1622). By using imagery from a variety of printed sources, Salom Italia achieved a perfect marriage of form and content, since the Book of Esther recounts the triumph of the Jews of Persia and includes an account of Mordecai's triumphal procession through the streets of Shushan, the capital. This episode was depicted by Rembrandt in an etching that was made in Amsterdam around 1641 and was probably known to Italia.

The original owners of this scroll would have understood the reference to triumphal entries in the decorative program. As they unrolled the scroll to follow the text, revealing one arch at a time, they would have been symbolically passing through each portal, thereby reenacting the triumph of Mordecai and of all Jews that is at the heart of the celebration of Purim.

EDB

REFERENCES
Kayser and Schoenberger, *Jewish Ceremonial Art*, no. 149; Kleeblatt and Mann, *Treasures of the Jewish Museum*, pp. 64–65; Mann and Gutmann, *Danzig 1939*, cat. no. 48, pp. 80–81.

Marriage Contract

Bride: Esther,
daughter of Mashiah son of Kadadad
Groom: Mordecai,
son of Judah son of Nasr

Isfahan, Persia, 1647

Ink, gouache, gold paint, and block
print on paper
32⅞ x 25 in. (83.5 x 63.5 cm)

Gift of Dr. Harry G. Friedman, F 3901

Marriage is one of the most important *mitzvot*, or commandments, in Judaism, and scriptures are replete with verses encouraging the union of man and woman. One of the essential elements of a Jewish wedding ceremony is the writing and transfer of a marriage contract, or *ketubbah* (plural, *ketubbot*). Originally formulated to protect a woman's rights in marriage, the *ketubbah* establishes the financial obligations of the groom toward his bride in case of divorce or death. Since the contract was to be a practical document understood by all parties, it was written in Aramaic, the lingua franca of the ancient world. Only the date was written in Hebrew. Although Aramaic has fallen into disuse, it continues to be the language of traditional *ketubbot* to this day. Most *ketubbot* are based on a traditional text; however, the terms of engagement and the decoration of the contract offer a glimpse into the lives of various communities as well as the socioeconomic status of particular families.

Ketubbot produced in the Near East are usually written on paper, and their decoration is strongly influenced by Islamic art in their lack of figures and the use of aniconic motifs. Persia was the main center of *ketubbah* illumination in the Islamic world. Moreover, since Muslim law also requires a contract in order to legalize a marriage, it was customary for Muslims in Persia to decorate marriage contracts. Persian Jews thus seem to have modeled their marriage contracts on those of the Muslims. While in Western centers of *ketubbah* illumination, such as Italy and Holland, decorated *ketubbot* were often elaborate and expensive documents written on parchment and mainly commissioned by affluent community members (see *ketubbah* from Vercelli, p. 121), in Persia and other Eastern Jewish communities illustrated marriage contracts were used by most Jews, regardless of their position in society. In fact, Jews in Persia were usually members of the lower social strata: metalsmiths, weavers, dyers, and petty merchants.

One of the two earliest decorated examples known from Persia, this contract is dated 1647 in Isfahan, home to one of the country's oldest Jewish communities. A second *ketubbah* from the same year, a humble example from the Kurdish town of Maragheh, in northwest Iran, belongs to a different decorative tradition, featuring a simple frame in black ink (the library of the Jewish Theological Seminary of America, no. 145). The scarcity of Persian *ketubbot* from this period might be explained by the harsh policies of Shah 'Abbas II (1642–66), who persecuted Jews and other minorities, including Armenians and Zoroastrians, with vehemence. Threatened with expulsion, many Jews were forced to convert to Islam. It has been remarked, however, that despite the hostile conditions, Jewish culture managed to survive, and at times even to thrive, with a number of fine illustrated Judeo-Persian manuscripts extant from the seventeenth century.

In this *ketubbah*, the text of the contract occupies the center of the page, while biblical verses form the inner and outer frames, including excerpts from the Book of Ruth (4:11), Isaiah (61:9–10), Proverbs (5:18; 31:10–12), and Psalms (128:3–6). Additional verses, part of a wedding poem often featured in more complete form in later *ketubbot* from Persia and Afghanistan, are inscribed above the main text. The design of early Persian *ketubbot*, with verses inscribed in large, painted letters, has been traced back to fragments of medieval decorated *ketubbot* found in the *genizah* of the Ben Ezra Synagogue in Cairo (a *genizah* is a repository of worn Hebrew texts that are "hidden" to prevent their profanation).

Unlike most later Persian *ketubbot*, which are usually painted, the decoration of this contract was created by a repeat of stamped patterns, a technique also used in a later *ketubbah* from Isfahan dated 1781 (Klau Library, Hebrew Union College, no. 702) and in some later examples produced in the Persian city of Hamadan. In this *ketubbah*, the outer decorative frame features a repetition of hunting motifs: above, a gazelle leaps toward the left; below, a powerful beast attacks a gazelle. Popular during the Safavid period, hunting became a beloved motif in the arts of Persia, from textiles to ceramic tiles. Konstanze Bachmann, paper conservator at the Cooper-Hewitt National Design Museum in New York, has pointed out that repeated stamped decoration, usually by means of carved wood blocks, is also found in Persian textiles from the medieval period onward.

CN

REFERENCES
Bier, *Woven from the Soul*, cat. nos. 7, 30–32, 34; Diba, *Iranian Wedding Contracts*; Sabar, *Ketubbah*, pp. 327–29, 332–33, no. 218; Sabar, "Origins," pp. 129–58; Sarshar, *Esther's Children*, pp. 63–74; Taylor, *Book Arts of Isfahan*, pp. 31–32.

Curtain for the Torah Ark

Simḥah, wife of Menaḥem Levi Meshullami

Venice, 1680–81

Silk: embroidered with silk and metallic threads, metallic fringe
85¹⁄₁₆ x 55⅛ in. (216.1 x 140 cm)

Gift of Professor Neppi Modona, Florence, through Dr. Harry G. Friedman, F 2944

This is an extraordinary Torah curtain because of its impressive size, beautiful workmanship, and unusual iconography. According to the dedicatory inscription at bottom center, the curtain was made

בשנת / ישא / ברכה / מאת ה׳

in the year 'He shall carry away a blessing from the Lord' (Psalms 24:5; chronogram for the year 1680–81),

מעשה ידי הכבוד׳ מר׳ שמחה אשת כמ מנחם לוי משולמי י״ץ

the work of . . . Simḥah, wife of . . . Menaḥem Levi Meshullami.

The dedication reaffirms the significant role played by Italian Jewish women in the creation of synagogue textiles, even among very wealthy and prominent families such as the Meshullami, one of the first Jewish families to settle in Venice.

The decoration of the border, a symmetrical flowering vine, is an elaborate version of a motif found on many smaller textiles such as Torah binders and reader's desk covers. Neither is the motif of the Tablets of the Covenant surrounded by a glory of clouds unusual; it is found on many Italian Torah curtains of the seventeenth and eighteenth centuries and is a Baroque convention for the presentation of a holy object or personage. On this curtain, however, the clouds are above a landscape. The Tablets emerging from the glory link it to a mountain, which is identified by another quotation from Psalms as "the mountain that God has desired for His abode" (Psalms 68:17). The reference in this passage is not to Mount Sinai, where the Tablets were received, but to Mount Moriah, on which the Temple was built. Thus the mountain on this curtain has a dual iconographic function: it is the locus for the giving of the Tablets and a link to the representation of Jerusalem below.

Only one other Torah curtain has similar decoration. Still the property of the Venetian Jewish community, its iconographic elements include Mount Sinai represented by three peaks on Byzantine paintings. The curtain was created by Stella Peragia in 1673. The greater detail and naturalism of the Peragia curtain and its earlier date suggest that it was the model for the Meshullami composition, in which the forms are more stylized and disjointed.

What is unusual about these two curtains is the detailed representation of Jerusalem, unique in Torah curtain iconography, but common on another type of seventeenth-century Italian Judaica, decorated *ketubbot*, or marriage contracts. Since the Italian Jewish marriage ceremony includes the recitation of Psalm 128, which mentions Jerusalem, and remembrances of the city's destruction conclude every Jewish wedding, depictions of the city were appropriate to the decoration of the contracts displayed at the ceremony.

The exact source of the curtains' representations of Jerusalem (distinguished by the elaborate towers at each juncture of the walls and by the main gates in the form of *aediculae*) has not yet been identified. There is no doubt, however, that its use on the curtain was inspired by the decorations of *ketubbot*, creating an iconographic link between two forms of Judaica prominent in the lives of women.
VBM

REFERENCES
The Jewish Museum, *Fabric of Jewish Life*, 1977, no. 3; Kayser and Schoenberger, *Jewish Ceremonial Art*, no. 5; Kleeblatt and Mann, *Treasures of the Jewish Museum*, pp. 70–71; Makover, *The Jewish Patrons of Venice*, no. 3; Mann, *Gardens and Ghettos*, pp. 276–77; Vilnay, *The Holy Land in Old Prints and Maps*, p. 32.

Hanging Lamp for Sabbath and Festivals

Johann Valentin Schüler (1650–1720)

Frankfurt, 1680–1720

Silver: case, repoussé, and engraved
22¼ in. high x 14½ in. diam.
(56.5 x 36.8 cm)

Jewish Cultural Reconstruction,
JM 37-52

By the sixteenth century, only Jewish homes continued to use the star-shaped lamps that had been popular throughout medieval Europe. Because of the strong sense of tradition that dominates Jewish life, these lamps were used well into the modern era—often with more elaborate designs and in finer materials than their medieval precursors. The basic form of the lamp, however, remained unchanged: a star-shaped container for wicks and oil suspended from a shaft; and, below, a catch basin for dripping fuel.

Johann Valentin Schüler fashioned this elaborate baroque lamp for a member of the Frankfurt Jewish community. Together with his brother Johann Michael (1658–1718), with whom he shared an atelier, Schüler also produced many other types of silver Judaica: Hanukkah lamps of various shapes, candleholders, spice containers for havdalah, Torah shields, and elaborate covers for prayer books. The works of both brothers are similar in style and often incorporate pieces cast from the same molds, so it is impossible to tell which Schüler was the author of an unmarked work. The Judaica of the Schüler brothers seem to have served as models for younger Frankfurt silversmiths such as Johann Adam Boller.

Above the radiating arms that form the star of this lamp rises a complex and intricately worked grouping of figures, animals, and objects. The cylindrical shape of the lower shaft, decorated with masks and spouts, evokes the design of medieval fountains in public squares. Guido Schoenberger suggested that the fountain symbolism was especially appropriate for Sabbath lamps, since the Sabbath is greeted as a "fountain of blessing" in "Lekha dodi" (Come my friend), a hymn of welcome to the Sabbath that was incorporated into the synagogue services of Frankfurt during the first half of the seventeenth century.

The small figures atop the "fountain" of the lower shaft were cast from stock molds and modified to fit the Jewish purposes of the lamp. Each holds aloft symbols of the holy days of the Jewish year. The figure bearing matzah and a matzah iron represents Passover; Sukkot is marked by a lulav and an etrog; Shavuot by the Tablets of the Covenant; Yom Kippur by the knife and chicken used in the *kapparot* (atonement) ceremony; Hanukkah by a menorah and an urn for oil; Purim by a grogger and scroll case; Rosh Hashanah by a trumpet and "Book of Life"; and the Sabbath by a flaming havdalah candle. Such symbolic figures appear on other types of Judaica made in Frankfurt during the eighteenth century to mark the times when the objects were used. The small figures of animals and zodiac symbols at the top of the shaft, as well as the rampant lion, appear on other works by the Schülers and their contemporaries.

In 1903, the lamp was transformed into a *ner tamid* (eternal light). Various additions were made, most of which were removed when the piece was acquired by The Jewish Museum, New York. Only the two flags held by the lion remain, because they bear an inscription recording the donation of the lamp by Mathilde Freifrau von Rothschild in memory of her husband: "Shimon, known as Wilhelm Freiherr von Rothschild."

VBM

REFERENCES
Mann, *A Tale of Two Cities*, no. 116; Kleeblatt and Mann, *Treasures of the Jewish Museum*, pp. 80–81; Mann, "The Golden Age of Jewish Ceremonial Art in Frankfurt"; Mann, *The Jewish Museum*, no. 108; Schoenberg, "A Silver Sabbath Lamp from Frankfurt-on-the-Main."

Pair of Finials

Maker: SIC

Mantua, 17th–18th century

Silver: cast, repoussé, engraved
24 in. high x 5 in. diam. (61 x 12.7 cm)

Gift of Samuel and Lucille Lemberg,
JM 20-64 a, b

In the cathedral of Palma de Majorca rest the oldest known pair of Torah finials, their possession by the church a vivid reminder of the Expulsion of the Jews from Spanish and Portuguese territories in the 1490s.

The earliest finials date to the fifteenth century. Some aspects of their decoration, like horseshoe arches, are local features that recall the age of Muslim rule on the Iberian Peninsula and the hybrid mudéjar art that developed as a result. Viewed from the perspective of later Judaica, the most significant feature of the *rimmonim* is their tower form, clear evidence of a Spanish tradition underlying the appearance of the same type in centers to which the Sephardim fled after the Expulsion.

Italy was one of these centers. In the sixteenth century, its ancient Jewish community was revitalized by the arrival of Sephardic Jews, who brought with them traditions of intellectual and cultural achievement, as well as unique literary and artistic genres. Secular and religious Hebrew poetry and the illumination of marriage contracts were part of the Sephardic artistic tradition, as was tower-form metalwork for synagogue and home use. Another Spanish custom brought by Sephardic Jews to their new homes was the practice of decorating the corners of the reader's desk in the synagogue with finials similar to those used to ornament the staves of the Torah scrolls. The large size of this pair of finials and their heavy weight suggest that they were used on a reader's desk rather than on a Torah.

The body of each *rimmon* is a three-storied hexagonal tower. Torus moldings mark the base and entablature of each story, and spiral pilasters are set on every corner. A balustrade runs in front of each story; its corners support urns of flowers set on scroll-shaped bases. The result is a complex architectural form that projects forward in space on several levels. The basic form is, however, obscured by urns with cast flowers and other applied ornaments that fill the arches, hide the balustrade, and overlay the spiral pilasters. The largest urn and flower ensemble serves as a finial.

The blurred outline that results, the obscuring of the boundaries of the object, and the richness of ornament find parallels in other Italian Baroque metalwork. A pair of lavish multistoried candlesticks made in Rome in the mid-eighteenth century show these same characteristics as well as the three-dimensional floral elements and *clipeus* motifs found on the *rimmonim*.

VBM

REFERENCES

Freudenheim and Schoenberger, *The Silver and Judaica Collection of Mr. and Mrs. Michael M. Zagayski*, no. 3; Kayser and Schoenberger, *Jewish Ceremonial Art*, no. 22; Kleeblatt and Mann, *Treasures of the Jewish Museum*, p. 88; Makover, *The Jewish Patrons of Venice*, no. 9; Mann, *Gardens and Ghettos*, no. 194; Parke-Bernet Galleries, *The Michael M. Zagayski Collection of Rare Judaica*, no. 239.

Hanukkah Lamp

Johann Adam Boller (1679–1732)

Frankfurt, 1706–32

Silver: cast, engraved, filigree, hammered, and gilt, with enamel plaques
17 x 14½ in. (43.2 x 36.8 cm)

Gift of Mrs. Felix Warburg, S 563

In the past, artists consciously modeled their new works on older ones. Artistic innovation occurred within prescribed forms. Therefore, it is always interesting to view a work in which an artist has taken a traditional genre and transformed it by virtue of his own originality. Such is the case with this Hanukkah lamp by Johann Adam Boller.

It belongs to a series of *menorot*, branched lamp stands decorated with knops and flowers according to the description of the biblical menorah (Exodus 25:31–40) but of a size suitable for home use. In Frankfurt, these *menorot* were first made by the Schüler brothers in the early years of the eighteenth century, and by Boller as well. All are closely related in form, proportion, and decoration. Cast figures of the apocryphal heroine Judith holding the head of Holofernes were set atop the center shafts, and additional cast figures of warriors, archers, rampant lions (often holding shields), animals, birds, and flowers surmount the oil containers and support the bases. Victor Klagsbald has suggested that these small figures may relate to the house signs of the Frankfurt ghetto.

Boller appears to have later rethought the type and created this Hanukkah lamp in which form and decoration are joined in a more dynamic synthesis. The rampant lion holding a shield, which appears on examples by the Schülers, has been greatly enlarged and made part of the shaft of the lamp, a combination of figure and shaft that appeared on German hanging lamps from the fifteenth century onward. In this case, the lion holds a shield engraved with a stag and a dove, probably an allusion to the names of the lamp's owners. Similarly, Boller invested the decoration with greater iconographic significance by changing the shape of the base from a rectangle to a domed octagonal form, to which are affixed four red-and-white enamel scenes from the life of Jacob: Rebecca's meeting with Eliezer (Genesis 24:17–27); Jacob's dream (Genesis 28:12–15); Jacob rolling the stone from the mouth of the well (Genesis 29:10); and Jacob wrestling with the angel (Genesis 32:24). These enamels lend a coloristic dimension to this work, which is innovative compared with other Hanukkah lamps of the series. Small colored enamel florets on the flowers of the branches and a lavish use of gilding expand the palette of the piece. Though based on a long artistic tradition with biblical sources and models in medieval manuscripts and metalwork, the second Boller Hanukkah lamp is a highly innovative and creative work.

VBM

REFERENCES

Kleeblatt and Mann, *Treasures of the Jewish Museum*, pp. 82–83; Mann, "The Golden Age of Jewish Ceremonial Art in Frankfurt"; Mann, *A Tale of Two Cities*, no. 121; Weber, "Splendid Bridal Gifts," p. 175.

Torah Crown

Lemberg (Lvov), Galicia, 1764/65–73

Silver: repoussé, cast, cutout, engraved, parcel-gilt; semiprecious stones; glass

19¼ in. high x 8⅝ in. diam. (48.9 x 21.9 cm)

Gift of Dr. Harry G. Friedman, F 2585

A close examination of the inscriptions and structure of this crown reveals that it was made and decorated in two phases. The longest inscription, on a gilt cartouche of the lower band, reveals that the older, lower section was given by a couple in honor of their sons:

זי׳ / הֹה האלוף ... / הר.../ משה בֹה / יצחק מענקֹס ...
זל... ואשתו... / רחל בת מ שמעון זל / עבור בניהם שיזכו
לגֹ׳ / לתורה ולֹה ולֹ׳מטֹ׳ו אֹס / לסֹדֹר ולפֹרֹט והֹיֹה
כׁ׳אׁשֹׂרׁ (!) / ירים משה ידו וגבר ישראל / לפֹק

T[his was] d[onated by] Rabbi . . . Moses son of the late R[abbi] Isaac Menkes, and his wife . . . Rachel daughter of the late Simon, on behalf of their sons, may they be worthy to r[aise them] to the Torah, to the m[arriage canopy] and to g[ood] d[eeds]. A[men], S[elah]. In the year (chronogram from Exodus 17:11=[5]525 [= 1764/65]).

The decoration of this lower portion largely consists of architectural and ornamental elements: pilasters and arches, fruits, rococo scroll and shell forms, and animals. Eight or nine years after its fabrication, a second donor added engraved silver dedicatory panels to the lowest tier in memory of his parents:

יזכור / אלֹקים את נשמת / אדוני אבי מורי הֹה / האלוף
המרומם מֹ׳ / שמעון בֹמ אברהם / זֹל בעבור שאני נודר /
זֹאת בֹעֹד הׁזֹכׁרׁיׁתׁ (!) / נשׁמׁתֹהׁ (!) / וֹתׁנׁצׁבֹׂהׁ / אֹס

May the Lord remember the soul of . . . my father . . . the late Simon, son of the late Abraham, for I vow this on behalf of the remembrance [sic] of his soul and M[ay his] s[oul] be b[ound up] in the b[onds of] eternal life. A[men], S[elah].

ואת אמי מֹוֹרׁ / החשובה והֹצֹ׳ נ : / החסידה מֹ זיסל /
בת מהוֹ ישראל / איסר זצֹל

And my mother . . . Zissel daughter of the late Rabbi Israel Isser.

The second donation, the upper section, is the most interesting portion of the crown. The cast griffins that support it are relatives of the heraldic, guardian figures found on the contemporaneous carved wooden arks of Galician synagogues. They support a circlet bearing a complete cycle of zodiac signs, each labeled in Hebrew. This astrological cycle has a long history in Jewish art from the period of the mosaic pavements of ancient synagogues, through medieval decorative arts and illuminated manuscripts, to printed versions of the same texts dating to the eighteenth century. Another possible influence on the iconography of the Lvov crown was the famous painted ceiling of the nearby Chodorów wooden synagogue, whose program included a zodiac cycle surrounding a central circle with a double-headed eagle, symbol of the Polish kingdom that ruled Galicia until 1772. (The same political symbol appears on the lower tier of the crown.) However, the symbols of the crown cycle differ markedly from those of the painted ceiling in both their forms and surrounding inscriptions, which suggests that the silversmith had another model, probably a printed prayer book.

By adding another tier and a dome, the second, unnamed donor created a crown whose complex structure reflects the multitiered architecture and furnishings of Galician synagogues of the seventeenth and eighteenth centuries. He also set a pattern that would be followed by numerous Eastern and Central European Torah crowns into the twentieth century.

V B M

REFERENCES

Grafman, *Crowning Glory*, pp. 267, 271; Kayser, "A Polish Torah Crown"; Kayser and Schoenberger, *Jewish Ceremonial Art*, no. 35; Kleeblatt and Mann, *Treasures of the Jewish Museum*, pp. 102–3; Roth, *Jewish Art*, p. 121 and fig. 114.

Curtain and Valance for the Torah Ark

Jacob Koppel Gans (G[old]s[ticker]?)

Bavaria, 1772–73

Velvet: cut and uncut, embroidered with
metallic and silk threads
Curtain: 84 x 64½ in. (213.4 x 163.8 cm)
Valance: 37½ x 67½ in. (95.3 x 171.5 cm)

Gift of Dr. Harry G. Friedman, F 1285 a, b

Since Jews were generally not allowed to join guilds in German-speaking lands before their emancipation in the nineteenth century, early signed works of ceremonial art made by Jewish artists are exceedingly rare, if one discounts works of folk art made by untrained craftsmen. This Torah curtain and matching valance are exceptions. The text of a cartouche at bottom left reads:

נעשה / ידי להתפאר / בע״זה יעקב קאפל / בן מה״ורר
יהודא / ליב ז״ל גנש גש׳ / היכשטטט

*"My handiwork in which I glory" (Isaiah 60:21)
. . . Jacob Koppel son of Juda Leib, of blessed
memory, Gans G[old]s[ticker]?, Hochstadt.*

Opposite the inscription is a cartouche that contains a chronogram indicating the date. The other personalized inscription appears at the top of the curtain and indicates the donor:

ר׳ יעקב קיצינגן ש׳ בן המנוח כ״ה ליב ק׳ / זל וזוגתו מרת הינדל
ת׳ בת האלוף והקצין כ״ה / טעבלי אולמא שלי״טא מפפערשא

*Jacob Kitzingen son of the deceased Rabbi Leib
K[atz], of blessed memory, and his wife Hendel
daughter of . . . Tevli Ulma . . . from Pfersee.*

In these inscriptions, the places of origin as well as most of the family names are those of towns in Bavaria, which suggests that the curtain was made there.

Indeed, this curtain and valance represent a late flowering of a type that had been established in Bavaria in the 1720s by another Jewish embroiderer, who signed his works "Elkone of Naumberg." The valance of a curtain made by Elkone for a synagogue near Augsburg (as is Pfersee) also bears three crowns (symbolic of Torah, priesthood, and royalty) and five vessels of the ancient Tabernacle, arranged in the same order and similar in form to those on Jacob Koppel Gans's work. Elkone may have been inspired by a series of valances with Tabernacle vessels made in Prague and Frankfurt during the second decade of the eighteenth century. His work, in turn, served as a model for that of Jacob Koppel Gans. It was Gans's original achievement to have closely integrated the decoration of the valance with that of the curtain by repeating the same symbols on both: the menorah, the crown, and the heraldic double-headed eagle.

VBM

REFERENCES
The Jewish Museum, *Fabric of Jewish Life*, no. 22, p. 12; Kayser and Schoenberger, *Jewish Ceremonial Art*, no. 9, a, b, pp. 28–29; Kleeblatt and Mann, *Treasures of the Jewish Museum*, pp. 108–9; Landsberger, "Old Time Torah Curtains," pp. 353–89, fig. 10.

Marriage Contract

Bride: Eleonora, daughter of
Benjamin Segrè
Groom: Mordecai, son of
Azriel Treves

Vercelli, 1776

Ink and paint on parchment
24¼ x 20 in. (61.6 x 50.8 cm)

Gift of Samuel and Lucille Lemberg,
JM 43-61

The custom of decorating the marriage contract, or *ketubbah*, was first practiced in the Middle East, most likely as a result of the public nature of the wedding ceremony, which included the reading aloud of the contract and the display of the dowry. These customs were also followed in pre-Expulsion Spain and were later observed in Italy by Sephardic exiles. The practice of commissioning decorated *ketubbot* flourished in Italy, probably because the public reading of the contract during the marriage ceremony became popular in the sixteenth century and because Italians had a tradition of decorated documents. Since Jews had been banned from the south of Italy by 1541—a law that remained in force for over three centuries—Italian contracts stem predominantly from the northern regions, with a few examples from central Italy.

In Italy, *ketubbot* were commissioned by all Jews, including Sephardi, Ashkenazi, Levantine (from the eastern Mediterranean), and Italian—descendants of the old Roman community. Written on parchment, they usually featured lavish decoration, inspired by both Jewish and Christian art. For instance, the use of an archway to frame the text, as seen in this fine example from Vercelli, can be traced to the title pages of Hebrew printed books—northern Italy was a main center of Hebrew printing—but may also be linked to local architecture or sculpture. Figurative representation was also common in Italian *ketubbot*, although for centuries, most Jews had shied away from it because of their stern interpretation of the biblical prohibition against graven images. The inclusion of human figures, some allegorical and others portraying biblical or genre scenes, reflects a high degree of acculturation.

Other popular motifs in decorated Italian *ketubbot* include the signs of the zodiac and, as seen here, the emblems of the two families. The adoption of unofficial coats of arms was widespread among wealthy Italian Jews, in imitation of the practices of the local nobility. Most *ketubbot* include a single shield, containing the insignia for both families, or just that of the groom, whose family usually commissioned the contract because he was obligated to furnish the bride with a *ketubbah*. This example, however, features two separate emblems, possibly because the bride belonged to a family of prominent scholars, including Benjamin Segrè

of Vercelli, who might have been her father. The coat of arms for the Segrè family—a rampant lion facing right with a Star of David—is featured at the center of the lower border. No less distinguished was the Treves family, to which the groom belonged and whose emblem—a rampant lion to the right of an apple tree—appears above the text at center, a prominent location, for the groom's family likely commissioned the document.

Issued in Vercelli, this *ketubbah* differs from other extant examples from the same Piedmontese city, characterized by an arcuated shape at bottom and a floral border. Although some Italian contracts depict the bride and groom, very few represent the wedding party—shown here in lavish costumes and hairdos—or the attendant musicians. Flirtatious interactions between various couples add a picaresque note, including a distinguished man with a cane peering through his spyglass at a lady at a window, at the upper right. A later example from Pesaro, dated 1853, at the Israel Museum (179/339), also features a gathering of musicians and elegantly dressed couples, but the figures there were cut out from printed sources, painted, and pasted onto the parchment, instead of finely rendered, as seen here. The extravagance of examples such as this one might have prompted Italian rabbis to repeatedly enact laws limiting the amount of money that could be spent on the decoration of a marriage contract.

The secular nature of this *ketubbah*'s decorative program, with figures of a musician and a young man elegantly dressed (perhaps a rendering of the groom?) in the niches often reserved for depictions of Moses and Aaron, indicates that it might have been the work of a Christian artist. Many other Italian examples, however, display a close relationship between text and image, with depictions of biblical scenes featuring heroes whose names were borne by the groom, the bride, or their fathers, with extensive use of Hebrew texts, attesting that they were decorated either by Jewish artists or by Christian makers under the strong guidance of their Jewish patrons.

CN

REFERENCES
Roth, "Stemmi," pp. 182–83; Sabar, *Ketubbah: The Art of the Jewish Marriage Contract*, pp. 79–89 and no. 29; Sabar, *Ketubbah: Jewish Marriage Contracts*, pp. 8–20, 202–4; Sabar, "The Use and Meaning of Christian Motifs," pp. 47–63.

Hanukkah Lamp in the Form of a Torah Ark

Maker: ZK

Brody, 1787

Silver: repoussé, pierced, appliqué, chased, cast, and parcel-gilt; copper alloy
27⁷⁄₁₆ x 16¹⁵⁄₁₆ x 4½ in. (69.7 x 43 x 11.4 cm)

Gift of H. Ephraim and Mordecai Benguiat Family Collection, S 260

Architectural motifs have a long association with the decoration of Hanukkah lamps, since the ancient Jewish practice was to place the lit lamp before the facade of a home or within a window facing the street. This elaborate and magnificent work is unusual in that the architecture represented is an interior structure and one that is quite specific. The backplate is based on the elaborate wooden Torah arks that once adorned Polish synagogues.

The wooden synagogues of Poland were masterpieces of the carpenter's art in their exterior structure as well as their interior decorations. The greatest attention was lavished on the major centers of interest during services: the Torah ark and reader's desk. Arks were often several stories high, their basic function as a cabinet for scrolls almost obscured by elaborate columned superstructures overlaid with vegetation inhabited by birds and animals. Two aesthetic principles dominated the creation of these arks: symmetry and *horror vacuii*, a fear of empty spaces.

The same principles appear in the ark on this lamp. Pairs of heraldic animals face each other across the central vertical axis. For example, griffins support a crown symbolic of the Torah, which is aligned with the meeting point of the ark doors. As on the actual wooden arks, there is a demarcation of treatment between the "structural" architectural members of the decor (columns and entablature), which are fairly plain in form, and the areas around them, which are overlaid with dense silver vegetation that contrasts with the gilt ground. It is this part of the decoration, filled with motifs as if the artist possessed a *horror vacuii*, that is most reminiscent of folk art. However, the training of the artist is evident in the graceful forms of natural life and in the inclusion of sophisticated motifs such as the rococo scrolls and cartouche at the bottom.

VBM

REFERENCES
Kayser and Schoenberger, *Jewish Ceremonial Art*, no. 138, p. 131; Kleeblatt and Mann, *Treasures of the Jewish Museum*, pp. 110–11.

Torah Finials

Heinrich Wilhelm Kompff
(active 1783–1825)

Kassel, Germany, 1797–99

Silver: engraved, 18 x 5 in. diam.
(45.7 x 12.7 cm)

Purchase: gift of Dr. Harry G.
Friedman, by exchange; the Judaica
Acquisitions Committee Fund; and
Frances and Hubert J. Brandt Gift,
1999-107 a, b

In a publication of 1931, this pair of finials (*rimmonim*) is described as being in one of the two Kassel synagogues. Nothing is known of their whereabouts from Kristallnacht (1938) until 1970, when the finials were purchased from a dealer.

According to their inscriptions, the finials were "a donation of Rabbi Zelig, son of Rabbi Feis of blessed memory, for the Torah scroll of the Benevolent Society in the year [5]559 [1798/99]." This inscription appears along the circular bases that were probably added to the finials shortly before they were purchased. Similar bases appear on a pair of finials in the form of a column topped by a flaming urn. This inscription indicates a practice known from rabbinic responsa, that individuals and communal societies often owned their own Torah scrolls and ornaments, which they deposited in the synagogue for their use on special occasions. The remaining inscriptions appear on the column bases: "It is a tree of life/ to them that grasp it (Proverbs 3:18); Benevolent Society; Torah and worship."

The unusual form of the finials reflects the late-eighteenth-century interest in antiquity and the vogue for classical forms in the decorative arts. An early precursor may be the columns designed by Johann Fischer von Erlach for the facade of Saint Charles Borromaeus in Vienna, built between 1716 and 1737. The same high podiums with moldings on the church columns appear on the finials, as do the winding spirals of the column shafts. Kompff also made other Judaica for the synagogue in Kassel: a second pair of finials (of which only one remains) and a Torah crown.

VBM

REFERENCES

Geschichte der jüdischen Gemeinde Kassel: Unter Berücksichtigung der Hessen-Kasseler Gesamtjudenheit, 1:25, fig. 14 (right); *Notizblatt der Gesellschaft zur Erforschung jüdischer Kunstdenkmäler*, p. 5.

Torah Finials

Master: E. R. or F. R.

British Colonies, probably North America or the West Indies, c. 1800

Silver: cast, cutout, parcel-gilt, engraved, and punched
17¹⁵⁄₁₆ in. high x 5⅝ in. diam.
(45.6 x 14.3 cm)

Gift of Jacobo Furman in memory of his wife, Asea, 1992-144 a, b

The mid-eighteenth-century discovery of ancient Pompeii, with its wealth of classical frescoes and objects, inspired a return to classical motifs and symmetry in European silver design and ornamentation. In England, one of the main centers of the neoclassical style, silversmiths created works with light, graceful shapes and delicate decoration. These *rimmonim* (Torah finials) exemplify the British neoclassical style of the late eighteenth century in their open, airy form, consisting of two cylindrical bands alternating with three tiers of classical palm leaves and sheaves. The effect of openness is further enhanced by the cutout roundels in the central band and by the simple engraved floral decoration that catches and reflects the light. This technique of decoration was commonly used for silver cruet stands, cake baskets, sugar bowls, and salt cellars,

as exemplified in the work of the Bateman firm and others. The Batemans produced several pairs of *rimmonim* that are similar in form and style to the pair shown here.

British neoclassicism disseminated to Europe and to the far-flung British Colonies, where it was frequently imitated. These *rimmonim* are probably examples of colonial silver, for their hallmarks are similar but not identical to those in the well-documented British hallmark system. There were no official assay offices or registries of silversmiths' marks in the colonies during this period, and silversmiths were free to mark their works as they wished. Many, particularly in the United States and Canada, chose to use "pseudo-British" hallmarks.

During the period when these *rimmonim* were fashioned, Jewish communities existed in the British (or formerly British) territories of the United States, Canada, and the West Indies. As little has been published on West Indian silver work, and even less on Jewish ceremonial silver from that region, these *rimmonim* may be rare and important examples of this genre.

S L B

REFERENCES
Braunstein, *Personal Vision*, no. 9; Furman, *Treasures of Jewish Art*, pp. 40–41; Kleeblatt and Mann, *Treasures of the Jewish Museum*, pp. 136–37.

Finials for the Torah Case

Cochin, India, 18th–19th century

Gold: repoussé, cutout, and engraved;
tin backing

Left: 8 in. high x 10¾ in. diam.
(20.3 x 27.3 cm)
Right: 7⁵⁄₁₆ in. high x 10⅝ in. diam.
(18.7 x 27 cm)

Gift of the Michael and Luz Zak
Purchase Fund, 1982-184 a, b

According to their tradition, the Jews arrived in Cochin, on the southwest coast of India, before 379 C.E. and maintained a vibrant community until the recent emigration to the State of Israel depleted their ranks. Over the centuries, the community assimilated many Indian customs, including a division into castes whose members did not intermarry and who maintained their own synagogues: the White Jews, the Black Jews, and the Freedmen (manumitted slaves and their offspring). According to a letter in the possession of Jakob Michael, the previous owner, these *rimmonim*, or finials for the Torah, belonged to the White Jews' synagogue; however, similar finials were also used by the Black Jews. The finial at right bears an engraved inscription reading: שלמה הלגואה נע, "Solomon Hallegua, m[ay he rest in] peace." The

Halleguas are a well-known family of Cochin Jews.

Though resembling each other in technique and form, these *rimmonim* are not a pair. They differ in size and in details of their decoration. It was the usual custom of the Cochin Jews to place a single *rimmon* like one of these atop the silver or gold case (*tik*) in which the Torah scroll is permanently stored. This custom differs from that of other Oriental and Sephardic communities, who always place pairs of *rimmonim* on their Torah cases.

Other unusual features of these finials are their material, thin sheets of gold affixed to base metal supports, and their decoration with bands of floral ornaments executed in repoussé. These aspects reflect local Indian influence. Thin plates of silver and gold attached to base metal supports are traditionally used by Indian silversmiths to decorate large objects like furniture. Their repoussé ornaments were often fashioned from the same molds used for more base metals such as copper and brass. Therefore, close parallels for the bands on these *rimmonim* appear on the backplates of copper and brass lamps made in southern India. The cutout relief on all these works creates an ornamental effect of light and shade, which enhances the decorative motifs engraved and chased on the metal. Finally, the conical finial of these *rimmonim* is another feature borrowed from Indian lamps. The finial shown on the right was originally one of a pair given to the Indian government during the Indo-Chinese War. It was later sold by the government and subsequently entered the collection of Jakob Michael.

VBM

REFERENCES
Christie, Manson, and Woods International, *Fine Judaica, English and Continental Silver, Russian Works of Art, Watches and Objects of Vertu*, no. 160; The Jewish Museum, New York, *Annual Report 1982–83*, pp. 6, 29; Kleeblatt and Mann, *Treasures of the Jewish Museum*, pp. 48–49.

Solomon Alexander Hart, R.A.

(English, 1806–1881)

The Feast of the Rejoicing of the Law at the Synagogue in Leghorn, Italy, 1850

Oil on canvas
55⅝ x 68¾ in. (141.3 x 174.6 cm)
Gift of Mr. and Mrs. Oscar Gruss,
JM 28-55

Nineteenth-century British artists, perhaps more than those of any other nation, traveled extensively throughout the Continent, North Africa, and the Near East supplying visual records of monuments, places, and people. This phenomenon resulted from the isolation of the British Isles and was a continuation of the eighteenth-century tradition of the Grand Tour, in which nobles and gentry frequently engaged the services of an accompanying watercolorist to document sites. The first Jewish member of the Royal Academy, Solomon Alexander Hart, following the lead of his countrymen—for example, J. M. W. Turner and David Roberts—visited Italy in 1841–42 and made an elaborate series of drawings of historical sites and architectural interiors, which he hoped to publish.

Although the publication of these works never came to fruition, the studies provided Hart with the basis for numerous future canvases. Three of his entries to the Royal Academy in 1850 demonstrate his likely use of these studies: *Interior of a Church in Florence; Interior, St. Mark's, Venice;* and *The Feast of the Rejoicing of the Law,* a view of the interior of the Leghorn (Livorno) synagogue. The inspiration for Hart's Italian tour, his proposed publication, and his depiction of ecclesiastical interiors may indeed have come from the example of the well-traveled and prominent British painter David Roberts, who was Hart's neighbor in London. Roberts had in 1837 published a portfolio of Spanish scenes, similar to Hart's later proposed Italian one, which included church interiors. Several of Roberts's interiors were shown at the Royal Academy between 1836 and 1850. In fact, Roberts exhibited three church interiors along with Hart's similar subjects at the same 1850 hanging at the Royal Academy.

One of Hart's works listed in the 1850 Royal Academy exhibition catalogue appears to be the painting now in the collection of The Jewish Museum. It may be based on an 1845 entry of the same title. Using one of the artist's few observations of a Jewish structure during his Italian tour, the work shows the interior of the magnificent synagogue in Leghorn, originally built in 1591. This interior is perhaps the foremost example of the lavish redecoration common to Italian synagogues in the eighteenth century. Hart captures a romantic vision of the exotic dress of his Italian coreligionists as they parade the scrolls of the Law on Simḥat Torah,

the feast of the rejoicing of the Law. This marks the end of the fall harvest festival, Sukkot, and is the holy day on which the yearly cycle of reading the Pentateuch ends, immediately beginning again with Genesis.

Hart's other Jewish subjects reveal his ability to cleverly use his artistic resources and his visibility at the Royal Academy to demonstrate Judaism's cultural currency. Yet in his long and distinguished submission of entries to the Royal Academy, he seems always to temper his Jewish themes with English and Christian ones. This sensibility to social and religious equity was triggered by the issue of civil rights for English Jews, which was debated by Parliament in 1833. Hart's aforementioned 1850 Royal Academy entries are examples of this balance in Christian and Jewish ecclesiastical interiors. Historical themes, so popular during the 1830s, could serve as an expression of his patriotism—for example, *Sir Thomas More Receiving the Benediction of His Father* (1836). He connects Englishness with Jewishness in *The Conference of Menasseh ben Israel and Oliver Cromwell.* Similar nationalistic sentiments pervade Hart's literary themes, which are chosen from masterpieces of English prose and poetry such as Shakespeare's *The Merchant of Venice* and Scott's *Ivanhoe,* whose central characters are Jewish.

NLK

REFERENCES
Goodman, *The Emergence of Jewish Artists in Nineteenth-Century Europe;* Ormond, "The Diploma Paintings from 1840 Onwards," pp. 56–57; Steyn, "The Complexities of Assimilation in the 1906 Whitechapel Art Gallery Exhibition 'Jewish Art and Antiquities' "; Ziegler, "Jewish Artists in England," pp. 1–2.

Doors for a Synagogue Book Cabinet

Persia, early 18th–early 19th century

Wood: painted
27³⁄₁₆ x 7¹³⁄₁₆ in. (69 x 19.8 cm)

Gift of Dr. Harry G. Friedman,
F 4012 a, b

As was true of many Jewish communities in Asia, Persian Jews enclosed their Torah scrolls in rigid cylindrical cases known as *tikim*. The use of a case such as this meant that the Torah was stored vertically and read in the same position. Ornaments for the top of the case could include silver finials for the staves and silver crowns, and the inside was either painted or lined with textiles. Persian *tikim*, not counting their staves or ornaments, range in height from 24 to 57 inches (61 to 145 cm). They could have been kept in an ark or in architectural niches, as is known from Isfahan.

The relatively large size of Persian *tikim* precludes these doors from having been used for a Torah ark. Many synagogues had additional book cabinets, which held the five scrolls read at various times during the year (Ruth, Esther, Ecclesiastes, the Song of Songs, and Lamentations), or prayer books for the cantor. Further, none of the framing inscriptions refer to the Torah explicitly, although some quotations are taken from Genesis. For all these reasons, it is unlikely that the doors were made for a Torah ark.

The type of decoration on the doors is typical of motifs used in Persian art for mirror frames, caskets, and other decorative objects. The same birds and flowers (cuplike roses, trefoil leaves, and a sprouting of long-stemmed leaves) appear on works dating between 1714 and 1847. The rigid symmetry of the compositions suggests a somewhat narrower dating, from the early eighteenth to the early nineteenth century.

VBM

Marriage Canopy

Ottoman Empire, 1867–68

Silk satin weave: embroidered with
metallic threads and spangles; fringe
64¼ x 53 in. (163.2 x 134.6 cm)

Gift of Eve, Robert, and Richard Arles
in memory of their husband and
father, Emile, 2000-89

The wedding canopy symbolizes the home established by the couple through their marriage. This example was made during the last years of Ottoman rule in the area that is today Bulgaria. Because the Ottomans had conquered this part of the Balkans in 1396, Bulgarian art was part of the larger cultural traditions of the empire. This can be seen in the deep color of the silk ground of the canopy and in its embroidery with gold threads. As is true of many Ottoman embroideries, worked areas alternate with voids, thereby allowing the color of the silk to be an integral part of the design and lending a sense of depth to the textile. The composition is also typically Ottoman: a large motif occupies the center and is balanced by smaller decorative elements composed of the same motifs that point diagonally toward the center.

Nevertheless, the trellis motif of the border and its symmetrical, isolated motifs suggest the influence of Italian art, which was strong in the Balkans because of the presence of Italian traders and settlers. In addition, the canopy is dedicated

לבתי היקרה מ׳ ויניזייאנה / רי ארייה מבת 5628

*For my dear daughter, Veneziana/ di Aryeh . . .
5628 [=1867/68].*

The daughter's name, based on the city of Venice, is typical of Italian Jewish female names. Family names were also based on cities of residence.
VBM

Torah Ark from Adath Yeshurun Synagogue

Abraham Shulkin (American, born Russia, 1852–1918)

Sioux City, Iowa, 1899

Pinewood: hand-carved, openwork, stained, and painted
10 ft. 5 in. x 8 ft. x 30 in. (317.5 x 243.8 x 76.2 cm)

Gift of the Jewish Federation of Sioux City, JM 48-56

All aspects of traditional Jewish life are based on the Torah—the first five books of the Hebrew Bible—and ongoing rabbinic interpretations. Handwritten on parchment, the Torah scroll is read in the synagogue in front of the congregation on the Sabbath and Mondays and Thursdays, and on holidays. When not in use, the scroll is usually housed in a Torah ark—a cabinet set in or against a wall, traditionally the one oriented toward Jerusalem.

In Eastern Europe, Torah arks were often made out of wood and decorated with elaborate carvings incorporating mythical and symbolic creatures as well as vegetal motifs. Stylistically, this Torah ark, made in Sioux City, Iowa, by Russian Jewish immigrant and amateur woodcarver Abraham Shulkin, shows a close connection to Eastern European wooden Torah arks. The iconography of the eagle and the traditional images of the Tablets of the Law and the hands opened in the priestly gesture were often featured in Eastern European arks from the eighteenth and nineteenth centuries, all of which were destroyed during World War II. The synagogue of Izabielin, in Lithuania, not far from Shulkin's native village of Kapulie in Byelorussia, had a wooden Torah ark featuring beautiful carvings of animals and vegetation, including sunflowers similar to those in Shulkin's ark. In the synagogue of Olkienniki, also in Lithuania, the elaborate wooden Torah ark featured a pair of blessing hands topped by a double-headed eagle.

In the late nineteenth century, nearly five million Jews lived in czarist Russia, the largest concentration of Jews in the world at the time. Political oppression, government-condoned anti-Jewish riots (pogroms), and economic need prompted more than two million Jews to immigrate to the United States between 1880 and 1924. Most new arrivals settled in large urban centers in the Northeast, but some ventured farther west in search of opportunities in the new country. A number of Jewish immigrants, primarily from the small Russian town of Kapulie, reached Sioux City, Iowa, where a few German Jews had lived since the late 1850s, when the city had just been settled.

By 1896, the Russian Jews had founded the congregation of Adath Yeshurun, erecting Sioux City's first Orthodox synagogue soon after. Members of the synagogue made many of its interior furnishings, including this magnificent Torah ark, carved by Abraham Shulkin. A father of twelve, and a peddler and junk dealer, Shulkin was a talented woodcarver who proudly inscribed his name in Hebrew on the ark in the area flanking the Tablets of the Law, above the rampant lions: "This is the handwork of Abraham Shulkin." Below the tablets are two cutout niches housing a pair of doves, underneath which is a Hebrew dedicatory inscription: "This Torah ark was donated by Simḥah, daughter of the esteemed David Davidson." Davidson, who owned the Davidson department store in Sioux City, provided the lumber for the Torah ark, which Shulkin accepted in lieu of payment. Wood was not as readily available in Sioux City as it had been in the forested woods of Eastern Europe.

The symmetrical openwork design of the carvings can also be compared with that of Eastern European papercuts. In fact, Shulkin's work method might have consisted of making a preparatory papercut, which he then used as a model for the woodcarving. Although no papercut model for the Adath Yeshurun Torah ark is known to have survived, an extant papercut by Shulkin might have been the source for some of the motifs featured in a second Torah ark he carved in 1909 for the Tifereth Israel synagogue of Sioux City.

CN

REFERENCES

Conner, *Remember When*; Kleeblatt and Wertkin, *The Jewish Heritage in American Folk Art*, p. 82 (no. 64) and pl. 2; Piechotka, *Wooden Synagogues*; Shadur, *Jewish Papercuts: A History and Guide*, p. 31 and pl. 11; Wischnitzer, *The Architecture of the European Synagogue*, pp. 125–47.

Hanukkah Lamp

Northern Morocco, late 19th–
early 20th century

Silver: engraved; brass: cast
$10^{13}/_{16}$ x $117/_8$ x 4 in. (27.5 x 30.2 x 10.2 cm)

Purchase: Judaica Endowment Fund
and Nash Aussenberg Memorial Fund,
1996-46

Most Moroccan Hanukkah lamps are made of brass; silver examples are much rarer. The more expensive silver material was commonly used for other personal Judaica, such as the boxlike containers for prayer shawls. Not only is the material of this Hanukkah lamp rare, but the decoration of the lamp likewise represents an unusual complex of elements. Engraved arabesques and whirling circular motifs are engraved all over the backplate, lending the impression of a rich textile. Three-dimensional gilt rosettes and bird appliqués are placed in the arches at the top and along the row of engraved rosettes. They serve to enliven the color scheme and emphasize significant elements of the design. These appliqués are often used on bracelets made in Morocco.

The most interesting feature of the lamp is the presence of anthropomorphic forms behind the oil containers, which represent a significant departure from the aniconic Islamic art of Morocco. These forms are similar to those found, even in the modern period, on Jewish tombstones in coastal cities that had been settled by the Carthaginians, the first invaders of Morocco, in the ninth–eighth century B.C.E. The form is derived from the Punic god Tanit but is here multiplied by the number of Hanukkah lights needed for the holiday. The arrival of European artists, such as Eugene Delacroix, in the first decades of the nineteenth century may have stimulated the use of figurative forms in the Jewish art of Morocco. The incorporation of anthropomorphic figures in this Hanukkah lamp reflects the Jewish community's wide-ranging affiliation with European culture in the nineteenth and twentieth centuries.

VBM

REFERENCE
Mann, *Morocco*, cat. no. 31.

Choker Necklace

San'a, Yemen, 19th–20th century

Silver: granulated, filigree, parcel-gilt, appliqué, engraved, and punched; glass

3⅞ x 22⅜ in. (9.8 x 56.8 cm)

Gift of Dr. Harry G. Friedman, by exchange, 1994-76

According to various accounts, Jews arrived in Yemen either during the time of Joshua or in the tenth century B.C.E. The first secure evidence for their presence is a series of grave markers dated four centuries later. Some documents from the Cairo Genizah of the tenth to the twelfth century refer to the Jews in southern Arabia, but it is only in the eighteenth century that the Jews of San'a, the capital of Yemen, began to record their history in the city and the surrounding region. Their long presence in Yemen ceased after the founding of the State of Israel, when the Jews of southern and central Yemen emigrated en masse, leaving only a small community in the north.

The departure of the Jews meant the loss of most of the craftsmen of Yemen, especially its silversmiths, a métier that Jews had practiced even prior to the Arab conquest in the seventh century C.E. The fine work evident in this necklace and the small, detailed forms that compose it are the marks of a long tradition of skilled silver-smithing. The choker consists of fifteen or more strands. This necklace was worn for weddings and festive occasions. The silversmith alternated silver and gilt octagonal and cubic beads to create a rich coloristic effect. The same beads decorate the *tadarif*, the triangular pieces that cover the ends of the strands of beads, again resulting in a color contrast that is enhanced by small colored glass stones. Characteristic of this type of necklace is the twisting of the strands in the middle.

In the Islamic world, jewelry worn by women represented their dowry and the wealth of the household. The great variety of forms and their ownership by all sectors of the Jewish community signify the importance of jewelry to Yemenite Jews. VBM

Max Weber

(American, born Russia, 1881–1961)

Sabbath, 1919

Oil on canvas
12½ x 10 in. (31.8 x 25.4 cm)
Promised gift of Joy S. Weber

Max Weber was one of the first American modernists and one of the few avant-garde artists to include religious subjects in his work. Emigrating with his Orthodox family from Bialystok, Russia, to Williamsburg, Brooklyn, at the age of ten, Weber studied art at the Pratt Institute under Arthur Wesley Dow (1857–1922) and taught art classes in Virginia and Minnesota before heading to Europe in 1905 to continue his artistic training. In Paris, Weber met several leaders of the avant-garde, including collectors Leo and Gertrude Stein and artists Henri Matisse, Pablo Picasso, and Henri Rousseau. In addition, he saw works by Paul Cézanne and the Fauves at the Salon d'Automne and was exposed to the Japanese prints, African sculpture, and pre-Columbian imagery that greatly influenced the direction of modern art in the early twentieth century.

Returning to New York in 1909, Weber brought with him works by Europe's leading artists, including Matisse, with whom he studied in Paris, and Picasso, whose Cubist influence made a significant impact on Weber's work. Considered the first American to work in a Cubist style, Weber gained recognition from important American artists such as Arthur B. Davies and had a one-person exhibition of drawings and paintings at Alfred Stieglitz's influential 291 gallery in 1911. His fractured, multiple-viewpoint images of contemporary urban subjects—such as the newly constructed Grand Central Terminal—met with criticism from the public but praise from within the artistic community.

Weber began to explore spiritual and religious themes in his work around 1917. A few years later, he became actively involved with a group of Yiddish writers called *Di Yunge*, contributing woodcuts, essays, and poems to their journal. *Sabbath* is one of Weber's early religious paintings that link a modern Cubist vocabulary with a traditional Judaic theme. The simplified, angular forms create a dynamic setting for a scholarly Sabbath discussion. While the two men in the foreground with their dark clothing and beards are traditional Orthodox figures, the women in the background would be as much at home in a bohemian salon as in a religious milieu. Weber's introduction of contemporary figures and an avant-garde style into a traditional religious theme offers a rarely seen modernist approach to Jewish imagery.

K L

REFERENCES
Baigell, "Max Weber's Jewish Paintings"; North, *Max Weber: American Modern*; North and Krane, *Max Weber: The Cubist Decade*.

Isidor Kaufmann

(Austrian, 1853–1921)

Friday Evening, c. 1920

Oil on canvas
28½ x 35½ in. (72.4 x 90.2 cm)
Gift of Mr. and Mrs. M. R. Schweitzer,
JM 4-63

Artists as stylistically and geographically diverse as Paul Gauguin in France, Fritz von Uhde in Germany, and Isidor Kaufmann in Austria often sought escape from the density, commercialism, and moral decay of the great urban centers of the late nineteenth century. Their search for simplicity and traditionalism led them to the folk society of the nearby countryside. Although formal religious practice was of diminished importance for some of these artists, their respect for the apparent peace and beauty of these more pious lifestyles drew each to observe his coreligionists: Gauguin was attracted to the Catholicism of the Breton peasants; von Uhde to the Protestantism in Germany; and Kaufmann to the Hasidic Judaism in neighboring Galicia, Hungary, and Poland.

Friday Evening depicts a lone woman seated beside a table prepared for the inauguration of the Sabbath. The two flickering candles on the heavily starched table linen indicate that she has already invoked the blessing that signals the beginning of the Sabbath. Her attire, including a folk headdress and embroidered bib, shows her conformity with Orthodox tradition concerning modest dress but also labels her provincial. The presence of candlelit sconces and a chandelier in the era of electricity further confirms a traditional and dated lifestyle. Comfortably furnished and immaculately clean, the spare but elegant room signals an upper-middle-class home, presumably in a small town or village. In fact, the background and trappings depicted in the painting are a quasi–stage set. It is the Sabbath room that Kaufmann designed for the old Jewish museum in Vienna in 1899, modeled on the many homes he visited in the eastern provinces of the Hapsburg Empire.

Is one to assume that the lonesome sitter awaits the return of her husband from synagogue? Or are we to surmise that Kaufmann, the urbane artist from Sigmund Freud's Vienna, may wish to suggest a state of psychological malaise? The isolation of the sitter in *Friday Evening* is typical of Kaufmann's treatment of the religiously devout. These individuals at first seem rapt in their ritual observance. Yet their eyes are often as diverted from their spiritual calling as they are averted from the viewer. They are lost in a reverie similar to subjects of the late-nineteenth-century northern Symbolist painters, who turned away from the material world of

Impressionism toward the inner world of mysterious, often unresolved, emotions.

Kaufmann left *Friday Evening* unfinished. This fact, coupled with the artist's substitution of canvas for his usual mahogany panels, suggests that the work may have been painted late in his career. Large passages of washlike application of paint in the unfinished areas, so pleasing to the contemporary eye, and the areas of evident underdrawing provide the viewer with the privileged glimpse of the methods of an artist renowned for his sleek, lustrous surfaces.

Kaufmann's meticulous depictions of religious study and ritual are not religious paintings per se. The works became popular with the increasingly assimilated and cosmopolitan Jewish bourgeoisie of fin-de-siècle Vienna. For Kaufmann's patrons, these paintings served a curious twofold purpose: they linked past and present, providing a representational connection with their ancestral heritage; and they served as yet another of the myriad, status-laden trappings of his clients' bourgeois lifestyles.
NLK

REFERENCES
Goodman, *The Emergence of Jewish Artists in Nineteenth-Century Europe*; Natter, *Rabbiner-Bocher-Talmudschüler*.

Mezuzah Cover of Mess'ud el-Carif

Morocco, 20th century

Silver: engraved and pierced
10¾ x 7 in. (27.3 x 17.8 cm)

Purchase: Judaica Acquisitions
Committee Fund, 1997-170

The Bible mandates that passages from Deuteronomy inscribed on a parchment scroll be hung on the doorposts of Jewish homes and Jewish-owned buildings. Surviving medieval Jewish homes in the kingdom of Aragon, Spain, still have small cavities carved out of the stone doorpost. The parchment was placed inside and covered by a protective device. None of these coverings survives from Spain, but the same form of mezuzah was used in Morocco by those Jews who descended from Iberian refugees, and late examples of their covers survive.

This example was used to cover the parchment in a door niche in Morocco in the home of Mess'ud el-Carif, whose name is cut out below the name Almighty in the top section. The remaining decoration is composed of arabesques of flowering vines that are enhanced by engraved details and set against cutout voids. Fitted with a (now missing) deeply colored textile on its underside, the mezuzah cover would have been greatly enhanced in its aesthetic affect, which was similar to that of contemporaneous prayer-shawl bags and *ajouré* Hanukkah lamps from workshops in Meknes.

VBM

REFERENCE
Mann, *Morocco*, cat. no. 33.

Synagogue Menorah

Gyula Pap (Hungarian, 1899–1983)

Bauhaus, Weimar, 1922

Brass
16½ x 16⅞ in. (41.9 x 42.9 cm)

Purchase: Hubert J. Brandt in honor
of his wife, Frances Brandt;
Judaica Acquisitions Committee Fund;
gift of Mrs. J. J. Wyle, by exchange;
Peter Cats Foundation, Helen and
Jack Cytryn, and Isaac Pollak gifts,
1991-106

The architect and designer Walter Gropius established the Bauhaus in 1919 as a school for art, design, and architecture in Weimar, Germany. It then moved to Dessau in 1925 and was finally located in Berlin. The Bauhaus was closed by Nazi authorities in 1933. The name of the school, derived from the word for a medieval mason's lodge, signified its emphasis on training within crafts workshops, in addition to artistic instruction known as the "teaching of form." In 1922, Gropius began to espouse the unity of art and technology and the reproducibility of works.

This seven-branched menorah by Gyula Pap for a synagogue reflects Gropius's evolving philosophy regarding design. Each of its forms is identical to others of the same type; all are sleek and functional and reproducible. A second example of Pap's menorah is in the Bauhaus archive in Berlin. Both *menorot* have seven arms, like the original lamp stand in the Jerusalem Temple, but lack the ornament of knops and flowers mentioned in the biblical description. Instead, the artistic effect of Pap's design comes from the harmonious proportions of all the parts and the repeated shapes—for example, the circular base that is echoed in the tops of the oil cups and in the semicircles of the arms. The high polish causes these similar forms to reflect in the base. *Menorot* like this one were placed in synagogues as reminders of the ancient Temple.

Born in Hungary, Pap moved with his family to Austria when he was thirteen. From 1920 to 1924, he studied metalworking with Johannes Itten at the Bauhaus. In addition to the menorah, Pap created a standing lamp for the common room at the school, as well as many lithographs and photographs. After the war, he served as professor at the University of Fine Arts in Budapest, until his retirement in 1962. VBM

REFERENCES
Mann, *The Jewish Museum*, no. 70; Wingler, *Das Bauhaus*, p. 109.

Wall Hanging

Berthold Wolpe (English, born Germany, 1905–1989)

Workshop of Rudolf Koch (German, 1876–1934)

Offenbach, Germany, 1925

Undyed handwoven linen; embroidered with dyed linen 106⅝ x 57 in. (270.8 x 144.8 cm)

Gift of Milton Rubin, JM 33-48

The elegant simplicity of this embroidered hanging was a product of the sophisticated partnership of an imaginative student, a knowledgeable master craftsman, and an enlightened patron: Berthold Wolpe, Rudolf Koch, and Siegfried Guggenheim, respectively. Its aesthetic appeal depends on the expressive design of its Hebrew letters, which inscribe the text of the grace after meals and the superb craftsmanship of the handweaving and embroidery.

Rudolf Koch became known primarily as a fine book designer and creator of new typefaces. His fascination with letters and words and his admiration of the Bible led him to design many Christian texts. Simultaneously, his longtime interest in medieval embroidery encouraged him to study handweaving, spinning, and dyeing. It was through these media that Koch's interest in decorative lettering would reach a new level of sophistication. By 1924, he had set up a textile workshop but had not yet received any commissions. Shortly after, commissions came from his longtime friend Siegfried Guggenheim. These resulted in five religious textiles for the Guggenheim home.

For this work, Koch drew on the skills of his twenty-year-old student and Guggenheim's coreligionist Berthold Wolpe to create a design based on Hebrew letters. Wolpe clearly was influenced in his modernization of Hebrew letters by his master's ideas about the stylization and simplification of Renaissance Latin typefaces. He also incorporated Koch's theory about the word as an almost self-sufficient means of decoration. The simplicity of this textile design and its reliance on traditional techniques also relate to the contemporaneous development of textile workshops of the early Bauhaus. Wolpe, who immigrated to England in 1935, is now famed for the excellence of his own typefaces and the more than 1,500 books and jackets designed for the firm Faber & Faber. His respect for the past led to creative adaptations of traditional techniques and designs. Wolpe acknowledged the influence of Koch, whose style had its origins in the Jugendstil, the German version of Art Nouveau, and in the numerous Arts and Crafts movements that spread across Germany in the late nineteenth and early twentieth centuries.

The symbiotic relationship of this creative trio led to further developments. It was Guggenheim's Jewish textile commissions that again encouraged Koch to produce a series of seven large tapestries based on both the Hebrew and Christian Bibles. These were intended as church decorations. At the same time, Wolpe produced another Jewish ceremonial work in a different medium for the Guggenheim dining room. Wolpe's copper ewer and basin of 1926 carry the Hebrew benediction for the ritual washing of hands before meals. Guggenheim could thus begin and end his meals using finely wrought contemporary works in the observance of traditional Jewish practice.

The triumvirate's efforts culminated with the Offenbach Passover Haggadah of 1927, published and edited by Guggenheim himself. The book used one of Koch's innovative Latin type designs for the German translation opposite Wolpe's Hebrew lettering of the original text. Woodcut illustrations by another member of the workshop, Fritz Kredel, further enriched the Haggadah. For Koch, the collaborative nature of the publication of this communal text added to its fundamental value.
NLK

REFERENCES
Guggenheim, *Rudolf Koch*; Victoria and Albert Museum, *Berthold Wolpe*.

בּרוך אתה יי אלהינו מלך העולם הזן
את העולם כלו בטובו בחן בחסד
וברחמים הוא נותן לחם לכל בשר כי
לעולם חסדו ובטובו הגדול תמיד לא
חסר לנו ואל יחסר לנו מזון לעולם ועד
בעבור שמו הגדול כי הוא זן ומפרנס
לכל ומטיב לכל ומכין מזון לכל בריותיו
אשר ברא וכן כתוב אתה יהו את ...ב...
ונאל תצריכנו יי אלהינו לא לד
מתנות בשר ודם ולא לידי הלואתם כי אם
אם לידך המלאה הפתוחה הקדושה
והרחבה שלא נבוש ולא נכלם לעולם
ועד הרחמן הוא ימלוך עלינו לעולם
ועד הרחמן הוא יתברך בשמים
ובארץ הרחמן הוא ... נסתנכבד
לדור עשה שלום שלום במרומיו הוא עשה
שלום עלינו ועל כל ישראל ואמרו אמן

Passover Set

Ludwig Yehuda Wolpert (American, born Germany, 1900–1981)

New York, c. 1978 (original design, Frankfurt, 1930)

Silver, ebony, and glass
10 in. high x 16 in. diam. (25.4 x 40.6 cm)

Promised gift of Sylvia Zenia Wiener, P.1.1997a–i

The aesthetic principles advocated by the Bauhaus in the 1920s—that form and function were mutually dependent, that fine design should be aimed at mass production, that ornament should be banned—pervaded international artistic thought for much of the twentieth century. At first considered radical by many, the numerous Bauhaus designs that are still produced today testify to their viable aesthetic and practical values.

Ludwig Wolpert is the first metalworker to apply these progressive principles to the fabrication of Jewish ceremonial art. His Passover service, a copy after a lost original designed in 1930, may be his masterpiece. Its conception and execution aptly express the ideas generated by the Bauhaus School, first during its years at Weimar and then in Dessau. Wolpert gleaned many of these concepts from his Bauhaus-trained teacher Leo Horowitz and also became aware of burgeoning Bauhaus design through publications and colleagues.

The form of this set is based on earlier, lavishly decorated examples. Following Bauhaus precepts of minimal embellishment and maximum visual effect, Wolpert pared the multilevel server down to its essential functions in a highly calibrated play with contrasting materials. Three circular tiers above a conforming silver base are joined at equidistant points by vertical ebony and silver mounts. Notched to support the glass shelves, the mounts double as handles. Horizontal silver bands that separate each tier slide open to reveal a space, within which the symbolic matzah can be placed. The cutout Hebrew inscription

כוס ישועות אשא ובשם ה' אקרא

I will lift the cup of salvation, and call upon the name of the Lord

appears on the glass-lined silver goblet. This receptacle holds the wine symbolically set aside for the prophet Elijah. Practical, industrially replicable, cylinder-shaped glass dishes, meant to contain the ritual foods, have been set into precious silver mounts.

The design of the tiered platter, aside from the cutout inscription, is founded entirely on the appeal of its high-contrast materials. Wolpert's inspiration for his combination of wood, glass, and metal may have come from Josef Albers's berry dishes and teacups of 1923–25. Yet Wolpert applies these ideas to an infinitely more complex object with a rationality and a thorough understanding of the relationship of weighted objects in three-dimensional space. This latter conception conforms with the thinking of Moholy-Nagy, an important teacher at the Bauhaus, who strove to derive uncompromising new forms that could also be mass-produced. Although the fabrication of this seder plate was too difficult for large-scale production, it was carefully replicated several times.

A substantial part of Wolpert's later work, including Hanukkah lamps, memorial lights, and *kiddush* goblets, was indeed designed for mass production. Ultimately, the artist successfully adapted Bauhaus philosophy to the production of well-designed ritual domestic wares still available today. NLK

REFERENCE
The Jewish Museum, *Ludwig Yehuda Wolpert: A Retrospective.*

144

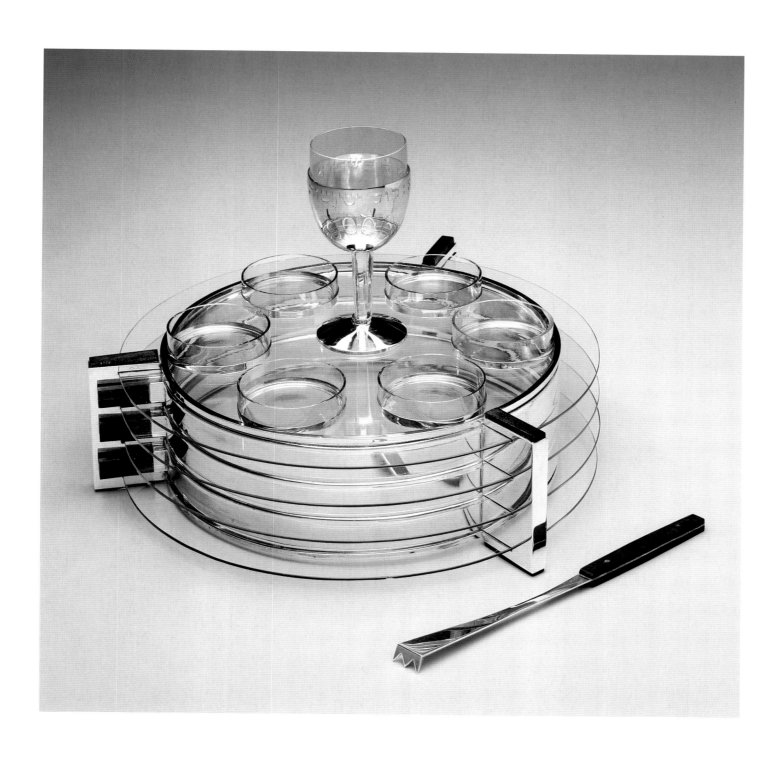

Hyman Bloom

(American, born Latvia, 1913)

Female Corpse (Front View), 1945

Oil on canvas
70 x 42 in. (177.8 x 106.7 cm)

Purchase: gift of Kurt Delbanco and Romie Shapiro, by exchange; Kristie A. Jayne Fund, 1994-599

Born in Brunoviski, Latvia, Hyman Bloom emigrated to America at the age of seven. In Boston's West End community, Bloom straddled the two worlds of his parents' Orthodox Judaism and the secular culture of urban life. He received his early artistic training from Harold Zimmerman at the West End Community Center and learned color theory and art history under Harvard professor Denman Ross. Bloom felt an affinity for the tragic sensibility of the Jewish expressionist Chaim Soutine and the personalized religious visions of the Christian mystic Georges Rouault. In his own quest for spiritual understanding, Bloom looked beyond Jewish tradition to the philosophies of Spinoza, theosophy, astrology, and the occult. Though hailed in 1954 by Willem de Kooning and Jackson Pollock as "the first Abstract Expressionist painter in America," Bloom never fully disavowed representation and kept a quiet distance from the New York School.

In *Female Corpse*, Bloom combines his private musings on the human condition and his anguish at the events of the Holocaust. In the early 1940s, scattered reports and photographs of massacred Jews mingled in Bloom's consciousness with broader philosophical inquiries on the nature of mortality. Beginning in 1943, Bloom made visits to the morgue at Boston's Kenmore Hospital to sketch autopsies. By focusing on a decomposing body on a dissection table, Bloom found a stand-in for the decomposing bodies in Europe, which he did not paint. Inspired by the haunting immediacy of Hans Holbein's *The Body of the Dead Christ in the Tomb* (1521) and the graphic lesions of Christ's body in Matthias Grünewald's Isenheim Altarpiece (1515), Bloom's life-size and surprisingly vertical presentation of the corpse forces the viewer into a confrontation with the brute reality of death.

Bloom renders the female body with a palette of yellows, reds, greens, and browns. Circular patches of impasto corrode the surface, representing gangrenous dead tissue. The painterly buildup of the rotting remains suggests not only decomposition but also smoldering. The pus-filled swellings might also be the blisters of a burned body, and the ruddy, bone-thin hands have the rawness of scorched skin. The fury of red and brown paint, culminating in an orange flourish at the right, suggests the encroachment of flames upon the swaddled corpse.

Yet to see nothing but death in Bloom's painting is to miss the dualities of his art. The sores are depicted in the form of cells, which constitute all forms of life. The white paint that engulfs the woman is not only a death shroud but also the amniotic sac that surrounds a fetus in the womb. And the segment of red and brown paint might be not only a perishing blaze but also a placenta—an infant's source of vitality. While depicting the isolation of death—a solitary corpse on his canvas—Bloom connects this state with the preternatural condition of human life. Just as the regeneration of life from death must be seen as a continuum, so does Bloom's painting chart the metamorphosis of artistic expression from tradition to innovation. The female nude (a subject belonging to a tradition of figurative art) is presented as a corpse, built up through gestural brush strokes and surrounded by amorphous partitions of colors. Bloom's painting, however, is neither an elegy for canonical representation nor a manifesto for a new abstraction but rather a meditation on the unceasing flow from old to new.

S N B

REFERENCES
Amishai-Maisels, *Depiction and Interpretation*, pp. 80–93; Dervaux, *Color and Ecstasy*, pp. 18–25; Thompson, *Hyman Bloom*, pp. 36–43.

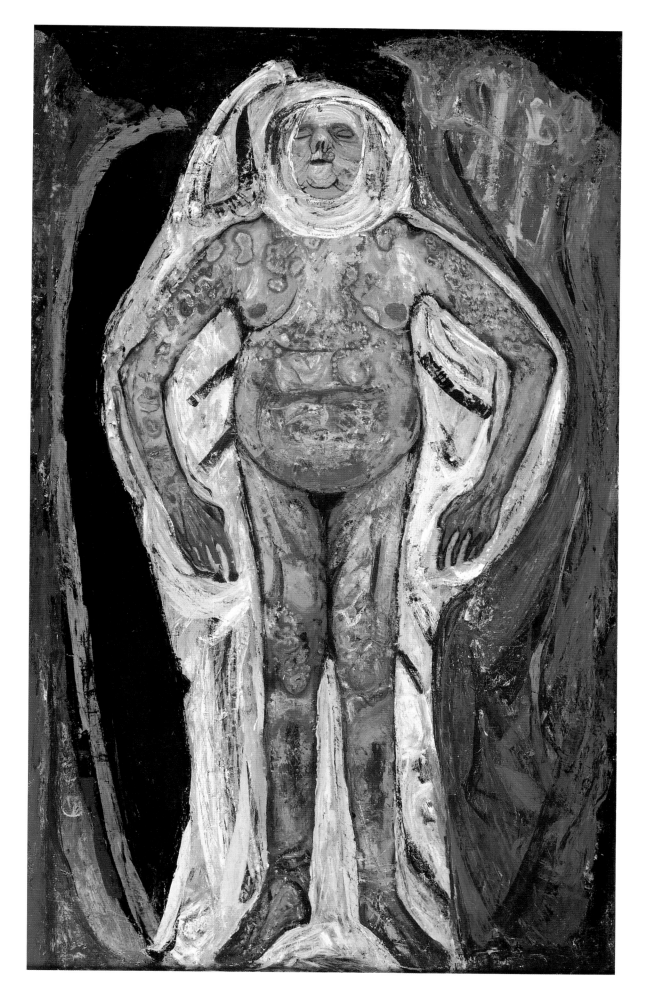

Jacques Lipchitz

(American, born Lithuania, 1891–1973)

The Sacrifice, 1949–57

Bronze
49½ in. high, 24¼ x 24¼ in. base
(125.7, 61.6 x 61.6 cm)

Gift of Mr. and Mrs. Albert A. List,
JM 16-65

Lithuanian-born Jacques Lipchitz arrived in Paris in 1909 and was confronted by an art world dominated by the stylistic revolution of Cubism. Three years later, he was introduced to Picasso and other Cubist painters and sculptors. His rapid absorption of the formal elements of that movement, including the influences of "primitive" art, led to his early successful sculptures of 1915–19, considered the first to use Cubist syntax. Those sculptures have been accorded a seminal place in the art of that period. A number of scholars have observed the humanizing aspects and personal immediacy in Lipchitz's manipulation of Cubism, a style that, in the hands of lesser artists, can become frigid or decorative.

For nearly a decade, Lipchitz developed new formal approaches to sculpture, including experimentation with solids and voids, as well as large-scale works. By the mid-1930s, his earlier austere, classically oriented formalism gave way to equally masterful works exhibiting expressionist modeling and a decidedly baroque sensibility. Likewise, his earlier focus on pleasurable themes from modern life—such as acrobats, harlequins, and still lifes—became transformed to heroic, often tragic themes from the Bible and classical mythology. These themes were often concerned with the major issues of man's struggle with the world, with others, and with himself. Lipchitz sought to distill the profundity of such subjects in a monumental scale while simultaneously striving for technical innovation.

One can best appreciate *The Sacrifice* (which Lipchitz considered his major work) by understanding its predecessors within his oeuvre—formally, thematically, and personally. The work takes a place in Lipchitz's ongoing focus on epic struggle, beginning with his *Jacob Wrestling with the Angel* of the early 1930s. The transformation of the biblical theme into a mythological one with his *Prometheus and the Vulture* series (1933–37) emerged in response to the oppressive threat of Nazism, which ultimately forced Lipchitz to flee France and seek refuge in America. Although Lipchitz had limited contact with the painters and sculptors of New York's Abstract Expressionist School—such as Mark Rothko and David Smith—there are nevertheless some striking connections between them. In fact, in 1946 the critic Clement Greenberg connected the scale, "bombast," and ambition of Lipchitz to then-emerging painter Jackson Pollock. The Abstract Expressionists and Lipchitz shared an emotive handling of media and were obsessed with classical and tribal myths. These attributes and their common focus on the tragic, changeless nature of human psychology were no doubt a response to the Zeitgeist of the epoch: the devastating realities of World War II and the Holocaust.

The iconographic precursor for *The Sacrifice* is Lipchitz's technically intricate and masterful *The Prayer* (1943), where he alludes to the curious, "primitive," and sometimes controversial ritual of *kapparot*—the custom of symbolically transferring personal sins onto an animal. *The Prayer* actually shows a disemboweled fowl, spewing forth guilty as well as innocent victims. The latter serves as a metaphor for the suffering of the Jewish people at that time.

The Sacrifice of 1949–57 expands upon this theme from a more optimistic perspective—in response to the end of World War II and the successful struggle to found the State of Israel. The lamb, a symbol that Lipchitz considers Christian, refers to his hopes for a peaceful coexistence between Judaism and Christianity. While the fragmented nature of *The Prayer* reflects his technical difficulty during its execution as it symbolizes the profoundly helpless moments during World War II, the artist has approached *The Sacrifice* with a forceful unity of spirit and majestic amplitude of form that express his renewed affirmation of life.

NLK

REFERENCES
Fineberg, "Lipchitz in America"; Greenberg, "Review of Exhibitions of American Abstract Artists," pp. 72–75; Lipchitz with Arnason, *My Life in Sculpture*, pp. 160–63, 178–83; Wilkinson, *Jacques Lipchitz: A Life in Sculpture*, pp. 141–42; Wilkinson, *The Sculpture of Jacques Lipchitz*.

Torah Curtain

Adolph Gottlieb (American,
1903–1974)

Millburn, New Jersey, 1950–51

Velvet: appliqué embroidered with
metallic thread
Upper section: 112¾ x 80½ in.
(204.5 x 286.4 cm)
Lower section: 121¾ x 81½ in.
(207 x 309.2 cm)

Gift of Congregation B'nai Israel,
Millburn, New Jersey, 1987-23a-d

A surprising number of commissions for ecclesiastical decoration went to major European painters and sculptors in the years following World War II—perhaps a response to the mediocrity of religious furnishings in the previous hundred years. Reestablishing the long tradition of using master artists in such projects, churches and synagogues commissioned Fernand Léger, Marc Chagall, Henri Matisse, Georges Rouault, and Henry Moore, among others, to execute stained glass, vestments, liturgical objects, and other embellishments.

Adolph Gottlieb's Torah curtain is an American expression of this revival. During the postwar boom in synagogue construction, sweeping redefinition of synagogue design began. Based on a modernist aesthetic, it rejected historical references. Many architects considered symbols appropriate only on liturgical objects in the sanctuary. Sparse decoration was standard practice.

In a bold step, Percival Goodman, architect for the Millburn synagogue, charged three emerging, avant-garde artists with commissions to decorate that building. Adolph Gottlieb, Robert Motherwell, and Herbert Ferber, each of whom has since become a major figure in the Abstract Expressionist movement, supplied a Torah curtain, a lobby mural, and an exterior sculptural relief, respectively. Gottlieb's design for the curtain (actually executed by the women of the congregation under the supervision of his wife, Esther) is a late example in the development of his influential pictograph paintings of 1941–53. It directly reflects these compartmentalized canvases, which in turn were influenced by the grid-based works of Mondrian and by the sectional arrangement of religious narrative cycles of the early Italian Renaissance. (See entry on Gottlieb's *Return of the Mariner* in this volume, pp. 56–57.)

The forms contained within Gottlieb's compartments, and the meanings of these forms, are related to unconscious expressions associated with African, Oceanic, and Native American art as well as with Carl Jung's writings about symbols and the "collective unconscious." Gottlieb's pictograph style was therefore easily adaptable to the creation of a ritual object using symbols of Jewish collective consciousness. In this curtain, he abstracts such basic elements of religious belief as the Tablets of the Law, the twelve tribes, the Temple, and the Ark of the Covenant. He also includes stylizations of objects developed for synagogue use (Torah mantles and Torah shields) and emblems that have become synonymous with Judaism (the Lion of Judah and the Star of David).

Gottlieb's pictographs have been noted for the frequent appearance of sexual references and his predilection for visual puns. In this Torah curtain, he intended the W-form pictograph at the lower right corner to represent a "breastplate" (a common term for Torah shield). It seems to depict the chain by which that ornament is hung over the Torah staves. There can be little doubt that these two pendulous shapes, generally associated in Gottlieb's work with female breasts, are an international pun on "breastplate." However, the serpentine outline can also be perceived as the artist's usual visualization of the male symbol. This combination of the male and female in one image is a common Jungian reference to the life force, and in this case embodies Gottlieb's ideas of the universality and continuity of human existence. It also relates to Jung's standard interpretation of the anima and animus as well as the dual readings of positive and negative spaces. Ultimately, this avant-garde adaptation of traditional symbols becomes an expression of the viable continuum of Jewish ceremony and community, a significant concept after the devastations of World War II and the Holocaust.
NLK

REFERENCES
Hirsch, *Adolph Gottlieb: A Survey Exhibition*; Hirsch, *The Pictographs of Adolph Gottlieb*; Kampf, *Contemporary Synagogue Art*; Wong, "Synagogue Art of the 1950s."

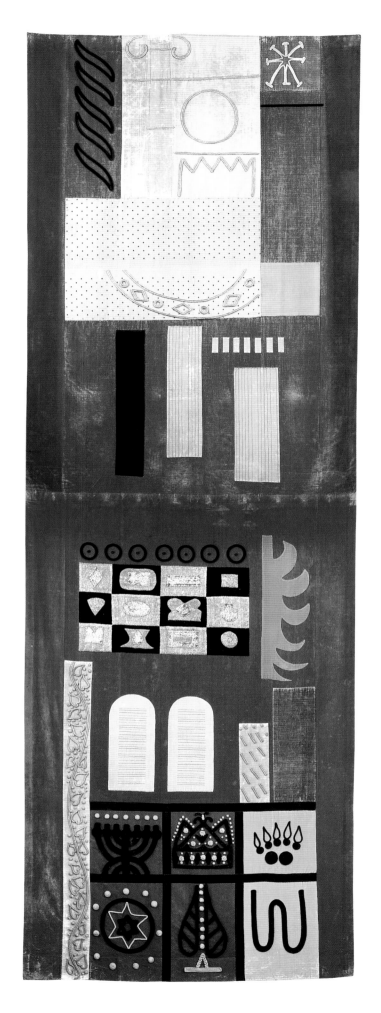

Ludwig Yehuda Wolpert

(American, born Germany, 1900–1981)

Fabric with inscription from *Ethics of the Fathers*, 1959

Designed for the draperies of Larchmont Temple, Larchmont, New York

Silk screen on fiberglass 64 x 48¾ in. (162.6 x 123.8 cm)

Gift of Betty Wolpert, widow of the artist, 1992-158

Many contemporary Jewish artists have contended with the challenges of creating ceremonial objects that conform to modern aesthetics. The trend first emerged among artists in Europe associated with the Bauhaus in Germany, who applied the school's principles to ritual objects, seeking to eliminate decoration that served no functional purpose and emphasizing the object's beauty through simplicity in form and line.

A pioneer of modern design of Jewish ceremonial art, Ludwig Yehuda Wolpert fulfills the ideals of the Bauhaus and the biblical concept "This is my God and I shall adorn Him." Born near Heidelberg to a traditional family, Wolpert cherished his Jewish heritage. Originally trained as a sculptor, Wolpert later studied metalwork with a silversmith who had taught at the Bauhaus in Weimar. It was there that Wolpert decided to devote himself to the creation of Jewish ceremonial art, applying the new forms and principles of Bauhaus design to his work. After the rise of Nazism, Wolpert immigrated in 1933 to Palestine, where he became professor and director of the metalcraft department at the New Bezalel Academy for Arts and Crafts in Jerusalem. His teaching stressed simplicity and functional purity of design.

In 1956, Wolpert helped establish and consequently came to direct the Tobe Pascher Workshop at The Jewish Museum in New York. For many years, this workshop was the only one devoted exclusively to the creation of modern Jewish ceremonial art. There was an immediate impact on Wolpert's designs when he began working and teaching at the workshop. Particularly, the use of new materials—aluminum, plastics, fabrics, and textiles—introduced variety and color into his work.

Wolpert's designs fit appropriately into the contemporary home and synagogue, fully realizing the Bauhaus idea of integrating a building and its contents. The principle of pure functionalism shows up most clearly in his large-scale synagogue pieces—unified images unadorned of extraneous decorations. Perhaps Wolpert's greatest contribution is his glorification of the Hebrew letter. As an artist knowledgeable in the Hebrew tradition, he had a kabbalistic love of the Hebrew alphabet. The significance of the Hebrew letter in Jewish tradition is profound; the letters are considered sacred objects for meditation by religious Jews. It is believed by devout Jews that the existence of the Hebrew alphabet predates the creation of the world. Wolpert's ceremonial objects display imaginative versions of the ancient calligraphy. His use of the letter, combined with his knowledge of the appropriate verse, invests his modern designs with an aura of tradition.

Wolpert used a frieze-like motif of stylized Hebrew letters as the embellishment of this fiberglass textile, woven for the draperies of the Larchmont Temple in Larchmont, New York. These repeating bands of text are actually a quotation from *Ethics of the Fathers* (5:23), a treatise of the Mishnah: "Be bold as a leopard, light as an eagle, swift as a deer, and strong as a lion, to do the will of Your Father who is in Heaven." Wolpert reapplied the same design for another fabric in 1959, seeking to realize another mandate of the Bauhaus—that of making fine design accessible to the masses. Wolpert believed that one-of-a-kind objects do not confer special importance, leading him to create designs that permitted reproductions in order to place them within reach of many. Thus, Wolpert successfully realized not only Bauhaus ideals but also the Talmudic tradition of *hiddur mitzvah*, the beautification of ritual.

LF

REFERENCES
The Jewish Museum, *Ludwig Yehuda Wolpert*; Kampf, *Contemporary Synagogue Art*, pp. 70–71, 149–50, 172; Kanof, *Jewish Ceremonial Art*; Spertus, "Ludwig Yehuda Wolpert, 1900–1981," p. 86.

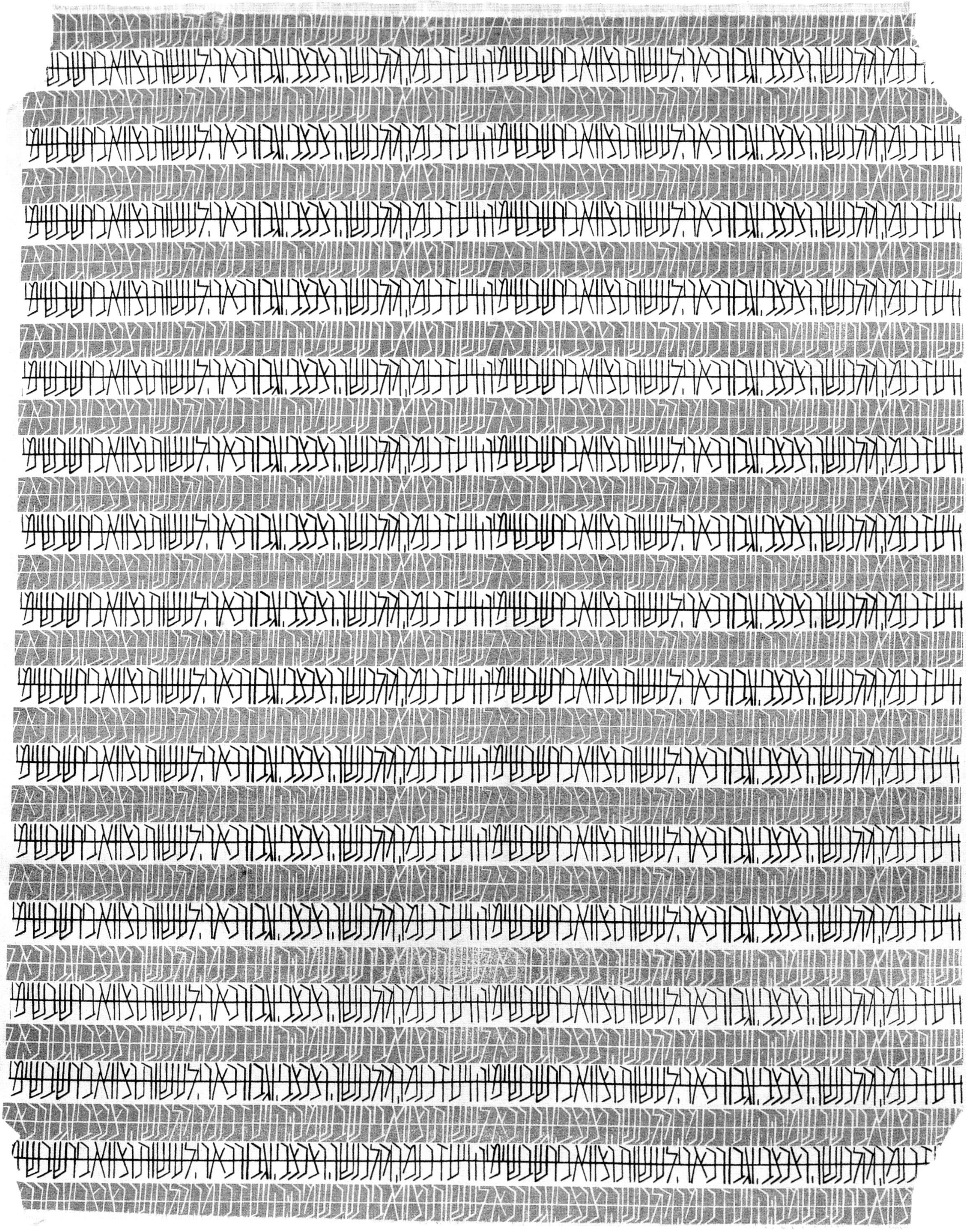

Torah Crown

Moshe Zabari (Israeli, born 1935)

New York, 1969

Silver: raised and forged; pearls
13½ x 15⅜ in. (34.3 x 39 cm)

Gift of the Albert A. List Family,
JM 85-69

This is not a Torah crown of the usual form, modeled on the regalia of kings and queens; the artist eschewed any association with crowns that were meant to be worn. Still, this work is a Torah crown in the sense that it is a unified ornament that encompasses both the staves of the Torah scroll and that includes some references to the traditional type of crown. Like the older examples, Zabari's work is a three-dimensional form that circumscribes space. Its three-dimensionality is underscored by pendant pearls, which establish successive points from which to measure the space defined by the form. When the crown is carried in procession, the pearls shake and the silver curves quiver to lend the kinetic sense that was conveyed on older crowns by pendant bells.

In the purity of its forms, in its emphasis on the beauty of materials, and in its avoidance of extraneous decoration, the Zabari crown conforms to the modernist aesthetic. It is also a totally modern work in its emphasis on function. Whereas on older crowns, the utilitarian tubes that fit the crown to the staves of the Torah are hidden beneath an ornamental exterior, on the Zabari crown they are in the open, an important element of the design. They draw attention to the staves, known in Hebrew as "trees of life," which, to the artist, are an important part of the Torah, second only to the parchment. He sees the crown as an ornament for the staves as much as an ornament for the scroll.

The exuberant curves of the Zabari crown link it to decorative arts of the 1950s and 1960s, when curved, organic forms dominated. At the same time, they express the sense of celebration traditionally associated with crowns, which are used in the larger world at times of pomp and circumstance and in many synagogues only on festivals. In recognition of the joyful character of the holidays, the crown replaced the finials used week after week, on ordinary Sabbaths.

VBM

REFERENCES

Encyclopaedia Judaica, 1975–76 yearbook, cols. 428–29, pl. 7;
Kleeblatt and Mann, *Treasures of the Jewish Museum*, pp. 194–95.

Leonard Baskin

(American, 1922–2000)

The Altar, 1977

Carved, laminated lindenwood
60 x 71 x 36 in. (152.4 x 180.3 x 91.4 cm)

Purchase: gift of Herman Tenenbaum and the Saul and Suzanne Mutterperl Bequest, in honor of Mildred and George Weissman, by exchange, 1984-142

Leonard Baskin's figurative art stems from his deep understanding of artistic and literary traditions of both Western civilization and Judaism. The ancient themes that he derives from biblical, mythological, and historical sources forcefully convey contemporary human dilemmas.

The representational nature of Baskin's sculpture and graphics has been noted as an anomaly within the prevailing Abstract Expressionist and Minimalist aesthetic under which he matured. Yet certain stylistic conventions and thematic issues associated with these movements have found their way into his art. Baskin must also be identified with the vital current of figurative art that continued to develop alongside abstraction in the postwar years.

For Baskin, meaning can be expressed only through the human figure. His realism is indeed a reductivist one; he pares his forms just as he condenses content. Art historian Irma Jaffe notes mortality, grief, suffering, and homage as main themes that inform Baskin's works. What at first appears as a pessimistic vision is filtered into an expression of renewal and hope through the artist's manipulation of emotions. His own words plainly confirm his artistic struggle to find universal meaning in tragic subjects: "The human figure is the image of all men and of one man. It contains all and can express all."

Monumental in scale, *The Altar* ranks as Baskin's most important wood carving. It is a highly refined synthesis of the metaphysical themes with those of the Hebrew Bible, all filtered through the artist's strong Jewish background. Out of this large mass of wood emerges the figure of the trusting Isaac, stretched out upon the altar where Abraham dutifully prepares to sacrifice him. Isaac's back fuses with that of Abraham, who faces the opposite direction, emotionally overwhelmed, but relieved. An angel's wings sprout between the two bodies, protectively shrouding the supine body of Isaac. We recognize Baskin's frequent trope of giving his biblical or mythical characters his own features, thus making Abraham and Isaac—and by extension, the symbolically represented angel—into self-portraits. As such, Baskin's sculptural union of each of the three ancient protagonists—Isaac, Abraham, and the angel—projects the analogous tripartite conflicts within his and every person's psyche that Freud characterized as id, superego, and ego.

As Baskin learned of the German concentration camps in the 1940s and began to come to terms with his own mortality, his paintings, sculptures, and poems were preoccupied with the subject of death. Although for many years he collected images and newspaper clippings that related to the Holocaust, he did not confront the topic directly until the 1980s, when he created a series of watercolors accompanied by Yiddish epigrams that embodied his emotions. In 1990, the Ann Arbor Holocaust Memorial Foundation commissioned Baskin to create a bronze monument honoring the victims of the Nazis. In 1994, this was sited on the campus of the University of Michigan. Baskin continued to delve into this subject and created a series of large-scale woodcuts, exhibited in 1998. The extraordinary efflorescence of his artistic interest in this devastating period of history and the proliferation of Holocaust museums and monuments influenced Baskin's turn to the theme. However, it is a logical extension of the attitudes that pervaded his oeuvre for nearly six decades. *The Altar* foreshadows Baskin's obsession with the Holocaust in his later, equally powerful works.

NLK

REFERENCES
Jaffe, *The Sculpture of Leonard Baskin*; Kennedy Galleries, *Leonard Baskin, Recent Work*.

Spice Container

Zelig Segal (Israeli, born 1933)

Jerusalem, 1986

Silver: cast
3¾ x 2½ x 3¾ in. (9.5 x 6.4 x 9.5 cm)

Purchase: Sanford C. Bernstein
Foundation Fund, 1995-72

Israeli artist, designer, sculptor, and metalsmith Zelig Segal has devoted his career to the creation of ritual objects. His ingenious approaches to ceremonial art are fresh, imaginative, and infused with deep understanding of Jewish tradition. Segal received his religious training in Jewish schools and studied metalsmithing and Judaica at Jerusalem's Bezalel Academy under Ludwig Wolpert and David Gumbel, two of the most influential artists in Jewish ceremonial design of the twentieth century. Segal graduated in 1954 and headed the school's Department of Gold and Silversmithing from 1964 to 1968.

For Segal, the design process is always a voyage of discovery, and he experiments freely. Simple, geometricized shapes and an aesthetic of refined simplicity characterize his work, which links the design sensibilities of today with ancient Jewish traditions.

The juxtaposing of negative and positive elements is a recurring theme in Segal's work. The artist finds myriad ways to express this concept—sometimes using the profiles of objects to create a plus/minus tension when they are placed near each other, and other times working with surface finishes to create differentiation. Segal's 1986 spice container employs both plain polished silver (the outer section) and textured silver (spice holder) to define the two principal elements of the piece. Spice containers are part of the ritual of havdalah, the ceremony that marks the end of the Sabbath. The

sweet smell of the spice is meant to recall the beauty of the Sabbath. Segal's creation is not only a spice container but a sculptural work of art. He fashioned the work by "folding" a piece of polished silver in half to create an open wedge shape. He hammered out rounded protrusions in each of the sides so that the spice ball could be placed within this wedge and hang suspended. The irregular surface finish of the silver spice ball attracts the eye as its rough textures and polished areas pick up reflections of light. Like the silver ball within, the Segal spice container seems suspended between contemporary sculpture and modern packaging and yet recalls Jewish tradition.

S R

REFERENCE
The Israel Museum, *In a Single Statement: Works by Zelig Segal.*

Harley Swedler

(American, born Canada, 1962)

Beron Mezuzah, 1991

Bronze: cast with a patina finish, sterling silver, stainless steel, and rolled glass

4⅜ x 2¼ in. (11.1 x 5.7 cm)

Gift of Edna S. Beron and Harley Swedler, 1992-31

The rich dialogue between ancient and modern, between tradition and innovation, is celebrated in contemporary Judaica objects such as the *Beron Mezuzah*, by Harley Swedler. Often housed in a protective case, a mezuzah is a scroll that is inscribed with the *Shema* (verses taken from Deuteronomy), a central prayer in Jewish liturgy that affirms the covenant between God and the Jewish people. This particular passage also obligates Jews to affix a mezuzah to the doorposts of their homes.

As with other ritual and ceremonial objects, contemporary artists continue to reinterpret the mezuzah, combining modern-day aesthetics with ancient traditions. Architect Harley Swedler comes from a traditional Jewish background and unites the Hebrew text with his professional training to create contemporary Judaica pieces. Using metals, joints, edges, and seams, Swedler creates what he calls "alternative Judaica" to explore notions of unity and boundaries within Jewish sacred writings and culture. In his mezuzah, the words "obligation" and "covenant" are etched into the glass that encases the parchment scroll, epitomizing the mezuzah text.

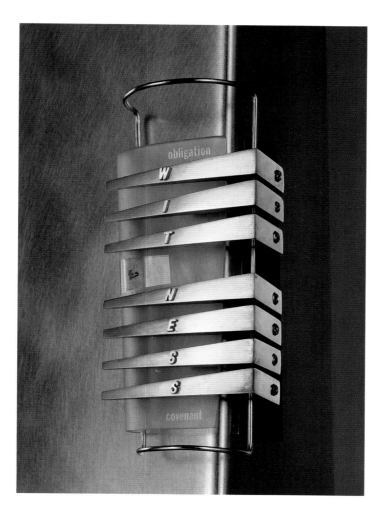

The form of the piece also reflects the spiritual essence of the text: the seven bronze ribs inscribed with the word "witness" correspond to the seven times that God's name is mentioned in the *Shema*, while the ribs represent the act of binding the text to the door.

A reflection of his Jewish heritage, Swedler's deliberate use of text underlines the purpose of the object and the history of the ritual. The incorporation of biblical references is the most dominant aspect of this mezuzah. By incorporating his culture, through text, into his art, Swedler is creating "Jewish art," which addresses, consciously or unconsciously, questions of Jewish identity.

The appearance of Conceptual Art in the 1960s gave legitimacy to the use of text within Jewish art, both high art and ceremonial. The text used in Conceptual Art tended to be general and intentionally ambiguous. The text utilized by Jewish artists, particularly by those making contemporary Judaica, is religious and culturally specific. Ludwig Wolpert, for instance, incorporated the Hebrew alphabet and biblical phrases into his Bauhaus-inspired Judaica (see p. 144). Here, Swedler continues that tradition. In English and in Hebrew, the artist uses sacred writings in his work, underlying the function of the piece with both text and form. Lines from the Torah become an inherent piece of the total form and the image, bringing to light the contemporary relevance of religious text and ritual in art and life.

LF

REFERENCES

Apter and Barnett, *Mezuzah*; The Jewish Museum, *Perpetual Well*; Whitehall Flagler Museum, *Tradition Today*.

Joel Otterson

(American, born 1959)

Unorthodox Menorah II, 1993

Mixed metal pipes, cast bronze, porcelain, and glass
28½ x 48 x 12 in. (72.4 x 121.9 x 30.5 cm)

Purchase: Judaica Acquisitions Committee Fund, Henry H. and Ruth Herzog, and Rabbi Louis Frishman gifts, 1993-216

A key component of Joel Otterson's art is the relationship between an object's function and its symbolic purpose; this ideological stance makes Otterson an ideal candidate for creating Jewish ceremonial objects. But despite his interest in the symbolic, Otterson never made a ritual object until 1991, after he visited Israel and became aware of the power of the menorah form. Otterson discovered that this ancient form could be understood on many levels: it has deep religious meaning and is connected with the story of Hanukkah; it is a symbol of the State of Israel and an essential presence in many Israeli homes; and it is even a favorite souvenir for tourists. Touring the large and impressive collection of Hanukkah lamps in the Israel Museum inspired him to make a special Hanukkah lamp entitled *Orthodox Menorah*, which is in a private collection. The Jewish Museum commissioned this second version in 1993. Otterson's lamp builds on traditional forms but follows the artist's quirky style, which reclaims objects from their everyday existence and reuses them in visually arresting and innovative new ways. One of the most striking elements of his lamp is the ornate armature of copper pipe fittings, which he welded together to form the menorah's branches. Copper pipes and soldering are a recurring theme in Otterson's work and recall the profession of both his father and brother, who were plumbers.

Otterson is a master of displacement—that is, juxtaposing unlikely elements to create surprising visual effects, such as the hypermasculine Hulk Hogan figure that crowns *Unorthodox Menorah II*. During Otterson's stay in Israel, he noted that cartoon characters had invaded the realm of ceremonial objects. Bart Simpson, the Smurfs, and the Peanuts characters were regularly emblazoned on yarmulkes (skullcaps) worn by Jewish boys. The playfulness and charm of this idea inspired the artist to choose Hulk Hogan for this lamp. He reasoned, "If they can make a Bart Simpson yarmulke, I can make a Hulk Hogan menorah." The cast glass image of Hulk might at first seem completely incongruous, but traditional Hanukkah lamps often featured a victorious figure, such as the biblical Judith, to suggest the victory of the Jews over their oppressors. The artist updated this idea with an image of the famous television wrestler.

Along with its spreading copper arms and triumphant Hulk Hogan figure, *Unorthodox Menorah II* features what appears to be a vintage ceramic lamp as a decoration for the main shaft. The base is a cast creation that the artist made to suggest the garish flower-covered ceramic lamps popular in the 1940s and 50s. Otterson uses this object as if it were a precious memento or souvenir. It is at once familiar and jarring but resonates with the story of an old lamp that kept on burning.

S R

Amy Klein Reichert

(American, born 1959)

Miriam's Cup, 1997

Silver: cast and hammered
4½ x 7⅞ in. (11.4 x 20 cm)

Purchase: Lorraine and Martin Beitler Foundation gift and Judaica Acquisitions Committee Fund, 1997-131

Passover, celebrated by Jews in the spring, is a weeklong holiday that commemorates the Israelites' redemption from slavery in Egypt, as told in the Book of Exodus. The injunction for every Jew to feel as if he or she had personally come out of Egypt is fulfilled through the seder, or ritual meal that traditionally takes place in the home on the first night of Passover (and second night in the Diaspora). The Haggadah, the liturgical order for the seder service as well as the term for the book containing this service, includes the recitation of the story of the Exodus from Egypt, which is accompanied by singing, discussion, and the eating and drinking of ritual foods. By participating in this ceremony, Jews reexperience the Exodus and reflect on its significance for their own lives and present circumstances.

Fully realizing the mandate to personalize the oppression of the Israelites and their flight from Egypt, a group of women created the first feminist seder in New York in 1976, connecting it to the history of women's liberation. Truly reinventing ritual, the feminist Passover seder and the women's Haggadah pay special tribute to the prophetess Miriam, sister of Moses, who, timbrel in hand, led the women of the Exodus in song and dance and provided the Israelites with a perpetual well of water during their wanderings in the desert.

Miriam's Cup is one of the first pieces of Judaica created by Amy Klein Reichert, an architect and exhibition designer. Exploring her own spiritual connection to Miriam and Jewish women's ritual,

the artist originally created the work for a groundbreaking 1997 exhibit of Miriam's cups by Jewish women artists. Influenced by the wave of American Jewish feminism and the reinvention of female-centered rituals, Reichert created *Miriam's Cup*, a functional piece of ceremonial art to be placed on the seder table as a symbol of Miriam as a source of sustenance and spirit for the Jewish people. During the seder, each participant drinks "living waters" (*mayim ḥayyim*) from the Miriam's cup after the recitation of a set of prayers devoted to her. Miriam, who safely placed Moses in a basket and sent him down the Nile river to be discovered by Pharaoh's daughter, was, throughout her life, associated with water. She led women in singing and dancing at the crossing of the Red Sea as they were led out of Egypt, and provided the Israelites with a miraculous "well" of water that followed her in the desert, drying up only when she died. As Reichert has stated: "What are the sounds of freedom? The wind rustling through grasses, the murmuring of exiles, desert sounds, a joyous song with a tambourine. Miriam's cup is a restless vessel, like her ancient well accompanying the people of Israel along their journey. It is heard as well as seen, its cymbals dancing in response to the slightest vibration of the table."
LF

REFERENCES
The Jewish Museum, *Perpetual Well*; Lipstadt, "Feminism and American Judaism," pp. 291–308; Umansky, "Spiritual Expressions," pp. 337–63; for a history of the first feminist seder: Broner, *The Telling*.

Kay Sekimachi

(American, born 1926)

Tzedakabako, 2000

Linen fiber, stenciling
10¼ x 5½ x 5½ in. (26 x 14 x 14 cm)

Purchase: Contemporary Judaica
Acquisitions Fund, 2000-76

San Francisco–born Kay Sekimachi is an internationally recognized fiber artist. Her work is noted for its innovative forms and delicate sculptural quality. A Japanese American, Sekimachi was sent, along with her mother and three sisters, to an internment camp in Topaz, Utah, under a 1942 order signed by President Franklin Roosevelt, which authorized the incarceration of more than 120,000 Japanese Americans. Ironically, the camp offered Sekimachi her first exposure to art. A fellow detainee and former university art instructor, Chiura Obata, began an art school there. Art supplies arrived for the students, and Sekimachi attended Obata's daily classes in drawing and painting.

After the war, San Francisco became a center for weavers, and it was there that Sekimachi developed her passion for the medium. She enrolled at the California School of Arts and Crafts to study with Trude Guermonprez, a major figure in weaving and textile arts, who had immigrated to the United States from Germany in the late 1940s. Guermonprez impressed upon Sekimachi the

almost limitless potential of the fiber medium, introduced her to intricate weaving techniques, and encouraged her to create nonfunctional works such as tapestries, wall hangings, and room dividers. In 1956, Sekimachi broadened her expertise through study at Haystack Mountain School of Crafts in Deer Isle, Maine, with the celebrated textile designer Jack Lenor Larsen.

Sekimachi's fascination with the box form began in the 1970s with an exhibition of miniature textiles at the British Craft Centre in London. For this exhibition, she created a small loom-woven box. She discovered that the form was highly suitable for a multiple layer weaving, a technique that integrates various layers of fiber to create surface patterns. Sekimachi found that the color scheme of black and natural was best for these box shapes, as it allows the viewer to see the form and not be distracted by color.

In 2000, The Jewish Museum commissioned Sekimachi to weave an alms container, which is used in homes and synagogues to collect money for Jewish organizations and charities. She entitled it *Tzedakabako*—a combination of the Hebrew word for righteousness (*tzedakah*) and the Japanese word for box (*bako*). Sekimachi produced the work on a tube and shaped and pressed the ends to create a box form with a folded top. She stenciled the Hebrew letters for *tzedakah* on the exterior and used a multiple layer weave in black and natural to create a pattern for the folded top.

S R

REFERENCES
Baizerman, "Interview with Kay Sekimachi"; The Jewish Museum, San Francisco, *Making Change*; Nathan and Mayfield, "Kay Sekimachi, the Weaver's Weaver."

Michael Berkowitz

(American, born 1952)

Fashions for the Millennium: Protective Amulet Costume, 2000

Stenciled satin
Jacket: 31 in. long (78.7 cm),
Skirt: 38½ long (97.8 cm)

Purchase: Dr. Joel and Phyllis Gitlin Judaica Acquisitions Fund, 2000-75

The power of ritual, the importance of the sacred word, and the search for mystery in everyday life are themes central to the work of Michael Berkowitz. Raised in an Orthodox Jewish home, Berkowitz developed a profound sense of the importance of religion and originally planned to become a rabbi. He later spent years exploring Buddhism, Eastern art, and folk art traditions. During these years of searching and study, Berkowitz became aware of the importance that words and sacred texts had in many traditions, including Judaism. He writes, "After years of being influenced by Asian art forms, I began to investigate my own religious heritage as a source of material for my work." The results of this reexamination produced a series of life-size cut-paper amulets and body-enveloping costumes emblazoned with Hebrew texts. Berkowitz com-

ments, "Many believe that the ancient Hebrew letters, being the sacred language in which God imparted his laws, have immense power . . . [a power] beyond the literal meaning of the words. . . . After all, *words* were the tools used by God to create the universe."

Fashions for the Millennium: Protective Amulet Costume is a wearable amulet that comes out of Berkowitz's exploration of the use of the word in artistic and religious contexts. Unlike traditional amulets, which were sewn on clothing or worn about the neck, Berkowitz's takes the custom of amulet protection to an entirely new level by enveloping the body in a costume stenciled with prayers. The mysterious, concealing aspect of the costume and the bright red stenciled Hebrew calligraphy create an unusual visual effect. Originally designed as a wedding dress for Berkowitz's wife, the costume is made from white bridal satin. Fabrication of the garment was delaying the marriage, so it was never actually worn for that event. The costume is composed of a number of components that completely veil the wearer from view. There is a two-part head covering, including a veil and hat. A shawl is worn about the shoulders, and leggings cover the ankles and feet. *Fashions for the Millennium: Protective Amulet Costume* was intended as part of a series of costumes that explore ideas of protection, healing, and spirituality.

The costume is covered with a series of inscriptions, primarily taken from the Book of Psalms. For example, the right sleeve bears the verse "God is your guardian. God is your shelter at your right hand" (Psalms 121:5), while the belt is inscribed "You have girded me with strength for the battle" (Psalms 18:40).

Berkowitz has written, "Like so many in our modern society, I have looked for new ways to find transcendence, new ways to be religious. I have found it in my art. Using the context of the religion of my birth and my ancestors, I have built upon that base."

S R

REFERENCES
Bendheim, "Demon Binding Charms: Michael Berkowitz"; Lauren, "Inner Life"; Mann, *Jewish Texts on the Visual Arts*, pp. 104–9.

Matthew McCaslin

(American, born 1957)

Being the Light, 2000

Lightbulbs, porcelain light fixtures, metal electrical conduit, switches, and metal receptacle box
62 x 44¾ x 10½ in.
(157.5 x 113.7 x 26.7 cm)

Purchase: Contemporary Judaica Acquisitions Committee Fund, and Judaica Acquisitions Committee Fund, 2001-14a-j

Since the early 1990s, Matthew McCaslin has created sculptures and site-specific installations featuring industrial electrical materials, clocks, fans, and video monitors. Grounded in the formal and aesthetic strategies of Process Art and Post-Minimalism of the 1960s and 1970s, his work invites the viewer to consider his or her own relationship to technology, nature, and time.

In 2000, McCaslin was invited to participate in *Light x Eight*, The Jewish Museum's biennial Hanukkah exhibition of works by contemporary artists who use light. Struck by the beauty and diversity of the museum's display of Hanukkah lamps, the artist created a site-specific piece that at once referred to the rich historical tradition of this ceremonial object while reimagining it for the twenty-first century.

McCaslin's signature vocabulary of industrial materials—lightbulbs, switches, and metal electrical conduit—is metaphorically relevant to the holiday. The artist sees industrial electrical hardware as a sublime material that lurks behind our walls, as ubiquitous as it is hidden, connecting us physically, culturally, and spiritually. Seeing the beauty of these industrial forms, the artist literally brings this infra-structure out of hiding "into the light," a most appropriate expression for Hanukkah, the Festival of Lights.

McCaslin's piece—both sculpture and Hanukkah lamp—plays with the combination of formal restric-tion and openness that he found so intriguing about this ritual object. On the traditional side, *Being the Light* follows some of the dictates for a Hanukkah lamp's configuration—eight lights, with a ninth act-ing as the *shamash*, or servitor, which kindles the other lights. The electrical system devised by the artist also cleverly reflects the traditional lamp: the *shamash* must be switched on before the other eight bulbs can be illuminated. In a final allusion to tradi-tion, the switches for the eight lights are arranged in a single row, echoing the form of the bench-style Hanukkah lamp.

However, McCaslin also playfully departs from tradition. Notably, the lights are not at a typical uni-form height, and turning on the switches in a row actually lights the bulbs nonsequentially rather than in the expected right-to-left order. Finally, at the same time that McCaslin is in dialogue with tradition, he also seems to be nodding at that most contemporary version of the Hanukkah lamp—the electric menorah that has become so popular in recent decades.

F W

REFERENCE
Bitterli and Wohlgemuth, *Matthew McCaslin: Works, Sites.*

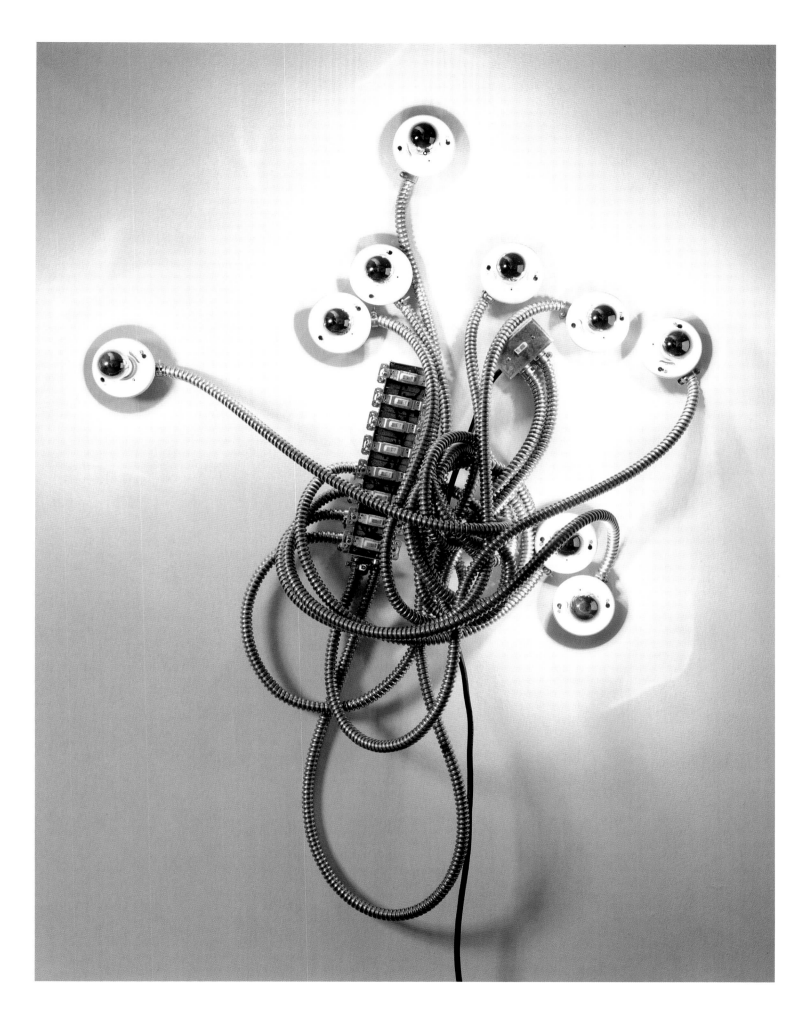

Society and Politics

Society and Politics

For Clement Greenberg and other prominent art critics of the 1950s and 1960s, an abstract art devoted to issues of form and style—and a "formalist" criticism that accentuated these issues—could serve as a spiritual release from the alienation of politics, industrialization, and mass culture. Over the past thirty years, however, many curators, art historians, and critics have come to view this allegiance to abstraction and formalism as limiting. They have attempted to see art and artifacts as part of a broader continuum of social, cultural, and political meaning, to place culture into the context of the society and politics that shapes and influences it.

The Jewish Museum's permanent collection—informed by the institution's mandate to bring together objects that tell the story of the Jewish people—exemplifies the interconnection between art, politics, and society. It encompasses a range of cultural expressions that speak to a history of oppression and struggle as well as to the role played by Jews in civilizations throughout history. These works in turn are placed into broader social context by permanent installations, such as *Culture and Continuity: The Jewish Journey*, and temporary exhibitions that refuse to view artworks as self-contained, hermetic objects.

The subject of antisemitism is one of the most important issues explored in the museum's collection. Samuel Hirszenberg's painting *The Black Banner* (1905)—a stark, uncompromising depiction of a funeral procession of terror-stricken Hasidic Jews—commemorates the tragic plight of Jews in Russian-dominated Poland at the turn of the twentieth century. El Lissitzky's *Had Gadya Suite* (1919) explores the issue of Jewish oppression through the abstraction of Russian constructivism, images informed both by the traditional seder verse, itself an allegory for the triumph of good over evil, and the contemporaneous victory of the Russian Revolution over the forces of greed and oppression. In *March of the Clowns* (1941), Albert Bloch, the only American member of the Blue Rider, an early-twentieth-century group of German avant-garde artists, paints a darkly comic fantasy image of the defeat of Hitler. William Anastasi's *Untitled (Jew)* (1987) superimposes the word "jew" (lowercase) across a large white-washed canvas. The understated elegance of the image at once belies and foregrounds the power of the word "Jew"—a word that has all too often served as the ultimate epithet of the antisemite. The National Jewish Archive of Broadcasting contains many radio and television programs devoted to the issue of antisemitism in a multitude of social and geographical contexts, from anti-Jewish sentiment in the American West of the nineteenth century on *Bonanza* (1959–73) to Archie Bunker's cantankerous, New York–style bigotry on *All in the Family* (1971–83).

Other works in the collection bear witness to the disposition of the Jewish people in societies throughout the world. The oldest glass burial-society beaker in existence, made for the

Jewish community of Polin, Bohemia, in 1691, similarly reflects the influence of Bohemian culture on the Jews of Prague. A silver tray from the early eighteenth century, fashioned by English silversmith John Ruslen, attests to the readmission of Jews to the British Isles in 1656, after a 350-year banishment. The elaborate, four-handled tray was commissioned by London's small Spanish and Portuguese community as an offering of respect to the lord mayor of London. An embroidered purse inscribed with the name of its owner, Abraham Cohen, is a poignant remnant of the life of a Jewish man who contributed funds to support the American effort in the Revolutionary War. Boris Schatz's introspective *Self-Portrait* (c. 1930), replete with ornate frame, reminds us of the Zionist artist's role in establishing the Bezalel School of Arts and Crafts in Jerusalem in the early twentieth century. In his four animated short films, *Drawings for Projection Series: Johannesburg—2nd Greatest City after Paris*; *Monument*; *Mine*; and *Sobriety, Obesity, and Growing Old* (1981–91), the artist and filmmaker William Kentridge makes a powerful statement about Jewish complicity, resistance, or ambivalence in South Africa at the moment of apartheid's demise.

The social and cultural issues of family, personal responsibility, and community resonate throughout the collection, especially in programs from the National Jewish Archive of Broadcasting. Dramas and situation comedies such as *The Goldbergs* (1949–56), *Brooklyn Bridge* (1991–93), *thirtysomething* (1987–91), *Seinfeld* (1990–98), and *Will & Grace* (1998–present) engage a range of controversial subjects, including intermarriage, infidelity, gay marriage, the religious education of children, and the concept of "family values." Other programs deconstruct the prevailing rituals of Jewish life, from Buddy Sorrel's hilarious midlife bar mitzvah on *The Dick Van Dyke Show* (1960–66) to Rhoda Morgenstern's marriage to her non-Jewish lover in an uproarious, anxiety-ridden civil ceremony on *Rhoda* (1974–78).

MB

Mortar

Joseph de Levis (1552–1611/14)

Verona, 1605

Bronze
5½ in. high x 6 5/16 in. diam. (14 x 16 cm)

Promised gift of the Zucker Family Collection in honor of Jean and Alfred Moldovan, P.1.1993

Although the names of other Jewish artists of the Italian Renaissance are known, Joseph de Levis is the only one to have left a recognizable body of work. He and his brother, both bronze casters in Verona, had a workshop that was later joined by their sons. Most of the pieces made by the de Levises were for general use in the home or in churches: bells, mortars, andirons, and the like. The few pieces with Jewish symbols or characters, such as a mortar with a menorah and a Hanukkah lamp with the figures of Judith, Holofernes, and Hasmoneans, were made by Joseph or his nephew Servo (1570–1616/27), both of whom remained Jewish, while all the other family members in the shop were baptized. Another indication of Joseph's Jewish loyalty is his signature on this and all other works: Joseph de Levis, instead of the usual Italian name Giuseppe. Jews avoided the latter name because of its Christian associations.

On the other side of this mortar is a medallion imitating a Roman coin with the profile of a crowned male head. During the Renaissance, men and women of culture sought to re-create Roman art forms and style, among them the antique coins struck by the emperors. Another Renaissance characteristic is the use of bronze, which became a popular medium for sculpture, both large-scale and small, and for decorative arts such as this mortar. The band of decoration that combines leaves and harpies is typical of the period. VBM

REFERENCE
Mann, *Gardens and Ghettos*, cat. no. 181.

Torah Shield

Germany, 1669

Silver: chased and engraved
4¹¹⁄₁₆ x 5⅝ in. (11.9 x 14.2 cm)

Gift of Dr. Harry G. Friedman, F 2653

This work is a relatively early example of a Torah shield, a silver plaque designed to indicate the reading to which the scroll was turned. The rabbis suggested that rolling the Torah out of sight of the congregation was preferable, to prevent the congregation from regarding the Torah as a mundane object. Once the scroll was turned to the correct lection and covered, some means of denoting when it was to be used was required. Rabbi Israel Petaḥiah Isserlein (1390–1460) criticized a common practice of his day—affixing small paper labels with the name of the reading to the scroll, claiming that the tags did not enhance the beauty of the Torah. By the early sixteenth century, Rabbi Isserlein's complaint was placated by the creation of silver plaques hung from the staves of the Torah scroll. The new custom is recorded by Antonius Margaritha in his *Ganz jüdisch Glaub*, published in Augsburg in 1530.

The form of this shield is not yet fully developed. Mature examples of Torah shields incorporate a box for small interchangeable silver plates inscribed with the names of readings: the Sabbath, the New Moon, the New Year, and so on. Later shields are also decorated with more complex iconography. This example bears only one Jewish symbol, the crown engraved "The Crown of Torah," and one indication of a reading.

Its inscription, however, is very interesting. The shield was dedicated in the name of "the boy Uriel son of Azriel, born under a good sign [*mazal tov*] on the holy Sabbath, the ninth of Sivan, [5]429 [June 8, 1669]. . . . May the Lord grant him to be raised to [knowledge of] the Torah, to the marriage canopy, and to g[ood] d[eeds]," a quotation from the circumcision ceremony that was also used in dedications on Ashkenazi Torah binders.

VBM

REFERENCE
Grafman and Mann, *Crowning Glory*, pp. 17, 77, no. 1.

Beaker of the Polin Burial Society

Bohemia, 1691

Glass: enameled
9¾ in. high x 5¼ in. diam.
(24.8 x 13.3 cm)

Gift of Dr. Harry G. Friedman, F 3211

This work is the oldest glass burial-society beaker in existence. Made for the Jewish community of Polin, Bohemia, it is an interesting example of Jewish acculturation through the adaptation of a Bohemian art form.

In 1584, the Hapsburg emperor Rudolf II moved his court to Prague. During his reign, the Bohemian capital became a center of Renaissance art and scholarship, attracting artists and scholars from all over Europe. Among them were specialists in the arts of cutting and painting glass. The popularity of decorated glass among members of the court influenced other groups—guilds, societies, and noble families—to commission similar pieces.

In another development during the second half of the sixteenth century, the rabbis of Prague worked at organizing the community in their care. In 1564, Rabbi Eliezer Ashkenazi formed the first modern burial society; its regulations were codified by the great Rabbi Judah Loew, known as the Maharal (c. 1525–1609). In effect, the Jewish burial societies of Europe performed some of the same functions for members as did the Christian guilds, caring for the ill, the deceased, and the deceased's family, leading the Jewish organizations to adopt some of the guilds' trappings and rituals. One of these was the custom of holding festive banquets at which the business of the society was enacted, new members were elected, and special emblems of the organization were displayed. Some examples are the large drinking vessels decorated with vignettes of members performing characteristic activities. A drink of wine from this cup was the ceremony by which new members were admitted to the society. It is in this artistic, social, and religious context that the Polin beaker must be placed. Its decoration features a frieze of burial-society members who are marching with a bier toward the cemetery. The accompanying inscription reads:

זאת הזכוכית / שייך לחבורה קדישא / דקברנים מקק
פאלין / דורן מנאי משה בהרר / יעקב פאלין חנוכה
תנב / לפק

This glass belongs to the Holy Society of Morticians of the holy community of Polin. A present from Moses, son of Rabbi Jacob Polin, Hanukkah [5]452 [December 1691].

The same elements (a frieze of figures and an elaborate inscription) appear on similar glasses through the nineteenth century and were imitated on the faience beakers favored by burial societies in nearby Moravia. Both types represent regional forms that differ markedly from silver beakers commissioned by Jewish burial societies in other parts of Europe.

VBM

REFERENCES
Altshuler, *The Precious Legacy*, pp. 156–57; Braunstein, *Le-Hayyim— To Life*, no. 45; Kayser and Schoenberger, *Jewish Ceremonial Art*, nos. 174–174a; Kleeblatt and Mann, *Treasures of the Jewish Museum*, pp. 62–63; Mann, *The Jewish Museum*, no. 129; Shachar, "Feast and Rejoice in Brotherly Love," no. 1.

John Ruslen

(English, active 1656–c. 1715)

Lord Mayor's Tray, London, 1708–9

Silver: repoussé and engraved
21⅜ x 26½ x 3¼ in.
(54.3 x 67.3 x 8.3 cm)

Gift of Mrs. Felix M. Warburg, JM 2-47

In 1656, Jews were readmitted to the British Isles, after a 350-year hiatus, through the joint efforts of Oliver Cromwell and the Dutch messianic scholar Menasseh ben Israel. The following year, London's small Spanish and Portuguese community established the Bevis Marks Congregation, still one of that city's major synagogues.

This four-handled tray represents the congregants' 100-year annual tradition of offering presentation silver to London's lord mayor. Beginning in 1679, silver trays were commissioned for the mayor and sent to him, lavishly filled with sweetmeats. Most of these gifts bear as a central motif the seal of the Bevis Marks Congregation—a Tent of Assembly in the wilderness, a guard at its entrance, the whole surmounted by a cloud of glory. Similar presentation pieces were also offered to the lord mayor by other minority groups, namely, the Dutch Reform and French Protestant churches.

This lord mayor's tray was fashioned by John Ruslen, a well-established English silversmith who had for twenty-eight years provided Jewish ritual objects for Bevis Marks. Aside from his five existing presentation salvers, records indicate commissions for a sanctuary lamp in 1682; a pair of Torah finials (*rimmonim*) in 1702; and the Hanukkah lamp of 1709, depicting Elijah and the ravens. The Dutch-influenced repoussé work and chasing of Ruslen's tray demonstrate the polarity of silver styles coexist-ing during Queen Anne's reign. The ornate, if *retardataire*, style of this tray was considered appropriate for royal commissions and presentation pieces. Its decoration contrasts markedly with the severity of most silver intended for domestic use during this period. This tray shows the continuing demand for opulent silver that followed the restoration of Charles II in 1660. Charles, who had been in exile in the Netherlands and France, returned, bringing with him a taste for Dutch Baroque and the regal style of Louis XIV. These tendencies were quickly adapted by English artisans.

Like the Jews, Huguenots also sought freedom and opportunity in seventeenth-century England. After 1685, Huguenot silversmiths began to arrive in London when the French revoked the Edict of Nantes, which had originally granted religious liberties to Protestants in France. These foreign craftsmen brought new stylistic elements and technical innovation to the repertoire of English silver and, not least, forced unexpected competition upon native silversmiths. The simplicity pervading most Queen Anne silver was due in part to the new regulations requiring higher silver content for plate and the consequent need to reduce the costs of fabrication. Contrary to these exigencies, the sumptuous Ruslen tray aptly demonstrates that the Bevis Marks congregants spared no expense to honor their lord mayor.

NLK

REFERENCES

Dennis, *English Silver*; Grimwade, "Anglo-Jewish Silver," pp. 113–25; Roth, "The Lord Mayor Salvers," pp. 296–99; Victoria and Albert Museum, *Anglo-Jewish Art and History in Commemoration of the Tercentenary of the Resettlement of the Jews in the British Isles.*

Purse of Abraham Cohen

United States, 1766

Wool: petit-point embroidery; silk taffeta

9½ x 8¾ in. (24.1 x 22.2 cm)

Purchase: Judaica Acquisitions Committee Fund, 1985-31

In eighteenth-century America, it was fashionable for both women and men to carry their valuables in purses in the shape of an envelope. Men's purses usually had two inner compartments on each side (as in this example), where they could store their correspondence or important documents as well as snuff or toothpicks, while those used by women usually had a foldover flap and only one compartment, where mirrors, combs, smelling salts, and other trifles were kept. Frequently worked on canvas, these purses were often embroidered with vivid colors and lined with colorful materials, contrasting with the solid colors used in clothing.

In Colonial and Federal America, where upperclass women were expected to count needlework among their accomplishments, an embroidered purse was an appropriate gift from a lady to her fiancé or husband. A typical design was the flamestitch, later known as bargello or Florentine stitch, consisting of shaded zigzag patterns in colored yarns. The fine petit-point embroidery with floral motifs of this purse, however, is rare. A second purse, probably made in New England and thought to date to the 1760s, is today in the Metropolitan Museum of Art collection (Rogers Fund, 42.62). Probably a woman's purse, embroidered in vivid colors, the design features a carnation that is similar to the central white-and-blue flower in The Jewish Museum purse. As seen in most extant examples, the design on the outside of the purse is aligned in two directions, so that when the purse is closed, the pattern faces the same way on front and back.

Occasionally, embroidered purses bore the owner's name and date, as seen in this example. According to family records, Abraham Cohen, whose name is inscribed on the purse, contributed funds to support the American Revolutionary War effort. As the purse was acquired in the area of Philadelphia, where it had been passed down the family for generations, it is likely that Abraham Cohen lived in that city, home to one of the oldest Jewish congregations in America, or in the area of Lancaster, where Jewish settlement is documented as early as 1715. Although no Abraham Cohen seems to be recorded in Lancaster around the 1760s, three men by that name were living in Philadelphia at the time.

Jewish communal life in Philadelphia may be dated from 1740, when a Jewish cemetery was established, and the Mikveh Israel synagogue building was dedicated in 1782. Given the 1766 date on the purse, the most likely owner would have been Abraham Eliezer Cohen. In the Mikveh Israel minutes for March 30, 1783, Abraham E. Cohen is mentioned as the new *shamash*, or beadle, for the synagogue. The duties of the *shamash* included: "to keep the *shull* [synagogue] and everything belonging to it clean and in good order, he is to make all the candles—light them when they are wanted, and see them properly out. He is to attend whenever there is prayers, and see the *shull* secured afterwards. . . . He is to attend all circumcisions, weddings and funerals."

Records for the Jewish cemetery of Philadelphia, as reported by Ruth Hoffman of Congregation Mikveh Israel, date Abraham Eliezer Cohen's death to 1786 and mention his gravesite, but no tombstone has been found.

CN

REFERENCES

Gostelow, *Art of Embroidery*, pp. 103–5, 167; Haertig, *Antique Combs and Purses*, pp. 170–72; Wolf and Whiteman, *The History of the Jews of Philadelphia*, pp. 124, 141.

Samuel Hirszenberg

(Polish, 1865–1908)

The Black Banner (Czarny Sztandar), 1905

Oil on canvas
30 x 81 in. (76.2 x 205.7 cm)
Gift of the Estate of Rose Mintz,
JM 63-67

The influence of social and political events on much of the art produced in the nineteenth century has been a topic for vigorous exploration since the late 1960s. French painters such as Courbet, Millet, Daumier, and Pissarro have become paradigms of the socially motivated artists whose images provide visual testimony to the grim realities of the peasants and the urban poor. Similarly engaged, Samuel Hirszenberg ranks as one of the first artists to expose the tragic plight of his fellow Jews in Russian-dominated Poland at the turn of the century. He showed such overt political statements as *The Wandering Jew* in the 1900 Paris exposition and *Exile* at the Paris Salon of 1905. *The Black Banner* was exhibited at the Salon of 1906.

One of Hirszenberg's many politicized statements, *The Black Banner* depicts masses of black-clad Hasidic men carrying a coffin. An open book strapped to the casket acts as the sole white relief on an exceptionally dark field. The stares of horror, shock, and fear far exceed those of mourning for the passing of any single soul. Two terrified faces staring out at us—the one on the left possibly the artist's self-portrait—recall the haunting expressionist visions of Hirszenberg's contemporary Edvard Munch.

The anguished emotions of Hirszenberg's multitudes and the painting's stirring motion echo historical events. The early years of the twentieth century witnessed the intensified devastation of Eastern European Jews through numerous pogroms that had begun in 1881. The Kishinev and Homel pogroms of 1903 and the notorious Zhitomir massacre in 1905 led to the deaths of thousands of Jews.

The year of *The Black Banner* coincides with the founding of the Union of the Russian People—a right-wing, rabidly antisemitic political movement. Armed gangs of the union, called "The Black Hundreds," carried out the pogroms. Their official newspaper was *The Russian Banner*, and the czar's financial support was dubbed "black money." Hirszenberg's title thus makes a blatantly cynical play on the nicknames of the union's crews and their propaganda vehicles and, by extension, suggests that the coffin bears the body of one of their victims.

Of the several contemporaneous paintings that may have inspired *The Black Banner*, one is Giuseppe Pellizza da Volpedo's *The Fourth Estate* (1898–1901), a work that Hirszenberg may have seen during his stay in Italy in the late 1890s. *The Fourth Estate* reflects Pellizza's socialist leanings and his observation of the desperate conditions of workers in his native town in Piedmont. It compares in both theme and format to Hirszenberg's *Black Banner*. The implied optimism of Pellizza's active, confrontational army of workers stands in contrast to Hirszenberg's masses, frozen in their placement on the canvas as well as in their emotional expressions, leaving little room for hope in the future.

An obvious source of inspiration for Hirszenberg is a French painting that by 1905 had become an icon. The resemblance of *The Black Banner*'s composition, subject, and tonality to Courbet's *Burial at Ornans* (1849) readily suggests the strong influence of this French masterpiece on that of the Polish artist. Yet contrasts between the two pictures are apparent. Despite Courbet's citizens' of Ornans resignation at the loss of one of their kin, they display a sense of security in a terrain that is assuredly theirs. Not so for Hirszenberg's minions; their panic-stricken faces are alienated from their surroundings. These wanderers float in a volatile limbo—the figures cut off just below the hip, their feet hidden from view. *The Black Banner* continues Hirszenberg's exploration of pogroms begun a year earlier in his widely published painting of 1904, *Exile*.

Given the artist's Zionist leanings, *The Black Banner* has, over the years, accrued Zionist interpretations, predominantly from Israeli historians. They focus their readings on the significance of the open book tied to the casket and find hope in the less harrowed expressions on the faces of the younger members of this exodus.

NLK

REFERENCES
Cohen, *Jewish Icons*; Goodman, *The Emergence of Jewish Artists in Nineteenth-Century Europe*; Haam, "Ueber die Kultur"; Kleeblatt, "The Black Banner"; Sandel, "Samuel Hirszenberg"; "Sie Wandern."

Boris Schatz

(Russian, 1866–1932)

Self-Portrait, c. 1930

Oil and resin on panel, in a repoussé
brass frame
30½ x 27 in. (77.5 x 68.6 cm)

Gift of Dr. Harry G. Friedman, F 4357

The son of a Lithuanian Hebrew teacher, Boris Schatz abandoned his traditional Jewish studies to devote himself to art. At an early age, he met the noted Russian romantic sculptor Antokolski, a coreligionist who encouraged the youth to study in Paris. By Schatz's twenty-second birthday, he was ensconced in the capital of the art world, where he trained along conservative academic lines. He quickly found acceptance in Paris art circles, and his Salon entries ultimately brought him acclaim. In 1896, he was summoned to Sofia, Bulgaria, as court sculptor to Prince Ferdinand. There he also founded Bulgaria's first Arts and Crafts school.

Schatz left Bulgaria in 1906 to establish the Bezalel School of Arts and Crafts in Jerusalem, his most renowned accomplishment. An early and ardent follower of Zionism, he had his own ideas about an artistic style suitable for a new Jewish nation. Through periods of prosperity and adversity, he ran the school for over twenty years, offering courses in thirty-five types of materials and techniques. Schatz sought to provide training and jobs for the generally impoverished native Jews and for the newer immigrants from Eastern Europe. The distinctive style he evolved—an eclectic synthesis of Oriental symbols executed in an academically based European manner—was his attempt to embody Zionism's ideological goals.

This self-portrait and its handmade frame, possibly created in America during a fund-raising campaign, documents the interrelationship of art and craft in the Bezalel School approach. Schatz himself—in a sober likeness that makes him look a decade younger than his years—sits surrounded by the products of the school. The work is rendered in dark earth tones, in a weak resinous medium on a reclaimed wood panel—a frugality no doubt learned in Palestine, where natural and manufactured resources were scarce. The finely wrought repoussé frame bears an inscription from the Song of Songs, loosely translated: "I am for my *people* and my *people* are for me," instead of the usual translation *beloved*, as an appropriate plea for his cause. The central medallion in the arched pediment of the frame bears the scene *Bezalel Creating the Holy Ark*, which is emblematic of the school's origin and mission. (In Exodus, the artisan Bezalel was appointed by Moses to supervise the construction of the Tabernacle, or tent sanctuary.)

Schatz's artistic philosophy can be viewed as an offshoot of the numerous Arts and Crafts movements in late-nineteenth-century England, Germany, and Central Europe. In reaction to the shoddy design and machine-made excesses of the Industrial Revolution, these movements stressed high-quality design and handworkmanship that reflected each nation's stylistic heritage. Paradoxically, Palestine, however, had neither a mechanized society to react against nor an inherent style from which to adapt. Schatz's attempt at the creation of a "Jewish" style conforms with nationalistic goals of other Arts and Crafts movements. Instead of slowing down production in favor of more thoughtful and authentic design, Bezalel's goal was to stimulate a modest industry with luxury products that could help define new lifestyles in Eretz Israel and be available for sale to the tourist trade.

NLK

REFERENCE

Shilo-Cohen, *Bezalel of Schatz, 1906–29*.

Rug

Ya'akov Stark (worked in the Land of Israel, died c. 1916), designer of letters

Avraham Baradon (worked in the Land of Israel, died 1949), rugmaker and metalworker

Bezalel School, Jerusalem, 1910–15

Wool: knotted
67½ x 30¾ in. (171.5 x 78.1 cm)

Gift of Maurice and Rachel Ahdoot to celebrate the life of Solly, 1995-96

The Bezalel School was founded by Boris Schatz in 1906, one of the founders of the Academy of Art (1866–1932) in Sofia. His goal was to develop a distinctive "Hebrew" style, as opposed to having Jewish artists work in diasporic styles. The use of Hebrew letters as decorative motifs was one of the elements of the new style. Foremost among the designers of alphabets was Ya'akov Stark, who combined Art Nouveau style with Islamic arabesques to create new alphabets. On this rug, the name of the workshop, Bezalel, Jerusalem, appears at the top. Similarly shaped medallions along the sides contain the phrase *eretz ha-tzvi* (land of the deer), a poetic reference to the Land of Israel. The circular medallions that separate the oblong ones are filled with a monogram spelling "Jerusalem." The vogue for interlaced letters lasted only until the 1920s, when it was replaced by inscriptions composed of separate letters.

The design of the central panel is based on the theme of the seven-branched menorah. Interlocking small lamp stands fill a trapezoidal field. In the corners are larger *menorot* drawn in an exaggerated version of Art Nouveau. Documentary evidence indicates that the design was the work of Avraham Baradon, who began study at Bezalel in 1906, working in the carpet department and later heading the department of damascene work.

VBM

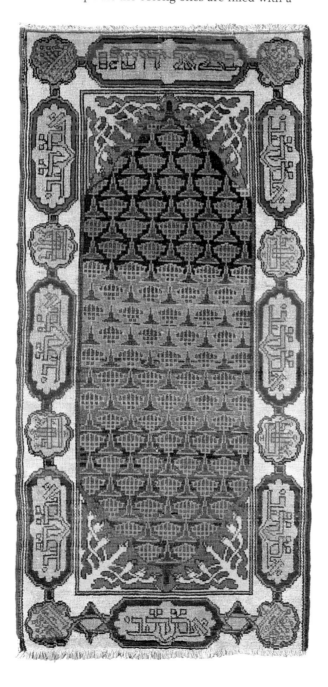

El Lissitzky

(Lazar Lisitsky) (Russian, 1890–1941)

Had Gadya Suite (Tale of a Goat): Cover and *Father Bought a Kid for Two Zuzim*, 1919

Lithographs on paper
10¾ x 10 in. (27.3 x 25.4 cm)

Gift of Leonard and Phyllis Greenberg, 1986-121 a, c

The *Had Gadya*, a charming ten-verse Aramaic ditty based on a German ballad, is chanted at the conclusion of the Passover seder. This song has been variously interpreted both textually and visually. Its verses describe a young goat, recently purchased by a father (made personal to each individual chanter by the pronoun "my" father). The goat is consumed by a cat, and the song continues to recount a succession of assailants until God destroys the final perpetrator, ending the vicious cycle. Generally considered an allegory for the oppression and persecution of the Jewish people, the various villains have been likened to aggressor nations in Jewish history. Yet God's triumph leaves hope for Jewish survival. The poem has been frequently illustrated as part of the Haggadah—the text for the seder ritual—a work that in itself was an illustrator's favorite because of its narrative simplicity and popular appeal.

El Lissitzky's folio of eleven printed illustrations, based on his 1917 watercolors of the same subject, is unusual for its lack of association with the text of the Haggadah. The *Had Gadya* derives mainly from the artist's involvement with pictures for Yiddish children's books executed between 1917 and 1919. El Lissitzky uses an architectural framework incorporating imaginatively designed, folk-influenced, modernist Hebrew typography as a border for each narrative sequence. The effect is a step in the development toward his classic, architecturally based abstraction. This culminates in El Lissitzky's remarkable artistic invention, which he referred to by the acronym PROUN (from the Russian words for "project for the affirmation of the new"). These later drawings, paintings, and geometric constructions became totally nonobjective, and soon El Lissitzky relinquished specific Jewish subject matter in a successful merger of art and architecture.

Sources for El Lissitzky's illustrations can be found in Jewish popular prints, Hebrew illuminated manuscripts, and the figurative style of Russia's famous painted wooden synagogues. His art also reflects his fascination with typography, Chagall's romantic Expressionism, and Suprematist avant-garde art. This combination of sources is a logical outgrowth of El Lissitzky's education and his maturing interests during the second decade of the twentieth century.

Denied admission to a Russian art school, El Lissitzky studied architecture in Darmstadt, Germany, where he is known to have become acquainted with that city's great Jewish masterpiece, the fifteenth-century Darmstadt Haggadah. He also made frequent trips to Worms, to study the architecture of its synagogue, then the oldest in Europe. When he returned to Russia in 1914, he soon became involved with the Jewish Ethnographic Society, which financed his expeditions to explore the Jewish art and architecture along the Dnieper River. There he was particularly moved by the fascinating architecture of the wooden synagogues and their imaginative and lushly painted interiors.

Although he exhibited his works in 1916 along with the first Suprematist works of the noted Russian constructivist Malevich, El Lissitzky continued for the next several years to illustrate children's books inspired by the folk motifs he had previously helped gather. In 1919 Chagall, head of the Vitebsk School of Art in Russia, offered him the position of professor of architecture. Chagall's resignation later that year brought El Lissitzky into closer contact with Suprematism through Chagall's successor, Malevich, the movement's originator.

The creation of the *Had Gadya* illustrations coincides with the year of the Bolshevik victory and prompted the popular notion that El Lissitzky saw the allegorical tale of survival and the triumph of good over evil as an analogue to the success of the Russian Revolution. If intentional, this is testament to *Had Gadya*'s universality—and its limitless potential for interpretation.

NLK

REFERENCES

Abramsky, "El Lissitzky as Jewish Illustrator and Typographer," pp. 182–85; Apter-Gabriel, "El Lissitzky's Jewish Works"; Debbaut, Soons, and de Bie, *El Lissitzky, 1890–1941*; Goodman, *Russian Jewish Artists in a Century of Change 1890–1990*.

Peter Blume

(American, born Russia, 1906–1992)

Pig's Feet and Vinegar,
1927

Oil on canvas
20 x 24 in. (50.8 x 61 cm)

Purchase: gift of David Kluger, by exchange; Miriam and Milton Handler Fund and the Charlotte Levite Fund in memory of Julius Nassau; Hanni and Peter Kaufmann, Gladys and Selig Burrows, Hyman L. and Joan C. Sall, and John Steinhardt and Susan Margules Steinhardt gifts, 1994-632

After World War I, a number of American artists turned to clarity and geometric precision either to glorify modern technology or, alternatively, to hark back nostalgically to the country's rustic past. At once elegant and impersonal, paintings of the postwar period depicted the smokestacks, factories, and skyscrapers of an industrialized metropolis as well as the barns and fields of an old-world, bucolic New England—the one a frank confrontation with the machine revolution, the other a fantasy of the calm that preceded it.

An artist who depicted the dynamism of the machine age as well as its pastoral counterpart, Peter Blume employed Precisionist sharp style and Surrealist associations of unexpected images to negotiate the place of Jewish identity in the context of the dominant culture. A Russian-born émigré raised in Brooklyn, Blume studied art at the Education Alliance, a settlement house on the Lower East Side sponsored by New York's Jewish community. His startling fantasy *Pig's Feet and Vinegar* was painted in 1927 in Exeter, New Hampshire, upon the artist's move from New York's "shtetl" environment to rural New England.

Blume's painting juxtaposes a still-life interior of pig's feet and a bottle of vinegar with a New England landscape in winter. The blatant presence of a symbol so impure in Jewish iconography puts Blume's confrontation with his Jewish identity (literally) on the table. It is possible that the offal and the wine gone rancid, placed in the interior of the painting, are expressions of the artist's discomfort with his religious and cultural identity—Judaism gone sour. The country outside, framed by the wooden cross of the window, represents the world of which he wishes to be a part. Yet the lugubriousness of the winter scenery hardly presents the outside world as seductive. What this landscape offers is a false promise, evoked by the unfinished house in the composition's center and the tree trunk that ends in a violent severing by the window frame. In an ambivalent confusion of "inside" and "outside," Blume renders not the countryside but the pig's feet as the seduction.

According to scholar Ismar Schorsch in a letter to The Jewish Museum about this painting, "Jewish tradition had long imagined the pig as a symbol of religious deception, displaying its cloven feet to persuade Jews that it was not counterfeit." There is most certainly a seduction at play. The pig's feet are depicted as to appear feminized: rather than the dead stumps of one of the most homely of animals, they appear as fleshly forms with pinkened tips, gracefully curved like a woman's hands, culminating in rosy points like her breasts. The disquieting presence of a symbol associated with deception encourages a reconfiguration of the earlier reading—indoor and outdoor are inverted. The pig's feet, seductive yet dangerous, may represent the temptation of America and assimilation. The barren countryside might thus serve as a representation of alienation, and the woman in the painting perhaps a figure with whom the artist empathizes—the immigrant who, from the outside, looks longingly toward the seduction within. But rather than indicate a clear narrative, Blume applies his dramatic technique with just enough restraint to call into play a variety of associations without resolving these conflicting possibilities. In a Surrealist, otherworldly landscape, in which pig's feet seem to float weightlessly above a table and trees and houses are left abruptly unfinished, Blume ambiguously juxtaposes inside and outside, barren and lush, alienation and seduction. Within the setting of New England—America's dreamland—Blume questions the Jewish artist's place in the American dream.

SNB

REFERENCES
Brown, *Inventing New England*; Chevlowe and Kleeblatt, *Painting a Place in America*; Harnsberger, *Ten Precisionist Artists*, pp. 55–76; Montclair Museum, *Precisionism in America 1915–1941*; Trapp, *Peter Blume*; Tsujimoto, *Images of America*.

Weegee

(born Arthur Fellig, American, 1899–1968)

Max is rushing in the bagels to a restaurant on Second Avenue for the morning trade, c. 1940

Gelatin-silver print
14¾ x 18⅞ in. (37.5 x 47.9 cm)

Purchase: Joan B. and Richard L. Barovick Family Foundation and Bunny and Jim Weinberg gifts, 2000-72

Weegee was a master at using his sharp, high-contrast images to capture glitzy, dynamic, and momentous occasions in all spheres, sometimes capturing the main event but often focusing on the spectators. His subjects included circus and ballet performances, Easter Sunday in Harlem, a murder at the cinema, a raucous night at Sammy's bar on the Bowery, and a Coney Island beach teeming with sunbathers. He depicts this New York as, in the words of art critic Max Kozloff, a "strip show gone bananas," often adding captions describing his adventures. The title for this photograph derives from a longer caption, in which Weegee indicates that his encounter with the "bagelman" occurred at six in the morning near the Consolidated Edison Company building on Fourteenth Street.

Calling his protagonist by his first name, Weegee alludes to a camaraderie with the workers with whom he regularly shares the deserted streets in the dead of night and the wee hours of the morning. He captures Max midstep as he looks and moves self-assuredly toward the fleeting glare of the photographer's flash. Weegee called his flash his "Aladdin's lamp," which allowed him to achieve what he referred to as "Rembrandt light" to describe the way that his glowing figures emerged from the darkness. Simultaneously, Max's almost sadistic expression—his half smile and vigilant eyes—makes him seem oddly menacing. Although the street is shrouded in blackness and the cement squares on the ground are obscured by enigmatic shadows and grime, Weegee creates a sense of place by hinting at the silhouette of a lamppost in the background. Today, you can still find originals as well as replicas of street lamps of this style, known as "bishop's crooks," lining the area around Union Square, where this photograph was taken, as well as in many other neighborhoods.

The police radio installed in his car gave Weegee his almost supernatural, Ouija-like ability to arrive at crime scenes before the police, likely earning him his nickname, although the name might also have derived from his early work as a photo assistant using a squeegee to dry prints. He was almost entirely self-taught. After several freelance assignments as a crime photographer, he became a staff photographer at *PM*, a left-leaning newspaper, in 1940. He became part of the first generation of what has become known as the New York School of photographers and was loosely affiliated with the Photo League, exhibiting *Weegee: Murder Is My Business* there in 1941. He often photographed in tandem with Lisette Model, who shared many of his subjects but often portrayed them in a more serious light. His candid depiction of his subjects and use of experimental techniques remained an integral part of his own work even later in life, when he moved to Hollywood and began creating distorted images of celebrities and consulting on special effects for films, including Stanley Kubrick's *Dr. Strangelove*. His legacy can be seen most vividly in his influence on the work of other photographers associated with the New York School, such as Diane Arbus, whose pictures often focus on individuals on the periphery of society.

JG

REFERENCES
Bar-Am, *Weegee the Famous*; Barth, *Weegee's World*; David Winton Bell Gallery, *Weegee: The Photography of Arthur Fellig (1899–1968)*; Kozloff, *New York: Capital of Photography*; Livingston, *The New York School: Photographs 1936–1963*.

Albert Bloch

(American, 1882–1961)

March of the Clowns, 1941

Oil on canvas mounted on Masonite
35⁹⁄₁₆ x 39⁷⁄₁₆ in. (90.3 x 100.2 cm)

Purchase: Oscar and Regina Gruss
Memorial Fund, 2001-42

In Albert Bloch's *March of the Clowns*, the ribbons of a maypole cascade alongside a startled effigy of Hitler that hangs from a swastika. On one of the corners of the Nazi symbol's four arms balances a gleaming Star of David. In 1941, at the height of World War II, Bloch brought to life his fantasy about the defeat of Nazi Germany in a darkly comical way. Amid an ephemeral atmosphere of swirling constellations parade a seemingly infinite procession of clowns that seems at once ecstatic, morose, and sinister. The leader of the band plays a bassoon, often called the "clown of the orchestra," that emits smoke, obscuring the viewer's vision of the figures and buildings in the background. Music played an integral role in Bloch's work, and one can almost imagine the racket created by the bassoon, drums, and trumpet. Bloch's wife once wrote in an unpublished letter to The Jewish Museum, "I never look at *March of the Clowns* without *hearing* the final variation of Brahms' *Variations on a Theme by Haydn*, a huge, glorious and victorious march ending the piece."

Bloch was the only American-born member of Der Blaue Reiter, or the Blue Rider, a group of artists founded by Wassily Kandinsky and Franz Marc in Germany in 1911. Bloch met these two artists upon his first visit to Munich, and they included six of his paintings in the group's first exhibition. The Blue Rider, which also included Paul Klee and August Macke, strove to express personal and distinct senses of spirituality through abstracted depictions of nature.

The politically charged subject matter and illustrational style of *March of the Clowns* may seem like a departure from the enigmatic works that pervaded the Blue Rider. However, Bloch's first foray into the visual arts was as an illustrator of so-called kindly caricatures of artists, performers, and writers—including Rudyard Kipling and Gustav Mahler—for the *Mirror*, a satirical paper in his hometown of St. Louis. He lived alternately in Europe and the United States until 1923, when he obtained a professorship in the Department of Painting and Drawing at the University of Kansas in Lawrence, which he held until his retirement in 1947.

Bloch painted *March of the Clowns* in 1941, while living in Kansas, and most likely before the United States entered the war. The parade's spectators are cartoon characters from the 1920s and 1930s, including Popeye, Olive Oyl, Krazy Kat, and Ignatz Mouse, all on the left side of the picture. In the foreground are characters that may be from the Katzenjammer Kids or Moon Mullins cartoons. Cross-cultural signs and symbols are strewn throughout the image. These include: an arch, historically a symbol of power and triumph; a cross, the icon of Christianity; a crescent moon and star, which have become the symbol of Islam; and festive-looking skeletons, often associated with the Mexican Day of the Dead. Perhaps the positions of the cartoon characters, so strongly identified with American culture, standing at the periphery of this procession of ghoulish creatures, mirror Bloch's feeling of isolation and powerlessness as he watched World War II unfolding overseas.

JG

REFERENCES
Adams, Conrads, and Hoberg, *Albert Bloch: The American Blue Rider*; Baron, Arntzen, and Cateforis, *Albert Bloch: Artistic and Literary Perspectives*; Sid Deutsch Gallery, *Albert Bloch (1882–1961): Paintings*.

William Anastasi

(American, born 1933)

Untitled (Jew), 1987

Oil on canvas
132⅛ x 132½ in. (335.7 x 336.6 cm)
Gift of the artist, 1987-115a-d

Untitled (Jew) appears to be a simple picture. It is composed of four equal-size canvases, each covered with deftly applied, impeccably controlled white paint. The snowy canvases butt closely together, leaving a cruciform shape at their juncture. The word "jew," spelled lowercase, is emblazoned across the top two canvases. Its off-center position gives the whole a Zen-like, Japonist sensibility. However, the provocative text on the surface of this spare, elegant painting denies the sensuality of the brush-work beneath.

Initially, Anastasi was drawn to the word "jew" because it could act as noun, verb, or adjective. But "jew"—given its associations with antisemitism—was simultaneously fraught with philosophic and social currency close to Anastasi's heart. For Anastasi, who is not Jewish, the term "jew" is the most charged word in the English language, having both positive and negative associations. On the one hand, it conjures great modern intellectuals—Freud, Schoenberg, Einstein, Kafka, and Marx—formative players of twentieth-century culture. On the other hand, the term reeks of ideas that are accusatory and denigrating, even violent.

With *Untitled (Jew)*, William Anastasi reconciles two seemingly contradictory artistic practices: painting and conceptual art. For Anastasi, painting remains both an instinctive activity and an intellectual construct. He thinks warily about what it means to make a painting. Yet he handles paint fluidly, intuitively deploying form, color, and facture in an autonomous manner that echoes his admiration of gestural abstraction and his obsession with James Joyce's stream of consciousness.

Anastasi began his career during the formative period for Conceptual Art, and many of his early works have become classics of this genre. These works play at the junctures of the real and the represented, the visual and the verbal. A breakthrough work—and one of Anastasi's most frequently discussed—remains his painting *Untitled (wall on a wall)*. Slightly smaller than the gallery wall itself, the painting depicts a simulation of the wall upon which it was hung, including air ducts and electrical outlets placed on the canvas in exactly the same proportion and position as on the wall itself. Installed at the Dwan gallery in New York in 1967, it has become one of the icons of art that challenged the classic, supposedly neutral, "white cube" gallery spaces. Like *Untitled (Jew)*, the 1966 *Untitled (wall on a wall)* is a heady conceit. A deceptively simple work, the earlier canvas stimulates aesthetic discourse about the definition and potential limits of a work of art. Such issues were crucial to the questioning about and reinvigoration of art during the sixties.

Following a quiet period in his career in the 1970s, Anastasi returned in the 1980s to an art world dramatically changed. He must have felt like a wanderer in uncharted terrain. Art's focus had moved away from the phenomenological and epistemological concerns so prevalent during the 1960s and 1970s preoccupations of Minimal, Conceptual, and Process Art and turned instead to an abiding focus on expressionist, narrative painting. Anastasi's picture of the word "jew" might be seen as a negotiation between painting, the medium of choice during the 1980s, and art relating to language, an important aspect of art in the 1960s and 1970s. *Untitled (Jew)* dismissed the representational, often agitated subject matter and paint handling typical of the early 1980s. Instead, it substituted a canvas freighted with linguistic, moral, and political meaning. Using the highly loaded word "jew" as a sole basis for creating a monumental picture, Anastasi enters the twentieth century's continuing struggle to deny assumptions about preconceived limits of painting.

NLK

REFERENCES
De Duve, "The Readymade and the Tube of Paint," pp. 110–21; Kalina, "William Anastasi"; McEvilley, *William Anastasi*, pp. 47–51; O'Doherty, *Inside the White Cube*.

jew

William Kentridge

(South African, born 1955)

Drawings for Projection Series: Johannesburg—2nd Greatest City after Paris; Monument; Mine; Sobriety, Obesity, and Growing Old, 1989–91

16 mm animated film transferred to videodisc, dimensions variable

Purchase: Mr. and Mrs. George Jaffin, Lillian Gordon Bequest, and Fine Arts Acquisition Committee Fund, 2001-12

Actor, director, set designer, puppeteer, printmaker, draftsman, and filmmaker, South African artist William Kentridge seems a consummate moralist. Trained as a political scientist and working as an artist, he reports feeling skeptical about political art. Kentridge's purposefully disjointed, highly personal narratives reverberate with references to the physical devastations and personal indignities associated with apartheid and the moral dilemmas that continue in its wake. His acute awareness of the South African predicament is rooted in his family history and its tradition of social engagement. More than a century ago, his ancestors emigrated from Lithuania to South Africa, and he is the son of two and grandson of three prominent lawyers. His father, Sydney Kentridge, represented the families of the Sharpeville victims, investigated Stephen Biko's death, and was involved in the Mandela trials.

The four animated films, *Johannesburg—2nd Greatest City after Paris*; *Monument*; *Mine*; and *Sobriety, Obesity*, and *Growing Old*, are the first in Kentridge's *Drawings for Projection* series. Each revolves around two central characters, Soho Eckstein and Felix Teitelbaum, who at first appear to be alter egos as they play out contradictory moral positions of white South Africans. In all four short animated films, Eckstein, the voracious, ruthless, self-indulgent industrialist, is shown as a stocky tyrant in his tight-fitting, pinstripe suit worn as a uniform. This character contrasts with Teitelbaum, the artist dreamer, who is disarmingly characterized as tentative, circumspect, and vulnerable. In fact, physically Teitelbaum is a self-portrait of Kentridge, and Eckstein is a portrait of the artist's grandfather. Together, these two Jewish antagonists play out the uncomfortable irony of a white Jewish minority in its privileged position in a racist society.

In the first three of these films, we see Eckstein amassing power and wealth at the expense of black South Africans who are essentially reduced to slave labor. Eckstein indulges his appetites, disregards his wife, abuses his workers, and devastates the South African landscape. While the thoughtful Felix wins the heart of Mrs. Eckstein, in *Sobriety, Obesity, and Growing Old*, she returns to her husband—the first instance in the continuing series where Eckstein begins to show pangs of remorse. "Magical" best describes the way Kentridge transforms the animate into the inanimate and vice versa—the way he morphs objects, people, and landscapes. "Terrifying" best expresses what they represent. The bleeding, wounded, and dead melt into the South African landscape; a cat turns into an atavistic stamping machine, its tail into the handle; a plunger coffee pot transforms into a pneumatic tube that descends hundreds of feet down a mine shaft; a microphone metamorphoses into a sprinkler. In subsequent films in the series, the two antagonists begin to take on each other's characteristics and morph into each other. Evidently, the collapsing together of the virtuous and the malevolent results from Kentridge's feeling that there are neither heroes nor innocents in the physical and social devastation that embodied apartheid South Africa but only victims.

Kentridge's animation technique is unique but simple; he calls his process "Stone Age." Capitalizing on his masterful draftsmanship, he creates large-scale charcoal drawings that he films in their process of transformation. Kentridge makes images and then erases them on the same sheet of paper, every day creating scores of changes to propel the visual narrative. His erasures leave traces of past images that contribute to the moody depictions and infuse them with a melancholic sense of lapsed time. This method—drawing, filming, erasing, and drawing anew—is a way of thinking, a means of writing, a method of questioning. Kentridge's drawings and films become metaphors—communal, national, and personal—that remain purposefully stranded at the intersection where memory meets history.

N L K

REFERENCES

Benezra, Boris, and Cameron, *William Kentridge*; Cameron, Christov-Bakargiev, and Coetzee, *William Kentridge*; Christov-Bakargiev, *William Kentridge*; Enwezor, "Truth and Responsibility."

Tina Barney

(American, born 1945)

The Trustee and the Curator, 1992

Chromogenic color print
28½ x 36¼ in. (72.4 x 92.1 cm)

Purchase: Horace W. Goldsmith
Foundation Fund, 2000-11

Tina Barney is best known for her large-scale color photographs of her family and friends in their affluent social milieu, taken over the past twenty years. Born into one of New York's elite Jewish families and raised in a grand Upper East Side apartment, Barney summered with her family in Southampton, New York, and Watch Hill, Rhode Island, along with other families whose social prestige extends for generations. The interpersonal relationships that take place in this familiar world of privilege are the subject of Barney's photographs.

Whereas paparazzi photographs of the wealthy focus on glamorous events that take place in the public eye, Barney's pictures capture casual, often private, moments from an insider's point of view. Her subjects include her extended family reading the Sunday *New York Times* in the kitchen of the summer cottage, her sister and niece dressed in bathrobes in a pink bathroom, and members of her social circle at the beach. These last images recall Lisette Model's photographs of the French Riviera in the 1930s. However, unlike Model's mocking critique of her elite subjects, Barney's photographs offer an intimate, yet coolly neutral, view of prosperity.

Working with a large-format 4 x 5 Toyo camera that requires a tripod, Barney arranges her subjects in their wood-paneled offices, summer cottages, and art-filled parlors so that the people in the pictures appear spontaneous and unposed. The casual atmosphere is not a product of candid photography but of the intimate relationship between the photographer and her subjects and settings. Like Nan Goldin, Barney is very much a part of the world she photographs, but her pictures relate closer to those of Cindy Sherman as staged tableaux.

In *The Trustee and the Curator*, two men in suits stand in the Robert Lehman Collection of the Metropolitan Museum of Art. Barney stated in an interview that the photograph depicts a curator of the Metropolitan Museum with her brother, a trustee of the museum. Barney and her brother are direct descendants of the Lehman family, founders of the investment banking house Lehman Brothers, as well as philanthropists and art collectors. Collecting art has always been a means of garnering social status. For many Jews in the early twentieth century, the acquisition of art contributed to the process of acculturation. Robert Lehman (1891–1969), like other serious Jewish collectors of his time, focused on European painting, particularly Christian art of the Italian Renaissance. Barney's photograph depicts the trustee with his hand raised—most likely a gesture of explanation, but similar to a posture of blessing typically associated with Christian iconography—and the artist has described his face as mirroring that of the Madonna behind him. In the photograph, the trustee becomes part of the iconography of the Renaissance paintings his family collects.

The photograph's intrigue is less about who the subjects are—they remain unnamed in the title, as Barney's subjects often do—but about the dynamic between the figures and the setting in the staged picture. The title does not indicate which figure is the trustee and which is the curator, nor where the photograph takes place. The photograph, then, is a tableau of a behind-the-scenes glimpse into the elite world of art collecting and philanthropy in the exclusive setting of a museum during nonpublic hours. Through the photograph, the viewer vicariously shares Barney's insider status.

K L

REFERENCES
Barney, *Friends and Relations*; Barney and Grundberg, *Tina Barney: Photographs, Theater of Manners*; Galassi, *Pleasures and Terrors of Domestic Comfort*.

R. B. Kitaj

(American, born 1932)

Eclipse of God (After the Uccello Panel Called Breaking Down the Jew's Door), 1997–2000

Oil and charcoal on canvas
35¹⁵⁄₁₆ x 47¹⁵⁄₁₆ in. (91.3 x 121.8 cm)

Purchase: Oscar and Regina Gruss Memorial Fund and the S. H. and Helen R. Scheuer Family Foundation, 2000-71

In 1989, R. B. Kitaj published his *First Diasporist Manifesto*, a terse, personal, and playful treatise in which he muses about what it means for an artist to create from the position of being an outsider, in particular that of a Jew. Equally important, he ruminates about the dynamic relevance of figurative art today as well as the modernist artistic and literary sources that continue to inspire him. Modern Jewish history—especially related to anti-Semitism and the Holocaust—is of paramount importance for Kitaj's textual and visual explorations. Dubbing his artistic movement "Diasporism," he deploys this shrewd terminology to underscore the paradox of his outsider condition.

Eclipse of God continues the artist's obsession with historical antisemitic imagery that he began years earlier with the impressive and monumental painting *The Jewish School (Drawing a Golem)*, of 1980. *Eclipse of God* also connects with his practice of reinterpreting Old Masters painters in contemporary artistic vocabulary. While the earlier work draws its racist imagery from a nineteenth-century popular print, the source *Eclipse of God* deploys is a predella panel from Paolo Uccello's Renaissance altarpiece *Miracle of the Profaned Host* (1467–68), commissioned for a church in Urbino. Uccello's original shows Christians breaking down the door to a Jewish family's home to rescue a host (a Eucharist wafer or bread) that had allegedly been purchased by the Jews, thrown into a fire, and begun to bleed. The "guilty" Jewish merchant and his family were ultimately burned at the stake for their alleged crime against Christianity. Strong religious and political motivations underlie Uccello's imagery, part of an anti-usury campaign that sought to replace Christian dependence on Jewish moneylenders with a new Catholic agency. Thus it portrayed Jews as heretical and faithless.

Kitaj carefully inverts the meaning of Uccello's work through his clever reformulation of details, drawing attention to the venomous hatred—the antisemitism—of the Renaissance original as well as the conflicting visual traditions that divide Judaism from Christianity. At the same time, Kitaj refers to opposing traditions within modern art in transforming Uccello's Jews into sympathetic characters through his expressionist handling of the figures. Against this, he opposes the pathos of the Jewish figures with calculating, geometric abstractions that delineate the angry Christian mob. The neck of the figure in the dark red coat with its back toward the viewer bears the word "god." Located on the side of the painting that depicts the Christians barraging the Jewish household, Kitaj's portrayal of God's back creates an ambiguous tension as it reveals his keen awareness of the Jewish interpretations banning representation of the deity. The inspiration appears to be the passage from Exodus 33:23 in which that author, speaking for God, mentions that He will never show His face, but can only be seen from behind. Kitaj's title *Eclipse of God* also acknowledges Martin Buber's eponymous text. By interpolating Buber's *Eclipse of God*, we realize that Kitaj uses this historical image as an exegesis about the absence of God during historical moments when the Jewish community's existence was threatened.

Kitaj often calls such a picture a "midrash" or a "responsa" to articulate the roles played by Jewish thought and traditions of interpretation in his art. He characterizes his diasporic works as: "[p]arable pictures—[with] their dissolution, repressions, associations, referrals, and sometimes difficulty, their text obsessions, their play of differences, their autobiographical heresies, their skeptical dispositions, their assimilationist modernisms, fragmentations and confusions, their secular blasphemies." Thus Kitaj paints a lively textual picture of the ever shifting, yet ever present connections between word and image, and between his use of literary and historical themes and their formal, painterly aspects.
NLK

REFERENCES
Kitaj, *First Diasporist Manifesto*; Morphet, *R. B. Kitaj*.

The Extended Jewish Family

The Goldbergs (1949–56), a first-generation immigrant family living an American Dream of upward mobility and assimilation, is the primary source for all later representations of Jewish families on television. After twenty successful years on radio, Gertrude Berg's tragicomic vision of an "average" family transferred to television. Perhaps with the exception of cooking, family is Molly Goldberg's raison d'être and the foundation that enables her to face the challenges of a middle-class housewife. In one episode from the first television season, Molly suspects that her husband is having an affair with an attractive forewoman at the dress factory. Molly confronts the alleged home-wrecker with questions: "What made civilization? What keeps it going in the right direction? Two people with love, devotion, and family." In Molly's universe, it was difficult to argue otherwise.

The 1950s family was also romanticized in *Brooklyn Bridge* (1991–93), but from a contemporary and more complex perspective. Gary David Goldberg's short-lived, critically acclaimed, and autobiographical series centers on Alan Silver, a precocious fourteen-year-old struggling with adolescence in ways unimaginable to Molly Goldberg's children. In the episode "War of the Worlds," Alan meets Katie Monahan, a smart Irish Catholic beauty. Neither the Monahans nor Alan's grandparents think the two should date outside their faith. In an effort to show common ground between their respective Irish and Jewish clans, Katie and Alan strategically arrange a meeting on neutral ground— a Chinese restaurant. *Brooklyn Bridge* is a nostalgic utopia with carefully drawn boundaries where Jewish families are able to coexist with other ethnic groups.

In contrast to the 1990s, positive portrayals of interfaith romance on television were taboo in the early 1970s. *Bridget Loves Bernie* (1972–73)—an update of the original 1922 Broadway play *Abie's Irish Rose*—tested the limits of a family sitcom and failed after one season. Bernie Steinberg, a Jewish writer/cabdriver, and Bridget Fitzgerald, an upper-class Catholic schoolteacher, fall in love despite their religious and economic differences. Responding to pressure from religious groups, CBS canceled *Bridget Loves Bernie* despite its sixth place in network television's top ten programs.

The "opposites attract" formula for television comedy continues today, but with a nod to sexual diversity. Although *Will & Grace* (1998 to the present) is unusual for its humorous approach to gay identity and culture, the series has garnered broad appeal for its sharp writing and talented cast. *Will & Grace* is a showcase for the most popular TV couple at the turn

left: Gertrude Berg (left) and the cast of
The Goldbergs.

above: David Birney and Meredith
Baxter in *Bridget Loves Bernie*.

of the twenty-first century: Will Truman, a WASP gay lawyer; and Grace Adler, a straight Jewish designer. The two share a long-term relationship as roommates, best friends, enemies, and even as potential coparents. The outrageous, alcoholic Karen, the flamboyant, childlike Jack, and Jack's son, Elliot, complete this unusual social group. In the episode "Star-Spangled Banter," Will and Grace choose different mayoral candidates based on their own ethnicity, gender, and sexual orientation: a Jewish woman for Grace and a gay man for Will. However, at a joint fund-raiser, political allegiances backfire as both candidates reveal their conservative and racist viewpoints.

Will & Grace can be categorized among the "friendship sitcoms" from the 1990s aimed at younger audiences. *Seinfeld* (1990–98), the most popular late-twentieth-century comedy about urban single young adults, eclipsed *Brooklyn Bridge* and other family sitcoms from television. Rather than possessing hereditary ties, *Seinfeld* concerns the close kinship of Jerry, Elaine, George, and Kramer, who play out bizarre and unhealthy family dynamics in this "show about nothing." In the final episode, the lead characters are on trial for breaking a "Good Samaritan" law in a small Massachusetts town. Based on testimony from former guest characters, the jury sentences the "New York Four" to prison for their malicious, selfish, immature, and greedy behavior. Rather than serving as moral compass, Jewishness occasionally lent itself to the show's humor but left audiences confused. The ambiguous ethnicity of *Seinfeld*'s characters was a subject of great debate among pop-culture fans who insisted that the show's ostensibly non-Jewish characters were coded with Hebraic sensibility.

Jews and their families have appeared irregularly in the history of television entertainment and, arguably, continue their presence at the turn of the twenty-first century. New York, a home for the alternative and the avant-garde, is the appropriate locus for varied definitions of family—nuclear, extended, invented—that reflect a new generation's changing attitudes toward tradition, religion, and sexuality.
AI

REFERENCE
Weber, "Goldberg Variations"; Shandler, "At Home on the Small Screen."

left: Cast of *Seinfeld*.

above: Louis Zorich and Marion Ross as the grandparents in *Brooklyn Bridge*.

right: Cast of *Will & Grace*.

Laugh Tracks and Tears: Depictions of Antisemitism on Television

Bonanza, "Look to the Stars,"
March 18, 1962, NBC, T1497

All in the Family, "Archie Is Branded,"
February 24, 1973, CBS, T725

Mary Hartman, Mary Hartman,
episodes 75 and 76, 1976, syndicated,
T2081–T2082

Skokie,
November 17, 1981, CBS, T699–T701

Beverly Hills 90210, "Hate Is Just a
Four-Letter Word,"
November 16, 1994, Fox, T1854

The memory of European pogroms and the Holocaust, as well as more contemporary forms of antisemitism, continues to shape television production. In the past forty years, images of anti-Jewish hatred have crossed all genres of fictional programming: situation comedy, made-for-TV film, teen drama, and even the Western.

Set in the post–Civil War era, *Bonanza* told the story of the Cartwright family, a prosperous all-male clan working on the Ponderosa Ranch, near Virginia City, Nevada. During its long and successful run on NBC, from 1959 to 1973, *Bonanza* offered several episodes examining the theme of racial and ethnic intolerance. "Look to the Stars" is an episode loosely based on the childhood of Nobel Prize–winning physicist Albert Abraham Michelson. Michelson's immigrant parents inform the Cartwrights that the schoolmaster has expelled their gifted son for disciplinary reasons. Ben Cartwright discovers that the schoolmaster is a bigot with prejudices not only against Jews but also against Chinese, Native Americans, and Mexican students. In this scenario, the minority families of Virginia City depend on Ben Cartwright, a school board member and respected pillar of the community, to pursue justice on their behalf.

Cartwright is a Hollywood archetype: the heroic WASP who rescues individuals disempowered and victimized by prejudice. The 1981 docudrama *Skokie* departs from this conceit by investing Jews with self-determination and agency. Based on a book by David Hamlin, former executive director of the Illinois American Civil Liberties Union, *Skokie* dramatizes the historical events of 1977 and 1978 in which a group of neo-Nazis demand the right to march in a predominantly Jewish suburb of Chicago. Holocaust survivor Max Feldman rejects the Anti-Defamation League's recommendation to ignore and "quarantine" these so-called hoodlums. *Skokie* was written by the Emmy Award–winning scenarist Ernest Kinoy and realized by his longtime associate Herbert Brodkin, who also produced the landmark miniseries *The Holocaust* (1978).

In the 1990s, the debate between free speech and hate speech was revived and dramatized in *Beverly Hills 90210* (1990–2000), a popular series about the lives of young adults in Los Angeles. Controversy erupts when the university's Black Student Union engages an African-American religious leader known for making antisemitic remarks to speak (the character was loosely based on Leonard Jeffries, a black-studies professor at the City College of New York). Surprisingly, it is a Holocaust survivor who is the

left: Cast of *Bonanza.*

above: Jean Stapleton and Carroll O'Connor in *All in the Family.*

right: Mary Kay Place as Loretta in *Mary Hartman, Mary Hartman.*

opposite, left: Danny Kaye (standing) as a Holocaust survivor in *Skokie.*

opposite, right: Cast of *Beverly Hills 90210.*

most open-minded about the situation. She encourages her granddaughter Andrea, one of the Jewish student leaders, to listen to what the speaker has to say before passing judgment on his politics.

During the 1970s, producer Norman Lear broke ground in situation comedy by examining controversial social issues such as racism and antisemitism. *All in the Family* (1971–83), the mother of Lear's subsequent progeny of hit spin-offs, centered on the bigoted New Yorker Archie Bunker. *All in the Family* attracted a diverse audience: some viewers praised the show's absurdist perspective on prejudice while others identified with Archie's intolerant opinions about race and religion. The episode "Archie Is Branded" is a provocative meditation on hate crime and the price of revenge. A radical activist from the "Hebrew Defense Association" offers to protect the Bunkers, who discover a swastika painted on their door. The Bunkers conclude that they have been mistaken for a Jewish family on the same block. Archie's liberal son-in-law argues against the activist's vigilantism and extreme tactics in the war against antisemitism. Archie, on the other hand, embraces his unlikely friend's vengeful philosophy. In one of the most shocking endings in sitcom history, the Bunkers hear an explosion, run to the front door, and discover

that a car bomb has detonated and murdered the activist.

Once again, Norman Lear unsettled audiences with *Mary Hartman, Mary Hartman*, a syndicated comedy about a brainless, braided housewife and her circle of family and friends in a mythical Ohio suburb. The show had a cult following, but its content (social satire) and genre (a situation comedy posing as a daytime drama) confused most television viewers. In a two-part episode, Mary's friend Loretta, an aspiring country-and-western singer, lands a gig on Dinah Shore's live talk show. Loretta spoils her chance at stardom by making offensive remarks about her host's Jewish producer. In her charming southern drawl, Loretta exclaims, "I couldn't believe that his was the people what killed our Lord!" Religious groups condemn the statements and a media frenzy ensues, leading to Loretta's public apology.

During the 1960s and early 1970s—the heyday of the civil rights movement—the subject of antisemitism served as a litmus test for addressing other forms of prejudice on television. Producers and audiences of network television were more comfortable examining antisemitism than racism, sexism, or homophobia.

AI

From Cradle to Grave to Screen: Jewish Life-Cycle Events

The Dick Van Dyke Show, "Buddy Sorrel, Man and Boy," March 2, 1966, CBS, T717

Rhoda, "Rhoda's Wedding," October 28, 1974, CBS, T158

Late Night with David Letterman, "The Bar Mitzvah of Barry Weil," September 24, 1982, NBC, T260-61

thirtysomething, "Prelude to a *Bris*," September 25, 1990, ABC, T1510

Northern Exposure, "Kaddish for Uncle Manny," May 3, 1993, CBS, T1708

The Dick Van Dyke Show, one of television's classic comedies, was essentially an autobiographical treatment of Carl Reiner's experience writing the programs *Your Show of Shows* and *Caesar's Hour*. The main character, Rob Petrie (played by Van Dyke), was a television comedy writer who lived in suburban New Rochelle, New York, with his wife (played by Mary Tyler Moore) and their son. In the episode "Buddy Sorrel, Man and Boy," Buddy's colleagues suspect him of having an affair or visiting a psychiatrist when he is elusive about his evening plans. In fact, he was sneaking off to a rabbi's apartment for bar mitzvah lessons. The subject of Jewish worship is treated here with extreme reverence. Petrie's minor faux pas, such as congratulating Buddy with "Shalom!" rather than "Mazel Tov," may have allowed a general viewing audience to identify with a character who was also unfamiliar with Jewish practice.

The enormously popular *Mary Tyler Moore Show* launched a number of spin-offs, based on the well-drawn characters in Mary's life. Her best friend, Rhoda, a funny and savvy Jewish woman whose mother is played by the redoubtable Nancy Walker, moves back to her native New York in the show *Rhoda*. The Emmy Award–winning "Rhoda's Wedding" was one of the highest-rated programs in television history. Though

Rhoda's unmarried state was long a source of anxiety for her mother, Rhoda's plan to marry her non-Jewish lover in a civil ceremony becomes the next source of Jewish mother/daughter repartee.

Taped in New York City, *Late Night with David Letterman* was remarkable as a self-parodying talk show. Its initial cult audience adored the irreverent host, the "Top 10 List," "Stupid Pet Tricks," and other absurd elements. In one episode, Letterman hosted the bar mitzvah reception of a young fan. To set the stage, comedian Robert Klein showed home movies of his bar mitzvah party, replete with Jell-O molds and a herring Ferris wheel.

Barry Weil's reception was allowed to take place in real time and shifted from foreground to background throughout the program. The contrast between the reverentially portrayed ceremony on *The Dick Van Dyke Show* and this gentle yet parodic exhibition of the absurdities and excesses of contemporary bar mitzvah parties is notable. Yet for its untraditional setting, Weil's reception includes all the traditional elements, from a candle-lighting ceremony to Barry's bar mitzvah speech.

The quintessential Yuppie drama *thirtysomething* focused on a circle of friends living in Philadelphia. In "Prelude to a *Bris*," Hope and Michael, an interfaith

left: Dick Van Dyke, Morey Amsterdam, and Carl Reiner in *The Dick Van Dyke Show*.

right: Valerie Harper and David Groh in *Rhoda*.

couple, struggle with the decision to circumcise their newborn son. Michael's discomfort with his Judaism leaves Hope confused about the necessity of a *bris*. In a prototypical argument (similarly played out over Hanukkah and Christmas in another episode), Michael confronts his attachment to—yet distance from—his own tradition when faced with having to justify his wishes to his Christian wife. This program triggered an enormous amount of discussion among viewers who related to the attempts to explore issues that face contemporary urban professionals, while not necessarily providing long-lasting resolutions to the conflicts.

Northern Exposure centered on native New Yorker Dr. Joel Fleischman, who was assigned to the remote town of Cicely, Alaska, to fulfill a medical-school financial-aid obligation. The popular series explored the trials and tribulations of the streetwise and ambitious Jewish doctor stranded in an isolated and eccentric hamlet. In "Kaddish for Uncle Manny," the death of Joel's uncle ignites a systematic search for a minyan of Jews throughout the area. Appreciative of Cicely's efforts, Joel nonetheless opts to recite the kaddish with his adopted community. While some viewers objected to a ceremony that included townspeople engaging in ritual gestures according to their own

respective faiths, the show represents a journey of discovery for Joel and reflects a trend among young American Jews to embrace Judaism, but on their own terms.

These programs illustrate a gradual change in the depiction of Jewish characters and practices on American television, from the reverence of the 1960s to the gentle self-parody of the 1970s to the more barbed satire of the 1980s to, finally, the deeply contemplative and ambivalent acceptance of the 1990s. AW

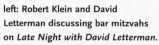

left: Robert Klein and David Letterman discussing bar mitzvahs on *Late Night with David Letterman*.

right: Rob Morrow and Janine Turner in *Northern Exposure*.

below: The "Prelude to a *Bris*" episode of *thirtysomething*.

Portraiture and Identity

Portraiture and Identity

The past half-century has seen a significant shift in the role and understanding of the individual, both in society and culture. The advent of movements dedicated to racial, sexual, and ethnic minorities (as well as organizations devoted to rights of workers, the elderly, the poor, or the physically challenged) has helped reveal the extent to which prejudice in mainstream culture has erased or diminished the voices of people considered less than equal. These movements embrace rather than fear difference—an attitude exemplified by cultural pride and an identity-based politics meant to embolden and protect minorities.

One consequence of identity politics has been the imperative to celebrate the individual—to allow the formerly oppressed or ignored to be heard over the official and often discriminatory voices of nation, society, and culture. The popularity of the memoir and autobiography in art, literature, and culture over the past twenty-five years represents one important example of this emphasis on individual empowerment through self-expression.

The voices and images of Jewish people reverberate throughout the museum's permanent collection—men and women often denied the right to speak for themselves in official histories and cultures. Its holdings cover a range of works devoted to portraiture and personal identity: portraits of both prominent and relatively unknown people; ritualistic and domestic objects that reflect the lives of Jewish individuals in places as disparate as Nome, Alaska, and Jerusalem; photographs and paintings of Jewish subjects in myriad cultural and social settings; and portraits, self-portraits, and Conceptual Art works that explore the nexus between Jewish and other identities, including women, people of color, and gay men and lesbians.

The collection is particularly rich in portraiture. Its representations of Jewish subjects offer an aesthetic window into their psychological, political, and cultural states and contexts. John Wesley Jarvis's *Portrait of Solomon Isaacs* (c. 1813) and Thomas Sully's *Portrait of Sally Etting* (1808)—images rich with exquisitely rendered details of clothing, hair, jewelry, and furniture—depict fashionable, wealthy Jewish Americans in early nineteenth-century New York and Philadelphia, respectively. Sculpture and paintings by Chana Orloff (*Portrait of Madame Peretz Hirshbein*, 1924), Larry Rivers (*Portrait of Vera List*, c. 1965), Alice Neel (*Portrait of Meyer Schapiro*, 1983), and Andy Warhol (*Ten Portraits of Jews of the Twentieth Century*, 1980) commemorate the lives of important twentieth-century Jewish cultural figures.

Other works depict historical subjects, images that document and offer insights into the nature and sensibility of the lives of Jewish individuals in different periods and geographic locations: an unusual artifact—a Rosh Hashanah greeting commissioned by an observant Jewish couple and manufactured in the centuries-old Inuit craft of walrus-tusk carving—speaks to one family's multicultural experience as pioneering Jewish settlers in Alaska in the late nineteenth century. Richard Avedon's photographic series *Jacob Israel Avedon* (1969–73) documents the final years of the artist's terminally ill father, a painful chronicle of the deterioration of the patriarch of a contemporary Jewish American family.

Finally, a number of works in the collection explore the intersection of cultural identities. Ross Bleckner's *Double Portrait (Gay Flag)* (1993) superimposes a Star of David onto a field of brightly colored stripes, a merger of two powerful icons—the abiding symbol of the Jewish people and the "rainbow" banner often used as a emblem of the gay rights movement—to allude to his own dual identity as a gay man and a Jew. Hannah Wilke's self-portrait *Venus Pareve* (1982–84) consists of a series of twenty-five hand-modeled sculptures of the artist's shapely, naked body rendered in brightly colored plaster of paris or chocolate. The work represents the late feminist artist's personal attempt to create a modern-day Jewish Venus, a symbol through which she questions a range of sexist and antisemitic stereotypes, from the dark-haired and seductive Jewess to the Jewish American Princess.

MB

Furniture Inlay

Lebanon or North Syria,
9th–8th century B.C.E.

Ivory: carved
1 x 1⅛ in. (2.5 x 2.9 cm)

Gift of Anna D. Ternbach, 1996-71

This diminutive ivory plaque representing a woman's face was originally an inlay in a piece of furniture, probably a bed or couch. Such inlays became particularly common in the Near East during the ninth and eighth centuries B.C.E. and were produced in one of three artistic "schools," in Phoenicia (modern Lebanon), northern Syria, and Assyria (modern Iraq). The Jewish Museum inlay is most likely of the Phoenician school, which combined elements of Egyptian and Near Eastern art in an elegant style. Here, the female figure wears an Egyptian wig, yet the scene in which she is represented has its origins in Near Eastern religious beliefs and practices. Based on other examples with this imagery, the original inlay was larger and included the frame and balustrade of a window. The motif of a woman looking out of a window, known from religious artifacts in Cyprus and Jordan from around the same period, has been associated with the cult of the goddess of love in several ancient Near Eastern cultures. For example, a Mesopotamian goddess, Kilulu, is described as "she who bends out the window." The custom of using virgins in sacred sexual rites was known in Phoenician cults of the goddess Ashtart, and it has been suggested that the motif of the woman at the window depicts the goddess or her representative gazing out provocatively from her chamber. Additionally, the crossed lines on the frontlet of The Jewish Museum ivory are thought to be Ashtart's symbol.

Numerous caches of these types of inlays, some still in the original beds or couches, have been found throughout the Near East and Mediterranean, from Iran to Spain. They were most often discovered in royal palaces and temples or in the graves of the wealthy. Considered highly valuable, they were frequently seized as booty and carted off to distant capitals. A large group of ivory inlays, including one depicting the woman at the window, were found at Samaria, the capital of the northern kingdom of Israel, and date to the same period as The Jewish Museum ivory. It was perhaps the close ties between Phoenicia and King Ahab, who married the Phoenician princess Jezebel, that enabled the acquisition of such expensive items by an Israelite king and his descendants.

SLB

REFERENCES

Barnett, *Ancient Ivories in the Middle East*; Merhav, *A Glimpse into the Past*, no. 36.

Medal of Gracia Nasi

Ferrara, 1557–58

Pastorino di Giovan Michele de'Pastorini (c. 1508–1592)

Bronze: cast, 2⅝ in. diam. (6.6 cm)

Gift of Samuel and Daniel M. Friedenberg Collection, FB 77

This medal is the earliest known example with a Jewish subject and a Hebrew inscription as well as an extraordinary historical document of one of the most prominent Jewish families of the sixteenth century. The Gracia Nasi portrayed here (originally Beatriz Mendes Beneviste [Grácia], 1540–1596) was the young wife of Samuel Nasci (c. 1522–1569?) and niece of the older Gracia Nasi (c. 1510–1569), a woman of extraordinary wealth and a key figure in dramatic events of international importance.

In the early sixteenth century, the family resided in Portugal, one of many new Christian families that had abjured Judaism in order to remain in the country after the edict of expulsion was promulgated in 1496. In 1541, the older Gracia Nasi, known originally as Beatriz de Luna, and her sister-in-law Brianda de Luna began an international odyssey that ended when the sultan of Turkey invited the family to settle in Istanbul. Earlier, from 1546 until 1553, they lived in Venice and then in Ferrara. Samuel Nasci married the younger Gracia (Beatriz), daughter of Brianda, in Ferrara in 1557. Shortly afterward, Samuel and his wife went to the Ottoman Empire.

This uniface medal was created by Pastorino de'Pastorini in 1557–58. At left is the sitter's name in Hebrew characters, and at right is a Latin inscription "A[nno] AE[tas] XVIII" (in the year of her age eighteen). During the Renaissance, medals became a significant art form as men and women sought to emulate the Romans of antiquity. In imitation of antique coins bearing portraits of Roman emperors, Renaissance rulers and church officials, as well as members of the lesser nobility and the bourgeoisie, commissioned idealized likenesses that expressed their *virtú* (character) and glorified their personalities. Generally, the individual was depicted in a bust portrait that gave an ennobled version of his or her appearance. The surrounding inscription identifies the sitter and may give additional information, as on this example. Since Gracia Nasi, the younger, is known to have been born in 1540, the inscription giving her age as eighteen indicates a date of 1557–58 for the medal.

Pastorino de'Pastorini was a well-known medalist who produced several similar portrait medals. Many of them show the subject surrounded by a beaded border and an inscription like those seen on Gracia Nasi's medal, but no other bears a Hebrew inscription. Since Pastorino never worked outside Italy, this medal must have been commissioned before the sitter left for Istanbul in 1558.
VBM

Thomas Sully

(American, born England, 1783–1872)

Portrait of Sally Etting, 1808

Oil on canvas
30 x 25 in. (76.2 x 63.5 cm)

Gift of William Wollman Foundation,
F 4610

Portraiture remained the predominant aspect of American artistic production for the increasingly prosperous population during the Colonial period and in the early years after the Revolution. Portrait painter Thomas Sully was but one of the many artists to record the images of America's minuscule Jewish community. In fact, the list of other major artists to receive Jewish commissions is quite impressive and includes Gilbert Stuart, Rembrandt Peale, and John Wesley Jarvis.

Here, Sully depicts thirty-two-year-old Sally Etting in the fashionable Roman-inspired clothing and coiffure of the neoclassical era, a style well suited to the ideology and aspirations of the Federal period of the early Republic. The sitter was born in York, Pennsylvania, to a family that would maintain civic and social prominence for generations. Her father, Elijah Etting, a trader whose clientele was largely Native American, was also a supplier to the Revolutionary army. He died when she was a child, and her family subsequently moved to Baltimore.

Sally Etting's highly successful brother Reuben, an important political figure in Baltimore and Philadelphia, may have commissioned this likeness of his maiden sister. Sully's journals noted a portrait of another Miss Etting, perhaps Sally's sister, and several portraits of the prominent Gratz family of Philadelphia, relatives of the Ettings. This latter group includes the 1831 portrait of the renowned social activist Rebecca Gratz, the purported inspiration for Sir Walter Scott's heroine of *Ivanhoe*. It may have been these Philadelphians who suggested Sully's service to the Ettings.

Sally Etting's portrait was executed just three months after the English-born Sully first settled in Philadelphia, the city that would become his home for the remaining sixty-five years of his long career. The perseverance, industriousness, and talent he demonstrated during his first year there enabled him to depart for London in 1809 to advance his artistic development. There, upon the recommendation of Charles Willson Peale, he studied with the eminent English-based American artist Benjamin West. After returning to Philadelphia early in 1810, Sully took up portrait commissions and within twenty years had become one of America's most prominent portraitists. In the words of the historian William Dunlap, Sully was the "prince of American portrait painters."

NLK

REFERENCES
Barratt, *Queen Victoria and Thomas Sully*; Brilliant, *Facing the New World*; Fabian, *Mr. Sully, Portrait Painter*.

John Wesley Jarvis

(American, born England, 1780–1840)

Portrait of Solomon Isaacs,
c. 1813

Oil on canvas
28¼ x 26⅝ in. (71.7 x 67.6 cm)

Purchase: gift of Mr. and Mrs. Jacob
D. Shulman and J. E. and Z. B. Butler
Foundation, by exchange; Estate of
Gabriel and Rose Katz Fund; and gift
of Kallia H. Bokser, by exchange,
1996-6

In the Colonial and Federal periods, portraits held a special significance in the homes of prosperous American Jews. These likenesses served their traditional purpose in asserting the subject's status and ensuring some measure of immortality. They also acted as daily reminders of family members distanced by geography. Most important, these portraits affirmed their sitters' identities as Americans in the open, democratic society to which they contributed. Like their Christian counterparts, Jewish patrons commissioned portraits from the most prestigious artists, such as Gilbert Stuart, Thomas Sully, and John Wesley Jarvis. The resulting images defined the esteemed position held by these members of the small but vibrant Jewish community.

Born in England, Jarvis was the most popular portrait painter in New York during the first quarter of the nineteenth century. He apprenticed with the engraver Edward Savage in Philadelphia before moving to New York, around 1802. Jarvis was prized for his faithfulness in delineating faces and his acuity in rendering character. He received commissions from many prominent Jews including the newspaper publisher and diplomat Mordecai Manuel Noah; and the war hero, later New York state assemblyman, Major Mordecai Myers. In Baltimore from 1810 to 1813, he executed portraits of Solomon Etting, a director of the Baltimore and Ohio Railroad, and his wife, Rachel Gratz Etting, a member of the well-known Gratz family of Philadelphia.

Solomon Isaacs was related to the most powerful, respected Sephardic families in America through his marriage to Elkalah Kursheedt, granddaughter of Gershom Mendes Seixas, "The Patriot Rabbi," and his sister Frances's marriage to the copper magnate Harmon Hendricks. (Seixas was one of the few clergymen invited to officiate at George Washington's inauguration and was a trustee of Columbia College.) Apprenticed to his brother-in-law, Isaacs learned all aspects of copper manufacturing, from appraising foreign metals to understanding the processes of refining and rolling. His expertise and ability to supervise engineers and mill hands led to a partnership with Hendricks, who reactivated the defunct Soho Copper Works in New Jersey. Isaacs was entrusted with Hendricks's long-standing account with Paul Revere & Sons. The firm also supplied Robert Fulton with copper for his pioneering steamboats and the United States Navy with copper sheathing for warships.

Posed on a luxurious armchair, Isaacs exudes the robustness and confidence of a young successful industrialist. Fashionably dressed, his white ruffled shirt and stock tie illuminate the olive complexion of his sensitively modeled face and serve as marked contrasts to his curly dark hair. Jarvis provides visual trappings of wealth to define his subject's social standing—a bamboo cane, the gold chain on his red pocket watch, and the extravagant chair with a carved lion. Although popular as a neoclassical decorative motif, the lion may allude to Solomon's biblical namesake and symbolize the Lion of Judah. The portrait may date from late 1813 or early 1814, to honor Isaacs's official partnership in the copper mill.

IZS

REFERENCES
Brilliant, *Facing the New World*; Dickson, *John Wesley Jarvis*; Kleeblatt and Wertkin, *The Jewish Heritage in American Folk Art*; London, *Portraits of Jews by Gilbert Stuart and Other Early American Artists*; Pool, *Portraits Etched in Stone*; Whiteman, *Copper for America*.

Jewish New Year's Greeting

Attributed to Happy Jack
(Inuit, c. 1870–1918)

Nome, Alaska, 1910
(date of inscription)

Walrus tusk: engraved; gold inset
10 in. long x 1 in. diam. (25.4 x 2.5 cm)

Gift of the Kanofsky family in memory
of Minnie Kanofsky, 1984-71

For 350 years, Jewish immigrants have brought to America their talent and drive to succeed, displaying entrepreneurship, patriotism, and often a great spirit of adventure. New opportunities combined with few restrictions allowed Jews to participate actively in the economic life of the United States. Jews also played an important role in the western migration by settling in less desirable areas. For example, the genesis of Alaska's Jewish community coincided with the purchase of the territory by the United States in 1867. It is believed that some Jews sailed there with the Russian fishing fleets in the 1830s and 1840s, but it was not until a Jewish-owned firm, the Alaska Commercial Company, secured the seal-fishing rights that known Jewish traders began making regular visits to the territory. In 1885, the first permanent Jewish settlers arrived in Juneau.

The Klondike gold rush of 1897, soon followed by another discovery of gold near Nome, brought thirty thousand miners, fortune hunters, and businessmen into Cape Nome. A number of Jews joined the immigration, and Inuits also sought a share of the bonanza. Several hundred of the latter rapidly established a market for native clothing, along with carved ivory figurines, cribbage boards, and other souvenirs.

This unusual Alaskan artifact combines the Jewish custom of sending Rosh Hashanah cards with the centuries-old Inuit craft of walrus-tusk carving, a tradition that developed quite separately from the whaleman's scrimshaw. However, with the arrival of the whalers in the nineteenth century, both Inuit carvers and scrimshanders expanded their repertoires as they exchanged techniques and materials. The complexity and diversity of Inuit subjects increased as more sophisticated interpretations displaced schematic figures and linear ornamentation. Inuit carvers quickly learned to copy illustrations or photographs in what is termed a "western pictorial style."

The most innovative and influential of the carvers was the Alaskan Inuit Angokwazhuk, known as "Happy Jack." He is credited with the introduction, after 1892, of the art of engraving walrus tusks with a very fine needle, which resulted in an almost perfect imitation of newspaper halftones and fabric textures. The carvers enhanced the incised lines by filling them with india ink, graphite, or ashes.

Most of the engraved walrus tusks are unsigned, but several closely resemble this carving. A cribbage board, for example, assumed to have been made by Happy Jack, is embellished with portraits of a couple separated by a nosegay. Even though he could not read or write, Happy Jack reproduced written inscriptions; one work included the full content of a Packer's Tar Soap label with its portrait, pinecones, and slogan. While some other native carvers also had the ability to copy the inscriptions and photographs provided by their customers, they lacked his consummate skill.

On this tusk, the artist has ably recorded the faces and attire of a religiously observant Jewish couple, believed to have run a store in Nome. The woman seems to be wearing a wig and is dressed in typical turn-of-the-century style. The man's beard is neatly trimmed; his top hat suggests a holiday or formal occasion. The Hebrew inscription delivers the traditional Jewish New Year salutation: "May you be inscribed for a good year, 5671 [1910]." In English is added: "Nome, Alaska."
A F

REFERENCE
Ray, "Happy Jack: King of the Eskimo Carvers."

לישנה מובה תכתבון

NOME, ALASKA

Elie Nadelman

(American, born Poland, 1882–1946)

Dancer, c. 1920–22

Cherry wood
28¼ in. high (71.8 cm)

Gift of William S. Rand in memory of
Muriel Rand, 1992-37

Elie Nadelman's iconic wood figures draw together classical forms influenced by Greek, Egyptian, and Renaissance sculpture with subjects and materials derived from American folk art. This confluence of high and low culture procured disdain in Nadelman's own day, yet today his genre figures are recognized as icons of modern American sculpture.

Born in Warsaw, Nadelman went in 1904 to Munich, where he saw fifth-century B.C.E. pediment sculptures from the temple at Aegina at the Glyptothek as well as polychrome late Gothic German sculptures and seventeenth- and eighteenth-century dolls at the Bavarian National Museum, all of which had an impact on his artistic style. The following year, he moved to Paris, where he became part of Leo and Gertrude Stein's artistic circle, meeting modern artists such as Pablo Picasso as well as critics, gallery owners, and collectors. During his seven years in Paris, he began sculpting in a classical style, and his drawings and figures were exhibited in several Salons d'Autumne and Salons des Indépendants, as well as the famous 1913 Armory Show in New York.

At the beginning of World War I, Nadelman went to America, where his classical heads and figures were very popular. Soon after his arrival, he married an heiress, and they began to collect American folk art, hoping someday to create a museum of their collection. Folk art, often made of painted wood and other quotidian materials, took as its subject the daily lives of common people. Nadelman began incorporating these themes into his cherry-wood works of 1918–24, with subjects such as a circus performer, a woman at a piano, and three versions of the sculpture *Dancer*, two painted and one unpainted. Most of his wood and plaster sculptures of this period were painted with color to delineate clothing and facial features. The Jewish Museum's unpainted *Dancer* retains the commonly held notion of classicism of his earlier unpainted wood and marble heads, although he may have intended to paint it as a variation of the other *Dancer* figures.

Nadelman's interest in popular culture extended beyond folk art to American vaudeville and circus. In his studio, he kept a photograph of the vaudeville dancer Eva Tanguay posed in a position similar to that of the *Dancer* sculpture. He also made a drawing entitled *High Kicker* (about 1917–19), perhaps of Tanguay. An additional source may have been the well-known painting *Le Chahut* (1890), by Georges Seurat, which depicts French can-can dancers kicking up their legs much like *Dancer*.

Nadelman's genre sculptures received harsh criticism from a public that had previously revered his classical works. His sculptures depicting contemporary life—from vaudeville performers to bourgeois types—were ridiculed by critics who felt that the artist was mocking high society. His chosen material, cherry wood, and his choice to paint many of the works may have irritated an audience that expected the restrained classicism of his earlier marble heads. Despite the criticism, Nadelman continued to work in this style, and his stylized genre sculptures were regarded as his best work only after his death.

K L

REFERENCES

Fort, *The Figure in American Sculpture*; Haskell, *Elie Nadelman*; Kirstein, *Elie Nadelman*; Ramljak, *Elie Nadelman*.

Chana Orloff

(French, born Ukraine, 1888–1968)

*Portrait of Madame
Peretz Hirshbein*, 1924

Bronze

24 x 14 x 9¼ in. (61 x 35.6 x 23.5 cm)

Gift of Erich Cohn, JM 91-64

*Portrait of
Peretz Hirshbein*, 1924

Bronze

25 x 18 x 11 in. (63.5 x 45.7 x 27.9 cm)

Purchase: Heinz Ksinski Bequest in memory of Joanna Ksinski, Miriam and Milton Handler Fund, and Fine Arts Acquisitions Committee Fund, 2003-12

In the early decades of the twentieth century, Paris acted as a magnet, attracting artists worldwide who came to study, pursue their art free from any traditional religious or ethnic restraints, and enjoy the cosmopolitan milieu. Among these foreigners was an extraordinary group of Jews, many from Eastern Europe, who made impressive contributions to French modernist art. By 1913, this contingent, known as the School of Paris, included Elie Nadelman from Poland, Marc Chagall from Russia, Jacques Lipchitz and Chaim Soutine from Lithuania, Sonia Delaunay-Terk and Chana Orloff from the Ukraine, and Amedeo Modigliani from Italy. These émigrés, who lived and worked in Montparnasse, forged strong personal and professional ties.

Orloff arrived in Paris in 1910 via Palestine, where her family had settled, and quickly entered the vibrant circle of artists in Montparnasse. By the 1920s, she was riding a wave of success as a leading portraitist to fashionable Parisians and the cultural elite. She absorbed the avant-garde tenets of Cubism and prevailing influences of classical and "primitive" art and distilled them into reductive, sinuous forms. Her elegant, highly stylized sculptures in wood and bronze, characterized by their simple volume, lyrical lines, and smooth rounded surfaces, brought her numerous portrait commissions.

In 1924, Peretz Hirshbein (1880–1948), a Yiddish playwright and novelist known for his pastoral romance *Green Fields*, commissioned Orloff to sculpt portraits of himself and his wife, the Yiddish poet Esther Shumiatcher (1899–1985). The couple had married in 1920 and traveled around the world for two years, a journey later chronicled in his book *Around the World* and her collection of poetry *In the Valley*.

Portrait of Madame Peretz Hirshbein displays the smooth surfaces and minimal detailing characteristic of the artist's work from this period. Orloff captures the intelligence and inner reserve of her subject and softens the severity of her high, angular cheekbones by slightly tilting her head. The artist conveys her continuing interest in fashion—she first worked as a sketcher with the couturier Paquin —by modeling the refined sailor-boy collar on Mme. Hirshbein's dress and the intricate, serpentine hair ornament. In the companion bust, *Portrait of Peretz Hirshbein*, the sitter's pronounced raised eyebrows, penetrating gaze, and firm mouth combine to emphasize the forcefulness of his character.

One year after executing these two powerful heads, Chana Orloff became a French citizen and was appointed Chevalier de la Légion d'Honneur. In her long, prolific career, she produced more than three hundred portraits of prominent European and Israeli artists, writers, and politicians.

IZS

REFERENCES

Chevlowe, *Paris in New York*; Grossman, "Restructuring and Rediscovering a Woman's Oeuvre"; Marcilhac, *Chana Orloff*; The Open Museum, *Chana Orloff*; Silver and Golan, *The Circle of Montparnasse*.

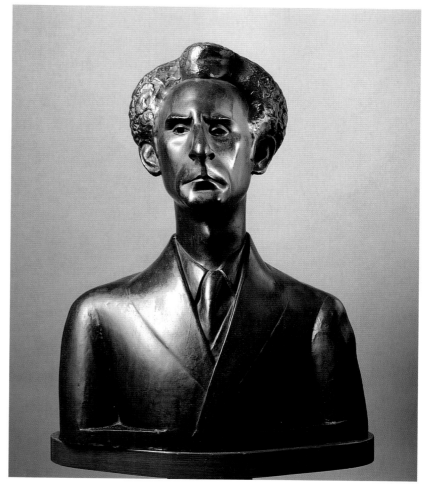

Gert Wollheim

(German, 1894–1974)

Untitled (Couple), 1926

Oil on canvas
39½ x 29½ in. (100.3 x 74.9 cm)

Gift of Charlotte Levite in memory of
Julius Nassau, JM 1990-130

As with so many artists of his generation, Gert Wollheim's art and politics were dramatically shaped by his experience on the frontline during World War I. Born into a wealthy Jewish family, Wollheim studied at the Art Academy of Weimar before serving on the battlefield, then settled in Düsseldorf after Germany's defeat. Fierce with antiwar rage and leftist politics, Wollheim participated in the experimental liberalism of *Das junge Rheinland* and the radical group *Aktivistenbund 1919*. From the trenches, Wollheim had sketched with graphic realism the contortions and anguish of a soldier's experience, and, based on these drawings, his paintings from the Düsseldorf years cried out against the social injustice of war. In 1925, Wollheim left the Rhineland for Berlin; this move also marked his emergence from the dynamic exuberance of Expressionism to a more sober study of everyday life. Fleeing the ascent to power of the National Socialists, Wollheim escaped to France in 1933. With the German conquering of France, he was arrested several times and confined in a variety of camps—some hard labor, others internment camps. In 1947, he immigrated to New York, where he died in 1974.

Painted in the middle of the Weimar period, the setting of *Untitled (Couple)* suggests the interior of a café, the lively sphere where the social boundaries of the new republic were tested. Yet Wollheim's treatment of his subject is static and cool—his posing of the couple is purposely theatrical. Against this backdrop, he examines the identity of these figures. The uncertainties about sexuality in Weimar Berlin were products of a society that enjoyed new freedoms but suffered deep unease. Debilitated and war-shocked, men faced a world of shifting female rights, while homosexual culture, bursting with experimentation, meant the obfuscation of traditional distinctions between man and woman. In his objective treatment of two figures whose sexuality is so deliberately ambiguous, Wollheim calls attention to the playfulness of this period as well as to the masquerade that thinly veiled the pervasive anxieties.

The woman on the right sports the closely cropped, slicked hair, penciled eyebrows, and white face powder fashionable with the *neue Frau*—the modern woman whose equal rights were at the foreground of the Weimar Republic's democratic debate. The style was especially popular among *Garçonnes*, lesbian women who favored this boyish look. The figure on the left, though seemingly, with sharp jawbone, a man, exemplifies another mode of Weimar lesbian fashion: butch women, known as *Bubis*, commonly wore fedoras, tuxedos, and penciled mustaches. Attentive to the details of this performance, Wollheim encodes his canvas with signs of gender disguise. The deliberately centralized position of two accessories—the dangling cigarette of the figure on the left, and the purposefully displayed monocle held by the figure on the right—highlights two appendages common to lesbians, both symbols of male sexuality: the cigarette holder, a device for extension; and the monocle, the "one eye" on a dangling string. The monocle functions by another means within the painting: at the center of the composition, it announces the theme of vision and deception. The monocle is a sign of attentiveness, commensurate with the *Neue Sachlichkeit* mission of objective recording of reality. Yet like the convex mirror at the center of Jan van Eyck's Arnolfini wedding portrait, the monocle doubles as an object that both defines and distorts. Together with the spectacles of the tuxedoed figure and the binoculars that dangle from his/her shoulder, the monocle completes a triumvirate of alternative seeing devices. In a painting whose subjects' identities are treated with such ambiguity, the presence of so many lenses calls into question the reliability of a seemingly straightforward viewpoint.
S N B

REFERENCES
Barron, *German Expressionism 1915–1925*, esp. pp. 81–97; Bilski, *War Resistance and Politics*; Gordon, *Voluptuous Panic*; Von Wiese, *Gert H. Wollheim, Phantast und Rebell*; Von Wiese, *Gert H. Wollheim, Monographie und Werkverzeichnis*.

Ilse Bing

(American, born Germany, 1899–1998)

New York—Me and the Elevated, 1936

Gelatin-silver print
7⅜ x 11⅛ in. (18.7 x 28.3 cm)

Purchase: Mr. and Mrs. George Jaffin Fund, by exchange, 2000-7

German photographer Ilse Bing made a brief visit to New York in 1936, during which she photographed the city's famous skyline. In *New York—Me and the Elevated*, Bing frames the Manhattan skyline within the diagonal lines of the elevated subway across the East River, her signature oblique angle giving the work the feeling of racing toward the midtown buildings—the six-year-old Chrysler building rising in the center—with the lower rooftops of the Queens residences below. Yet the viewpoint is not from aboard the train, but from the stationary platform where the photographer and her camera are reflected in a round mirror. By placing herself within the frame, Bing draws our attention to the relationship of the photographer to the city. She is an outsider who has placed herself within the city's framework.

Bing was born into an affluent Jewish family in Frankfurt at the turn of the century, receiving early instruction in art and music as part of her bourgeois upbringing. In 1920, Bing began her studies at the University of Frankfurt in mathematics and physics, later pursuing a doctorate in art history. As part of her dissertation research on the German architect Friedrich Gilly (1772–1800), Bing began taking pictures of his neoclassical buildings. By 1929, she had abandoned her studies in order to become a professional photographer.

The 1920s and 1930s in Germany produced a vast outpouring of photographic creativity, with work influenced by artistic movements such as Dada and Surrealism, Bauhaus, and New Objectivity. Women photographers, including Bing, Florence Henri, Germaine Krull, and Lotte Jacobi, were at the forefront of avant-garde photography. Mass culture at this time was permeated by an interest in art photography as well as photojournalism, commercial photography, and scientific photography. Advances in photographic technology made this possible. Perhaps the most significant change was the 1926 advent of the Leica, a small portable camera that worked with the newer, faster 35 mm film, allowing for more direct, spontaneous photographs that could be taken indoors without a flash. Bing was a pioneer of the new camera, and the Leica became her signature tool for the next twenty years.

Bing began her career by supporting herself with commercial work and was one of the few female photojournalists at the time. Inspired by the photographs of the Bauhaus-trained Florence Henri in a 1929 exhibit of modern photography at Frankfurt's art club, Bing decided to leave Frankfurt for Paris. Often focusing her camera on architecture, Bing's photographs reflect her youthful fascination with architecture, geometry, and harmonic composition. Constructivist and Bauhaus styles were of interest to her, but she preferred straight photography to the photographic manipulation associated with the Bauhaus.

During her 1936 New York visit, Bing was approached to work for the fledgling *Life* magazine, but she turned down the offer and returned to Paris, where she married musician Konrad Wolff. In 1940, Bing was sent to an internment camp by the Vichy government. In 1941, she and her husband immigrated to New York, where, although she became a United States citizen, Bing maintained a sense of isolation within her urban environment. K L

REFERENCES
Barrett, *Ilse Bing: Three Decades of Photography*; Edwynn Houk Gallery, *Ilse Bing, Vision of a Century*.

David Bomberg

(English, 1890–1957)

Hear, O Israel, 1955

Oil on wood
35½ x 27½ in. (90.2 x 69.9 cm)

Purchase: Oscar and Regina Gruss
Charitable Foundation Fund, 1995-33

The most creative artists in the early years of the twentieth century in England were immigrants. The earliest were Warsaw-born painter Alfred Wolmark and the sculptor Sir Jacob Epstein, who was from New York. Younger Jewish artists were to follow, most notably David Bomberg, who was born in Birmingham in 1890 and brought up in London's East End. He, along with Mark Gertler, Bernard Mininsky, and Jacob Kramer, was part of an extraordinary generation, all with foreign origins, that was active in London during the early years of the twentieth century.

Created two years before Bomberg's death, the monumental image *Hear, O Israel* can be seen as a devastating final self-portrait, and it stands as one of the great artistic autobiographical statements. Its title refers to the *Shema*, a biblical declaration of God's unity: "Hear, O Israel, the Lord our God, the Lord is One," which devout Jews recite twice a day. *Hear, O Israel* is an outstanding example of Bomberg's late expressionist style and is regarded as one of the most important religious paintings in twentieth-century British art. It depicts a shrouded man, probably the artist himself, passionately clasping the Torah. Painted with thick strokes and intense color, the semi-abstract figure is submerged in personal pain and despair, reflecting the artist's own disillusionment caused by the long period of neglect suffered in the latter part of his life.

During his early years, Jewish life in the East End of London was a powerful source of inspiration for Bomberg's work. The son of Polish immigrants, Bomberg was fortunate to receive a scholarship to the Slade School of Art in London. Although the Cubist and Futurist movements were seriously considered by Slade students, Bomberg always resisted being labeled and had no desire to associate formally with any artistic group. Initially, he developed a style characterized by the use of angular, abstract forms to give expressive force to his representational subjects. Using actual East End sites and events, he developed a flat, geometrical style. However, he never eliminated the human form or physical description.

World War I brought military service and personal losses for Bomberg, and during this period he shifted from pure skeletal forms to the rich flow of paint and color to create forms of a deeply expressive nature. In 1923, the artist received funds from a Zionist organization to record the pioneering work in Palestine, where he remained until 1927, producing remarkable studies of Petra and Palestine. From that time until the end of his life, his style changed, and he began to employ an expressionist manner and heavily impastoed paint to give greater force to his forms.

The scant recognition and long period of neglect suffered by Bomberg during the last thirty years of his life, along with his unwillingness to accept compromises in his career, contributed to his final bitter years and may be attributed to the highly individual and disturbing nature of his work. This was to be rectified by critics such as Richard Cork, who, thirty years after Bomberg's death said, "Bomberg can now be seen as one of the most rewarding and prescient painters Britain has produced in the modern era." Subsequent memorial exhibitions and written evaluations have secured this reputation and evaluation. Successive public exhibitions and critical acclaim have redressed the common attitude of great appreciation for his earlier constructivist period over the later series of family portraits, landscapes, and final tragic autobiographical statements.
SG

REFERENCES
Cork, *David Bomberg*, p. 321; Rachum, *David Bomberg in Palestine, 1923–27*; Spencer, "Anglo-Jewish Artists: The Migrant Generations"; Sylvester, *Bomberg: Paintings, Drawings, Watercolours, and Lithographs*.

Larry Rivers

(American, 1923–2002)

Portrait of Vera List,
c. 1965

Paint, charcoal, wood, tape, Plexiglas,
and aluminum window frame
32 x 27 x 4 in. (81.3 x 68.6 x 10.2 cm)

Gift of Vera G. List, 1984-21

Painter, sculptor, printmaker, poet, and musician Larry Rivers (born Yitzroch Loiza Grossberg) created works of distinguished versatility that enabled him to synthesize elements from the visual, literary, and performing arts. He was a jazz saxophonist before he took up painting, at the encouragement of two artist friends. His roots in improvisational jazz, with its anti-establishment ideology and inventive thematic variations, would later inform his paintings and mixed media constructions. He served briefly (1942–43) in the U.S. Army in World War II, and he studied with Hans Hofmann in 1947–48 in New York and Provincetown, Massachusetts. Rivers abandoned his initial Abstract Expressionist style after seeing Pierre Bonnard's retrospective at the Museum of Modern Art in 1948 and applied his drafting skills to figurative subjects related to his personal life and everyday surroundings. At a time when painters rejected representational imagery, Rivers's return to figuration came from his refusal to cut ties to the figurative masters of the past, seeking to situate himself among them by assimilating key aspects of their creative legacy. His 1950s works, with their sketchy paint application, combined elements of painting and drawing. In the 1960s, Rivers was criticized for appropriating themes and imagery from the work of Old Masters; however, his seemingly irreverent references stemmed from his obsession with examining history, particularly his own artistic and cultural heritage. This would culminate in the large-scale works *History of the Russian Revolution: From Marx to Mayakovsky* (1965) and *History of Matzah (The Story of the Jews)* (1982–84).

Vera G. List (1908–2002), a life trustee of The Jewish Museum, was an active collector and champion of contemporary art. In Rivers's *Portrait of Vera List*, the artist immortalized his patron without idealizing her. One of Rivers's early three-dimensional assemblages, this work is roughly fashioned and retains his characteristic gestural brushwork. Through the convention of portraiture, Rivers engaged in a dialogue with his artistic forefathers, while updating their traditional practices with new materials and techniques. In this half-length portrait, the collage elements, which include painted pieces of wood, Plexiglas, and torn sheets of graph paper, were applied on top of and behind the panes of a storm window to create a disjointed portrait of List. Rivers exploited the window's sliding panes, which can be moved to reveal different images. On the one hand, Rivers literalized the notion that a painting is like a window, offering a view into an imagined pictorial world; however, he did not adhere to the conventions of illusionistic painting. The work's composite views and fragmentation of the sitter's facial features and body parts prevent a coherent reading of the person depicted. This use of collage and fragmentation shows the artist's affinity with earlier avant-garde movements, such as Dada and Cubism, while the innovative use of materials and mixed media, as well as the conflation of high and low culture, coincides with the chief concerns of the contemporaneous Pop Art movement. This portrait conveys the deftly complex yet unfinished qualities of Rivers's distinctive style.

G G

REFERENCES

Harrison, *Larry Rivers*; Hunter, *Rivers*; Rivers, with Brightman, *Drawings and Digressions*; Rivers, with Weinstein, *What Did I Do?*; Rosenzweig, *Larry Rivers*.

Richard Avedon

(American, born 1923)

Jacob Israel Avedon, 1969–73

(printed 1980)

One of a portfolio of seven gelatin-silver prints
17 x 17 in. (43.2 x 43.2 cm)

Purchase: Sara and Axel Schupf, Jack and Judith Stern, and Hyman L. and Joan C. Sall Funds, 1993-168.7

Hailed early in his career as a fashion photographer extraordinaire, Richard Avedon now reigns as one of the most important portraitists of his generation. Known for his iconic images of celebrities from the worlds of art, literature, and politics, he has also directed his camera toward the downtrodden and the mentally ill and has made these anonymous figures equally commanding and empathetic. His meteoric rise in the fashion world resulted from innovative images photographed while working for *Harper's Bazaar* in the 1940s and 1950s—an ascent reflected in the 1957 movie *Funny Face*, partly inspired by his career and for which he acted as visual consultant. (The photographer in the film, played by Fred Astaire, is named Dick Avery.) However, portraits have always been Avedon's passion. His preoccupation with faces started with his assignment at age nineteen in the merchant marine, taking identification photographs of thousands of servicemen.

The artist's portfolio of seven photographs of his terminally ill father, *Jacob Israel Avedon*, taken from 1969 through his terminal illness until his death in 1973, represents a stunning anomaly in his oeuvre. In this series, chronicling the deterioration of a patriarch, Avedon approaches an intensely personal subject and makes it universal. Set against a white background, the sitter reveals himself unflinchingly to the spectator's gaze. Characteristically, the artist employs no effects to soften his subject's vulnerability. He does not flatter or cajole his father, but waits for the defining moment. He uses his signature white wall, no props, no complimentary lighting, no constructed poses to distract the camera from capturing his father's raw emotions of fear, pain, and resignation. In these photographs, Avedon confronts not only his father's mortality but his own and ours.

Born in Russia in 1889, Jacob Israel Avedon endured a difficult childhood in America, including several years in a Jewish orphanage. After studying at the College of the City of New York, he taught elementary school in Hell's Kitchen. In 1917, he and a brother opened a women's retail shop on Fifth Avenue, which lasted until the Depression led to its closing in 1930. Later, he moved to Sarasota, Florida, where he began a new life as a stockbroker. His biography reads as a classic narrative of the struggles of an American Jewish immigrant.

That struggle ends with his son's study of man's inevitable frailty. When asked how he felt about taking photographs of his dying father, Richard Avedon replied that these images represent "what it is to be any one of us."

IZS

REFERENCES
Hambourg, Fineman, and Avedon, *Richard Avedon: Portraits*; Livingston and Gopnik, *Richard Avedon*; Rosenberg, "Portraits: A Meditation on Likeness."

Nan Goldin

(American, born 1953)

Self-portrait in blue bathroom, London, 1980

Silver dye bleach print
27¾ x 40³⁄₁₆ in. (70.5 x 102.1 cm)

Purchase: Horace W. Goldsmith
Foundation Fund, 2002-28

Self-portrait in blue bathroom, London is part of *The Ballad of Sexual Dependency*, Nan Goldin's well-known photographic series, that originally toured clubs, museums, and galleries as a slide show set to music. Captured over ten years beginning in 1976, this body of work focused on the drug culture, sexual relations, and intimate moments in the everyday lives of the group Goldin called her tribe, in New York's East Village. The photographs from *The Ballad of Sexual Dependency*, published as a book of the same title in 1986, constituted a record of countercultural life before the overwhelming reality of the AIDS crisis entered the public consciousness. For Goldin, who in her later work confronted the impact of AIDS on the lives of her close friends, this series was a testament of both love and loss.

Goldin's scenes in *The Ballad of Sexual Dependency* are often convivial but are overwhelmed by self-indulgence and debauchery: a figure preparing to use drugs, two men embracing on the beach amid cans of Budweiser, or a couple having sex in an unkempt apartment. Candidly portraying outsiders, she emerged from the lineage of Lisette Model, who captured almost ethnographic studies of the disenfranchised, and Diane Arbus, who addressed her subjects with empathy, though often emphasizing their marginalized status. Goldin, a documentary photographer, had a real-life intimacy with her subjects, many of whom would have been considered depraved by the mainstream public.

The self-portrait in The Jewish Museum's collection was the first in a series of photographs from *The Ballad of Sexual Dependency* depicting Goldin's friends studying themselves in the mirror. The soundtrack for this segment of the slide show was a 1967 song by the alternative rock band Velvet Underground. It began: "I'll be your mirror/Reflect what you are, in case you don't know/I'll be the wind, the rain and the sunset/The light on your door to show that you're home." In Goldin's other mirror images, she focuses on her subjects being consumed with their likenesses. In this case, however, Goldin identifies with the camera itself, and her ethereal reflection stares back at it, and therefore at the viewer, rather than at her own face. Unlike some of her more explicit depictions of her subjects performing ablutions, Goldin's image hovering in the background resembles an early Christian icon: a metallic frame surrounds her face, and her illuminated skin glows against an azure wall.

In many of Goldin's works, she follows her friends into their showers and bathtubs. For her, purity and tenderness lie not in the cleansing that occurs in the bathroom but in her subjects' ability to make themselves vulnerable to her and her camera. In this self-portrait, the bathroom itself assumes center stage. The sanitizing objects—bottles of Dettol antiseptic, bathroom cleanser, and a loofah sponge propped at the side of the bathtub—exacerbate the harsh atmosphere created by the coarse walls that overwhelm the picture. The bathroom becomes a site of self-examination and physical manipulation, and it is within these intimate surroundings that Goldin reveals herself.

JG

REFERENCES

Goldin, *The Ballad of Sexual Dependency*; Goldin, *The Other Side*; Kozloff, *New York: Capital of Photography*; Sussman, *Nan Goldin: I'll Be Your Mirror*.

Andy Warhol

(American, 1928–1987)

Sarah Bernhardt, from Ten Portraits of Jews of the Twentieth Century, 1980

Portfolio of ten silk-screen prints
and colophon
Each 40 x 32 in. (101.6 x 81.3 cm)

Promised gift of Lorraine and
Martin Beitler, P.1. 2001.1-10

"I'm starting pop art," declared Andy Warhol in 1960, never dreaming, perhaps, how ineradicably he would be identified with the style. Popular imagery, much of it taken from advertisements, had been explored as early as 1956 in England by Richard Hamilton in a small collage entitled *Just What Is It That Makes Today's Homes So Different, So Appealing?* representing a trendy, middle-class living room inhabited by nearly nude figures cut from magazine ads. Advertising, both in the print media and on television, was ubiquitous, and reproducible art was central to the adman's campaign. It was Warhol's affinity for reproducibility that gave him a place in cultural history.

Educated at Carnegie Tech in the 1940s, Andrew Warhola, one of four children of Czechoslovakian immigrants who settled in a working-class neighborhood of Pittsburgh, was trained in the European Bauhaus tradition. He arrived in New York in 1949 at the age of twenty-one and was almost immediately employed as a commercial artist. Determined to be acknowledged as a painter, in the early sixties he began experimenting with an unusual technique of portraiture that combined photo silk-screening and painting. He purchased a black-and-white pub-

licity photograph of Marilyn Monroe, cropped it, enlarged it, outlined the shape of her head and shoulders on a large canvas, painted the eyelids, lips, and face in garish colors, and then applied the silk-screened photograph slightly off-register.

Marilyn Monroe (1962) was a historic success. In later portraits, Warhol added large cubes of color that were complementary to his sitters' faces and outlined certain features with sketchy brush strokes. A certain ambiguity remained, however: is the purpose commemoration or advertisement? Warhol claimed utter indifference, yet he perceived the numbing effect of our overexposure to car crashes, race riots, and electric-chair executions as well as the media's power to deify celebrities.

The *Ten Portraits of Jews of the Twentieth Century* was commissioned by dealer Ronald Feldman. Warhol recorded the series in his diary on August 29, 1979: "I haven't been told for sure yet who's in it. . . . think they were considering Bobby Dylan but I read that he turned born-again Christian." In the end, it included French actress Sarah Bernhardt; Gertrude Stein, Golda Meir, the Marx Brothers, Franz Kafka, George Gershwin, Sigmund Freud, Albert Einstein, Martin Buber, and Louis Brandeis. The artist used archival or existing photographs, instantly recognizable but "jazzed up": they are poster-size, big enough to be seen clearly across a gallery. Blocks of hot blue, turquoise, red, pink, orange, yellow, and green underlie their faces; brush strokes dart around eyebrows, lips, and hair.

When the portfolio and the related paintings were exhibited at The Jewish Museum in September 1980, the project was harshly criticized as "vulgar," "tawdry," and exploitative of its Jewish subjects. Yet there is something in the luminous eyes of Franz Kafka under intense blue slashed by lightning-rod yellow, in the handsome profile of George Gershwin squared by hunter green, in the zany movement of the Marx Brothers' triplicate heads, in Sarah Bernhardt's youthful gaze through luscious red and pink that leads one to believe that Warhol was not as uninvolved as he claimed—that he admired his "Ten Jewish Geniuses," as he called them.
VV

REFERENCES
Bockris, *The Life and Death of Andy Warhol*, p. 97; Bourdon, *Warhol*, pp. 124–25, 384–85; Hackett, *The Andy Warhol Diaries*, pp. 236–37, 279; Livingstone, *Pop Art*, pp. 34–38, 116–18.

Hannah Wilke

(American, 1940–1993)

Venus Pareve, 1982–84

Plaster of paris
Each 9⅞ x 5³⁄₁₆ x 3⁵⁄₁₆ in.
(25.1 x 13.2 x 8.4 cm)

Purchase: Lillian Gordon Bequest,
2000-20a-e

Hannah Wilke, a leading artist in the feminist art movement that began in the 1970s, worked to change the status and perception of the female body and to present a female point of view. Throughout her oeuvre, Wilke used her own naked body as the subject of her artwork. Through this process, she became one of the first female artists to question the societal construction of female sexuality, explore popular culture's attraction to that sexuality, and reveal the ways that this attraction is based on visual appearance and stereotypes of beauty.

Venus Pareve is a set of twenty-five sculptural self-portraits, hand-modeled by Wilke and then cast in plaster of paris or edible chocolate. Five of them are in the collection of The Jewish Museum. In *Venus Pareve*, Wilke creates an image of her body in order to comment on the ways that the female body gets viewed, consumed, adored, and scorned by society. The viewer gazes at multiple representations of Wilke's attractive and well-proportioned body from the thighs up. However, the artist confidently returns the gaze as she proudly displays her breasts and pubic area, thus complicating notions of objectification. Wilke's repetition of her own image twenty-five times confronts notions of female narcissism as well as emphasizes how beauty becomes standardized, stereotyped, and often exclusive. Culture's obsession with prescribed standards of female beauty is further underscored by the incorporation of the term "Venus" in the work's title, likening Wilke to the quintessential sexual object in Western art. On a number of occasions throughout her oeuvre—for example, in *Venus Envy* (1985), *Venus Basin* (1972), and *Venus Cushion* (1972)—Wilke uses the title term "Venus" as this metaphor to challenge the notion that there is an ideal beauty that women must attain. The use is perhaps most poignant in Wilke's last works, the *Intra-Venus* series (1992–93), in which she photographs her naked body ravaged from lymphoma, her body bloated and her head bald from chemotherapy.

In *Venus Pareve*, Wilke's metaphor does not end simply with the ways that the naked female body has been idealized and looked at as an object of pleasure. The use of edible chocolate as the material for some of the sculptures becomes an analogy to the female body and the feminine itself as well as a means to examine male power and female vulnerability. Chocolate evokes desire, obsession, eroticism, pleasure, and sensuality. It also evokes notions of guilty pleasures, forbidden fruits, and dieting to maintain a Venus-like status. Further, the contrast between the plaster and the chocolate sculptures accentuates chocolate's malleable and transitory nature (as it will melt and disintegrate over time), again challenging notions about the permanence and malleability of woman herself.

The term "pareve" in the title signifies that Wilke's self-portraits do not portray an ordinary Venus, but rather a Jewish Venus. In its most simple meaning, "pareve" modifies the type of chocolate that Wilke uses for her sculptures: it is considered neutral, neither meat nor milk. By casting a sculpture of herself in pareve chocolate, Wilke not only indicates that she is Jewish but also confronts a stereotypical notion of the dark-haired, seductive Jewess as well as another stereotype of the Jewish female: the narcissistic Jewish American Princess. Further, the use of "pareve" in the title calls into question the artificial differences that have been constructed between Jewish and non-Jewish women. J L

REFERENCES
Frueh, "Hannah Wilke"; Kreuzer, *Hannah Wilke*; Wilke, *Intra-Venus*.

Alice Neel

(American, 1900–1984)

Portrait of Meyer Schapiro, 1983

Oil on canvas
42 x 32⅛ in. (106.7 x 81.6 cm)

Purchase: S. H. and Helen R. Scheuer
Family Foundation Fund, 1995-111

Alice Neel's depiction of the art historian Meyer Schapiro stands at the end of a long line of psychologically penetrating portraits. Born four years before Schapiro, Neel adamantly pursued a career of figurative painting against the dominance of abstraction. By isolating her sitters in the comfortable setting of her studio and applying an expressive use of color, Neel sought to capture the individual characteristics of the public personalities that peopled her bohemia.

In 1983, Neel turned her unflinching eye to a man renowned for his penetrating gaze. Schapiro sits cross-legged with hands folded in his lap, his thin frame filling the armchair. To the pathos of his face Neel adds gray wisps of hair touched with falling light, which suggests a halo of luminescence. His expressive eyes are widened by the raising of his thick brows; the careful delineation of the wrinkles on his forehead proclaims the act of seeing as an act of will. His lips are parted; he is about to speak. The painting is a conversation between an eighty-three-year-old woman and a seventy-nine-year-old man, between two people who had been moved by but had outlived the political ideals of the thirties, between an artist and a critic who, whether looking at a person or a work of art, combined shrewd analysis of the historically conditioned with visionary understanding of the uniquely individual.

Meyer Schapiro was born in Lithuania in 1904 and at the age of three moved to the United States, where he and his family settled in the predominantly Jewish community of Brownsville, Brooklyn. As a professor of art history at Columbia University, Schapiro was mentor to a number of famous artists, historians, and critics. He was a prolific writer, and his boundless interest was variously captured by the ecstatic tensions of a Romanesque portal, Courbet's empathy for the French peasant, the psychological implications of Van Gogh's boots, and Cézanne's apples as sublimated desires. Yet Schapiro never proclaimed a single theory or methodology. His genius as a critic was to consider the contributions of Marx, Freud, and feminism—but never to be burdened by their molds—and to carry the understanding gained from looking at contemporary art when considering the ancient. His self-appointed task as art historian was to erode conventionally held notions about the limitations of particular periods in art. Schapiro revealed in the seemingly formulaic dogmatism of early Christian art the vivacious spirit of the individual craftsman. And in the supposed self-absorption and isolation of the expressive modern artist, he exposed engagement with the social world. While deeply involved with the political potential of art, at the core of Schapiro's review is the artist, a human being, with protests, visions, desires, and fears, whose limning of color and form is an act of freedom.

In his fifty years as adviser and trustee of The Jewish Museum, Meyer Schapiro added significant dimension to the museum's mission. At a time when Jews in America were asserting their influence on the art world, Schapiro encouraged the museum to present cutting-edge contemporary art. To expose the reciprocal relationship of old and new, to recognize in ancient ceremonial art the dynamic force of spiritual expressionism, and to read in the avant-garde new utterances of traditional values and ideas: this was the gauntlet that Schapiro threw down in the late 1940s. In its collections and programs, The Jewish Museum continues to embrace the challenge of Meyer Schapiro's dynamic dialectical approach.

SNB

REFERENCES
Allara, *Pictures of People*, pp. 72, 131–32; Epstein, "Meyer Schapiro: A Passion to Know and Make Known"; Kuspit, "Meyer Schapiro's Jewish Unconscious"; Miller and Cohen, "A Collision of Cultures: The Jewish Museum and the Jewish Theological Seminary"; Temkin, *Alice Neel*.

Robert Wilson

(American, born 1941)

The Golem, 1987

Papier-mâché made from Chinese and Japanese newspapers, glue, and metal frame support

79 x 29 x 21 in. (200.7 x 73.7 x 53.3 cm)

Purchase: Dr. Jack Allen and Shirley Kapland Fund, 1993-275a-f

The Golem is at once a sculpture, a costume, and a set design. This is not out of the ordinary for the objects that Robert Wilson uses in his theater productions. His intention is that they not be mere decorations but rather works of art in their own right. Most of Wilson's sculptural works to date are based on theater designs, props, and furniture. *The Golem* is a life-size papier-mâché sculpture made from Chinese and Japanese newspapers and was worn by an actor playing that character in Wilson's 1987 production entitled *Death, Destruction, and Detroit II* at the Schaubühne in Berlin. The golem appeared onstage, enclosed in the stiff hat and overcoat that was held together at the back with laces. Another character, possibly a rabbi, dressed in typical Eastern European Jewish garb, cut the lacings and removed the costume to reveal the actor-as-golem inside wearing the same (but this time real) hat and overcoat.

According to Jewish legend, the golem is an artificial being created by magic. Based on the idea that life can be fashioned from dead matter, the myth of the golem dates back to the kabbalah, the code of Jewish mysticism, which is as old as the Bible. The most well-known golem story is about the one created in the sixteenth century by Rabbi Loew, the famous Talmudic scholar from Prague. Rabbi Loew fashioned his artificial being out of clay and gave him life so that he would protect and save the Jews in Prague from those who wanted to destroy them. However, the golem became unruly, interpreting all commands too literally, so the rabbi was forced to destroy his beloved creation.

Wilson is known as a master in experimental theater, reinterpreting and deconstructing classic grand opera and dramatic literature, so that the viewer may consider these works in a new light. He has produced these plays in collaboration with many notable personalities, including Allen Ginsberg, Philip Glass, Lou Reed, and Susan Sontag. Wilson's trademark is rearranging and juxtaposing words and disparate objects to create new meanings and connections. *Death, Destruction, and Detroit II* is the middle work in a trilogy, the first of which was staged in 1979. The four-hour play was based on the writings—stories, letters, and diaries—of Franz Kafka, who, like Rabbi Loew, was from Prague. This "Kafkaesque" production did not follow a simple narrative, but was a series of text and images on nine separate stages. The presence of the golem character in the play evoked free associations about creation and civilization—the magical power to create a being from dust mirrors God's ability to create human life. The golem's first movements were guided by humans bearing sticks, evoking a robot, thereby raising larger questions about the choices that people make, the influences on those choices, and ultimately on free will.

J L

REFERENCES
Fairbrother, *Robert Wilson's Vision*; Shyer, *Robert Wilson and His Collaborators*; Stearns, *Robert Wilson*.

Ross Bleckner

(American, born 1949)

Double Portrait (Gay Flag), 1993

Oil on canvas
108⅛ x 72¼ in. (274.6 x 183.5 cm)

Purchase: Estate of Francis A. Jennings Fund in memory of his wife, Gertrude Feder Jennings, 2000-15

After the radical puritanism of Conceptualism and Minimalism reduced art to the bare bones of phenomenology in the 1960s, and neo-Expressionism recovered a gestural, figurative painting in the 1970s, a "post-abstract abstraction" took root in the following decade. As a part of this latter revival, loosely referred to as Neo-Geo, Ross Bleckner aligned himself with the late modernist tradition of demystification in painting.

Beginning in the 1980s, Bleckner began to appropriate various styles of painting, such as Op Art and the hard-edge abstraction of the 1950s and 1960s, and started to make vertical stripe paintings. While he simulated the distinctive character of serious abstract composition, Bleckner sought to reinvest such work with narrative elements. In *Double Portrait (Gay Flag)*, for example, he adopts both the form and scale of abstract modernist painting, but incorporates into its ostensibly subjectless imagery the rainbow colors of the "gay flag." Moreover, while alluding to the Pop Art precedent of Jasper Johns's flag series, Bleckner introduces another symbol within his symbolic striped pattern, a Star of David —in order to herald his cultural as well as sexual identity—which he paints in three-dimensional low relief, ambiguous but discernible at the top center of the work. Similar dualistic strategies inform numerous other works, such as *Count No Count*, where the artist invokes the veil of art historical reference in his use of patterns of polka dots to comment on late-1960s abstraction, only to reveal in title and abstract design the additional allusion to AIDS and the critical reference to T cells. Such painting functions as a pastiche of late modernism and contemporary life—as Bleckner inflects the act of appropriation with an autobiographical twist.

By engaging a stylistic form that had decades earlier, with Ad Reinhardt, for example, been emptied of a referential subject, Bleckner negotiates abstraction's exhausted state, realizing that such formalism could be personalized, made disjunctive, reconstructed. Thus Bleckner, along with painters such as Peter Halley and Philip Taaffe, and with the help of a booming art market, resuscitated a medium that had been declared dead by the art-critical establishment. With such painting, Bleckner straddles the fence of twentieth-century painting: invoking the vocabulary of abstraction while critiquing the claims of early modernism art to communicate subliminal and even mystical truths through nonrepresentational art. Bleckner has acknowledged this dialectical position: "The making of art is an act of deception. . . . It's a decoy act. My paintings flirt with belief, both undermining it and establishing it. Essentially, I'm degrading the sublime."

In identifying his subject as both painterly and one integrally tied to his identity as gay and Jewish, Bleckner defines himself as a painter who contravenes the pure imagery of late modernist abstraction and its rigid formalism and dismissal of metaphor. More important, by infusing abstraction with provocative and questioning references to issues of identity and history, the artist takes the ambiguity of perception in Op and Pop Art and grounds it in the real world.

M K

REFERENCES
Audiello, "Ross Bleckner"; Bleckner and Paparoni, "A Veil of Light"; Rosenberg, "The City Influence"; Wei, "Talking Abstract."

Elaine Reichek

(American, born 1945)

A Postcolonial Kinderhood,
1994

Mixed media
Dimensions variable

Purchase: Melva Bucksbaum, Mr. and
Mrs. Nathan Shaffran, Joan Kaplan
gifts; Fine Arts Acquisitions
Committee Fund; Agnes Gund and
Daniel Shapiro, Cheryl and Henry
Welt, Paula Krulak, Toby Devan Lewis,
and Henry Buhl gifts, 1997-195

As first-generation American Jews, Elaine Reichek's parents became middle-class Americans, a cultural transformation that took form in the details of their 1950s Brooklyn house. In her multimedia installation work *A Postcolonial Kinderhood*, Reichek explores the pressure to embrace the image of the American as promoted in popular culture and the reality of her family's cultural difference.

Reichek approaches her art anthropologically, examining colonialism and Western representations of the "other." In 1993, she adapted her methodology to her own history: the Jewish experience in postwar America. Re-creating her childhood bedroom, Reichek displays her parents' acquisition of the American dream through colonial-style furnishings. The artist created a room that illustrates the struggle between these two worlds, using a combination of handmade and store-bought furnishings, including a canopy bed, washstand, wrought-iron lamp, fire screen, braided rugs, and family photographs. As Reichek says, "The re-creation of my childhood bedroom explores the idea of decor as a means of Americanizing, of 'passing,' and of connecting people to a past they wished was their own."

In addition to the colonial-style trappings of Americana, Reichek embroidered quotations about the dilemma of growing up Jewish in postwar America onto tiny samplers that she sewed herself. A quotation from the artist's daughter reads: "The parents of Jewish boys always love me. I'm the closest thing to a shiksa without being one." The apparent innocence of the benign sampler is undermined by the embarrassing statements that appear on them. For example, her linen towels carry the monogram "J.E.W." The civilized, "WASPY" tradition of mono-

gramming, in conjunction with such loaded terminology, confronts the viewer with an intense irony, allowing Reichek to reveal the inherent racism within a supposedly civilized culture as well as the unease that Jews themselves have with the label "Jew." By investing samplers, which possess a traditional and particular iconography, with her own phrases and images appropriated from friends, relatives, and American maxims, Reichek subverts the original intention of the samplers, disrupting the content, and disclosing how histories are as much about what they exclude as what they include.

In late-eighteenth- and early-nineteenth-century America, the making of samplers was a device through which young, mainly Christian, girls learned the alphabet, practiced their handiwork, and stitched conventional images as well as told stories embedded with traditional feminine values. Carrying a particular narrative, samplers and tapestries, long considered functional and decorative, successfully capture Reichek's idea of acculturation, "women's work," and cultural ideology. Inscribing new voices onto the samplers, Reichek re-creates history and retells their stories.

The labor-intensive and lengthy method of hand-knitting everything herself relates to the historical and temporal aspect of Reichek's subject and addresses the relegation of embroidery to the realm of "craft" rather than "art." Focusing on the domestic, Reichek's work emphasizes a female perspective; the samplers evoking a woman, at home, practicing her stitches. Through embroidery, Reichek exposes how messages, pervasively hidden in images, are reiterated and passed through culture and media, within a coded system. The immediate comfort of her work—the knitting, furniture, tactile wools—tricks us into complacency. We feel we're seeing what we expect to see. Yet after a few moments, one begins to see the subtext—the claustrophobic, anxious nature of the room, and the disturbing, embarrassing words and phrases. Reichek employs her own culture—the dominant culture—to confront hidden oppressions within its systems. Jewish Americans are at once the dominant culture and the "other."

LF

REFERENCES
Grey Art Gallery, *Elaine Reichek*; Handler, *Elaine Reichek*; The Jewish Museum, *A Postcolonial Kinderhood*; Kleeblatt, *Too Jewish*.

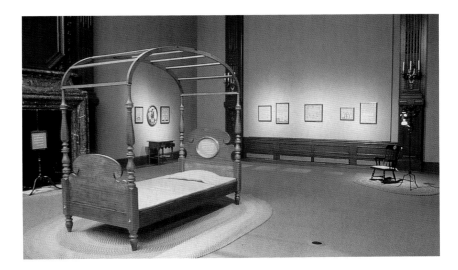

During the Time of Life allotted me,
Grant me, good God, my Wealth and Liberty;
I beg no more; if more thou'rt pleas'd to give,
I'll thankfully the Overplus receive.
My Art hath taught, my Fingers skill,
To quote all this, without a quill
Without a Pen, these words I wrought;
And finished with an Artist's thought.
When I am dead, and in my Grave,
My Friend's in Hand, my work may have.

Elaine Reichek
1993

I NEVER THINK ABOUT BEING
JEWISH
UNTIL I LEAVE NEW YORK.
.... PAUL TANNENBAUM

Bibliography

Full references follow for works cited in entries.

Abrahams, Edward. *The Lyrical Left: Randolph Bourne, Alfred Stieglitz and the Origins of Cultural Radicalism in America*. Charlottesville: University Press of Virginia, 1986.

Abramsky, Chimen. "El Lissitzky as Jewish Illustrator and Typographer." *Studio International* 172, no. 882 (October 1966): 182–85.

Ackerman, A., and S. Braunstein. *Israel in Antiquity*. Exh. cat. New York: The Jewish Museum, 1982.

Adams, Henry, Margaret C. Conrads, and Annegret Hoberg, eds. *Albert Bloch: The American Blue Rider*. Munich: Prestel, 1997.

Albers, Anni. *Anni Albers: Selected Writings on Design*. Middletown, Conn.: Wesleyan University Press, 2000.

———. *The Woven and Graphic Art of Anni Albers*. Washington, D.C.: Smithsonian Institution Press, 1985.

Allara, Pamela. *Pictures of People: Alice Neel's American Portrait Gallery*. Hanover, N.H.: University Press of New England, 1998.

Alloway, Lawrence, and Mary Davis MacNaughton. *Adolph Gottlieb: A Retrospective*. New York: The Art Publisher, in association with the Adolph and Esther Gottlieb Foundation, 1981.

Altshuler, David, ed. *The Precious Legacy: Judaic Treasures from the Czechoslovak State Collections*. New York: Summit, 1983.

Amishai-Maisels, Ziva. *Depiction and Interpretation: The Influence of the Holocaust on the Visual Arts*. New York: Pergamon, 1993.

Antin, Eleanor, and Henry Sayre. *Ghosts*. Winston-Salem, N.C.: Southeastern Center for Contemporary Art, 1996.

Apter, Lauren, and Amanda Barnett, eds. *Mezuzah: The 2002 Philip and Sylvia Spertus Judaica Prize*. Exh. cat. Chicago: Spertus Museum; Spertus Institute of Jewish Studies, 2002.

Apter-Gabriel, Ruth, ed. "El Lissitzky's Jewish Works." In *Tradition and Revolution: The Jewish Renaissance in Russian Avant-Garde Art, 1912–1928*. Exh. cat. Jerusalem: Israel Museum, 1987.

Attie, Shimon. *Sites Unseen—Shimon Attie: European Projects: Installations and Photographs*. Burlington, Vt.: Verve, 1998.

Audiello, Massimo. "Ross Bleckner: The Joyful and Gloomy Sides of Being Alive." *Flash Art* 183 (summer 1995): 112–15.

Baal-Teshuva, Jacob, ed. *Chagall: A Retrospective*. Southport, Conn.: Hugh Lauter Levin, 1995.

Bacon, Lenice Ingram. *American Patchwork Quilts*. New York: William Morrow, 1973.

Baigell, Matthew. "Max Weber's Jewish Paintings." *American Jewish History* 88 (Sept. 2000): 341–60.

———. "Segal's Holocaust Memorial." *Art in America* 71, no. 6 (summer 1983): 134–36.

Baizerman, Suzanne. "Interview with Kay Sekimachi." In *Nanette L. Laitman Documentation Project for Craft and Decorative Arts in America*. Smithsonian Archives, July 26, 30, and August 3, 6, 2001.

Bar-Am, Micha. *Weegee the Famous*. Exh. cat. Tel Aviv: Tel Aviv Museum of Art, 1990.

Barnett, Richard D. *Ancient Ivories in the Middle East and Adjacent Countries. Qedem* 14 (Jerusalem: Institute of Archaeology, Hebrew University, 1982).

Barney, Tina. *Friends and Relations: Photographs by Tina Barney*. Washington, D.C.: Smithsonian Institution Press, 1991.

Barney, Tina, and Andy Grundberg. *Tina Barney: Photographs, Theater of Manners*. Zurich: Scalo, 1997.

Baron, Frank, Helmut Arntzen, and David Cateforis, eds. *Albert Bloch: Artistic and Literary Perspectives*. Lawrence, Kan.: Max Kade Center for German-American Studies, University of Kansas; Munich: Prestel, 1997.

Barratt, Carrie Rebora. *Queen Victoria and Thomas Sully*. Exh. cat. New York: Metropolitan Museum of Art; Princeton, N.J.: Princeton University Press, 2000.

Barrett, Nancy C. *Ilse Bing: Three Decades of Photography*. Exh. cat. New Orleans Museum of Art, 1985.

Barron, Stephanie. *German Expressionism 1915–1925: The Second Generation*. Los Angeles: Los Angeles County Museum of Art, 1988.

Barth, Miles, ed. *Weegee's World*. Exh cat. New York: International Center of Photography; Boston: Little, Brown, 1997.

Barzel, Amnon. *Art in Israel*. Milan: Giancarlo Politi Editore, 1988.

David Winton Bell Gallery. *Weegee: The Photography of Arthur Fellig (1899–1968)*. Exh. cat. Providence, R.I.: Brown University, 1995.

Bendheim, Fred. "Demon Binding Charms: Michael Berkowitz." *The Lancet* 355 (March 18, 2000).

Benezra, Neal, Staci Boris, and Dan Cameron, eds. *William Kentridge*. Exh. cat. Chicago: Museum of Contemporary Art; New York: New Museum of Contemporary Art and Harry N. Abrams, 2001.

Benison, Saul, and Sandra Otter. *Interviews with Ben Shahn.* Columbia University Oral History Research Office. New York, October 29, 1956, and January 5, 1957.

Berger, Maurice, and Andy Grundberg. *James Casebere: Model Culture, Photographs 1975–1996.* San Francisco: Friends of Photography, 1996.

Berman, Russell A. *Cultural Studies of Modern Germany: History, Representation, and Nation-hood.* Madison: University of Wisconsin Press, 1993.

Bier, Carol, ed. *Woven from the Soul, Spun from the Heart: Textile Arts of the Safavid and Qajar Iran 16th–19th Centuries.* Washington, D.C.: Textile Museum, 1987.

Bilski, Emily D. *War Resistance and Politics: Düsseldorf Artists 1910–1945.* New York: The Jewish Museum, 1990.

Bird, Jon, Jo Anna Isaak, and Sylvére Lotringer. *Nancy Spero.* London: Phaidon, 1996.

Bitterli, Konrad, and Matthias Wohlgemuth, eds. *Matthew McCaslin: Works, Sites.* Ostfildern bei Stuttgart: Cantz, 1997.

Bleckner, Ross, and Demetrio Paparon. "A Veil of Light: Ross Bleckner." *Tema Celeste* 21 (July–September 1989): 52–54.

Bockris, Victor. *The Life and Death of Andy Warhol.* New York: Bantam, 1989.

Bourdon, David. *Warhol.* New York: Harry N. Abrams, 1989.

Braunstein, Susan L. *Le-Ḥayyim—To Life! Cups of Sanctification and Celebration.* Exh. brochure. New York: The Jewish Museum, 1984.

———. *Personal Vision: The Jacobo and Asea Furman Collection of Jewish Ceremonial Art.* New York: The Jewish Museum, 1985.

Brilliant, Richard. *Facing the New World: Jewish Portraits in Colonial and Federal America.* Exh. cat. New York: The Jewish Museum, 1997.

Broner, E. M. *The Telling.* San Francisco: Harper San Francisco, 1993. Includes *The Women's Haggadah,* by E. M. Broner and Naomi Nimrod, 1992.

Broude, Norma, and Mary D. Gerrard, eds. *The Power of Feminist Art: The American Movement of the 1970s, History and Impact.* New York: Harry N. Abrams, 1994.

Brown, Dona. *Inventing New England: Regional Tourism in the Nineteenth Century.* Washington, D.C.: Smithsonian Institution Press, 1995.

Brown, Susan. *American Studio Ceramics, 1920–1950.* Exh. cat. Minneapolis: University Art Museum, University of Minnesota, 1988.

Cameron, Dan, Carolyn Christov-Bakargiev, and J. M. Coetzee. *William Kentridge.* London: Phaidon, 1999.

Carboni, Massimo. "Fabio Mauri." *Artforum* 29, no. 8 (April 1991): 135–36.

Cavigga, Margaret Maddox. *American Antique Quilts.* Tokyo: Sufunotomo, 1981.

Chagall, Marc. *My Life.* New York: Da Capo, 1994.

Chevlowe, Susan. *Common Man, Mythic Vision: The Paintings of Ben Shahn.* New York: The Jewish Museum; Princeton, N.J.: Princeton University Press, 1998.

———, ed. *Paris in New York: French Jewish Artists in Private Collections.* Exh. cat. New York: The Jewish Museum, 2000.

Chevlowe, Susan, and Norman Kleeblatt, eds. *Painting a Place in America: Jewish Artists in New York, 1900–1945: A Tribute to the Educational Alliance Art School.* New York: The Jewish Museum, 1991.

Christie, Manson, and Woods International. *Fine Judaica, English and Continental Silver, Russian Works of Art, Watches and Objects of Vertu.* Sales cat. New York, October 25–26, 1982.

Christov-Bakargiev, Carolyn. *William Kentridge.* Exh. cat. Brussels: Société des Expositions du Palais des Beaux-Arts de Bruxelles, 1998.

Clark, Garth, and the Everson Museum of Art. *A Century of Ceramics in the United States, 1878–1978.* New York: E. P. Dutton, 1979.

Codognato, Mario. "Fabio Mauri." *Artforum* 34, no. 4 (December 1995): 97.

Coffey, John W., II. *Moshe Kupferman: Between Oblivion and Remembrance, Paintings and Works on Paper 1972–1991.* Raleigh: North Carolina Museum of Art, 1991.

Cohen, Elisheva, ed. *Moritz Oppenheim: The First Jewish Painter.* Exh. cat. Jerusalem: Israel Museum, 1983.

Cohen, Richard I. *Jewish Icons: Art and Society in Modern Europe.* Berkeley: University of California Press, 1998.

Compton, Susan P. *Marc Chagall: My Life, My Dream: Berlin and Paris, 1922–1940.* Munich and New York: Prestel, 1990.

Conner, Susan M. *Remember When . . . Personal Recollections and Vignettes of the Sioux City Jewish Community 1869–1984: Based on Oscar Littlefield's History.* Sioux City, Ia.: Jewish Federation, 1985.

Conroy, Sarah Booth. "Earth, Fire and Love: The Natzler Touch." *Los Angeles Times,* September 20, 1981.Cork, Richard. *David Bomberg.* New Haven, Conn.: Yale University Press, 1987.

Curtin, Michael. *Redeeming the Wasteland: Television Documentary and Cold War Politics.* New Brunswick, N.J.: Rutgers University Press, 1995.

Debbaut, Jan, Mariëlle Soons, and Caroline de Bie, eds. *El Lissitzky, 1890–1941: Architect, Painter, Photographer, Typographer.* Exh. cat. Eindhoven, Netherlands: Municipal Van Abbemuseum, 1990.

De Duve, Thierry. "The Readymade and the Tube of Paint." *Artforum* 24, no. 9 (May 1986): 110–21.

Dennis, Jessie McNab. *English Silver.* New York: Walker, 1970.

Dervaux, Isabelle. *Color and Ecstasy: The Art of Hyman Bloom.* New York: National Academy of Design, 2002.

Sid Deutsch Gallery. *Albert Bloch (1882–1961): Paintings.* New York, 1988.

Diba, Layla S., ed. *Iranian Wedding Contracts of the Nineteenth and Twentieth Centuries.* Exh. cat. Teheran: Negarestan Museum, 1976.

Dickson, Harold E. *John Wesley Jarvis: American Painter 1780–1840.* New York: New York Historical Society, 1949.

Dubow, Neville. *Imagining the Unimaginable: Holocaust Memory in Art and Architecture.* Cape Town: University of Cape Town, 2001.

Enwezor, Okwui. "Truth and Responsibility: A Conversation with William Kentridge." *Parkett* 54 (1998/99): 165–70.

Epstein, Helen. "Meyer Schapiro: A Passion to Know and Make Known." *Art News* (May 1983): 61–85; (summer 1983): 84–95.

Fabian, Monroe H. *Mr. Sully, Portrait Painter: The Works of Thomas Sully (1783–1872).* Exh. cat. Washington, D.C.: Smithsonian Institution Press for the National Portrait Gallery, 1983.

Fairbrother, Trevor, ed. *Robert Wilson's Vision.* New York: Harry N. Abrams; Museum of Fine Arts, Boston, 1991.

Fineberg, Jonathan. "Lipchitz in America." In *Lipchitz and the Avant-Garde: From Paris to New York*. Ed. Josef Helfenstein and Jordana Mendelson. Exh. cat. Krannert Art Museum and Kinkead Pavilion. University of Illinois at Urbana-Champaign. Seattle: University of Washington Press, 2001.

Fort, Ilene Susan. *The Figure in American Sculpture: A Question of Modernity*. Los Angeles County Museum of Art; Seattle: University of Washington Press, 1995.

Fox, Howard N., ed. *Eleanor Antin*. Los Angeles County Museum of Art, 1999.

Freudenheim, T. L. "A Persian Faience Mosaic Wall in the Jewish Museum, New York." *Kunst des Orient* 5 (1968): 39–67

Freudenheim, T., and G. Schoenberger. *The Silver and Judaica Collection of Mr. and Mrs. Michael M. Zagayski*. Exh. cat. New York: The Jewish Museum, 1963.

Frueh, Joanna. "Hannah Wilke." In *Hannah Wilke: A Retrospective*. Ed. Thomas H. Kochheiser. Columbia: University of Missouri Press, 1989. Pp. 41–49.

Furman, Jacobo. *Treasures of Jewish Art*. Southport, Conn.: Hugh Lauter Levin, 1997.

Galassi, Peter. *Pleasures and Terrors of Domestic Comfort*. New York: Museum of Modern Art, 1991. Distributed by Harry N. Abrams, New York.

Garrels, Gary, ed. *Sol LeWitt: A Retrospective*. Exh. cat. San Francisco Museum of Modern Art; New Haven: Yale University Press, 2000.

Geschichte der jüdischen Gemeinde Kassel: Unter Berücksichtigung der Hessen-Kasseler Gesamtjudenheit (1931).

Gidal, Tim. *Jerusalem in 3000 Years*. Cologne: Könemann, 1999.

———. *My Way*. Jerusalem: Museon Yisrael, 1995.

Gilbert, Barbara. "Earth and Spirit: Otto Natzler at 80." Hebrew Union College, Skirball Museum, Los Angeles, September 17–December 31, 1987.

Glicksman, Hal. *Wallace Berman Retrospective*. Los Angeles: Fellows of Contemporary Art / Otis Art Institute, 1978.

Goldin, Nan. *The Ballad of Sexual Dependency*. Ed. Marvin Heiferman, Mark Holborn, and Suzanne Fletcher. New York: Aperture, 1986.

———. *The Other Side*. Ed. David Armstrong and Walter Keller. Exh. cat. New York and Berlin: Scalo; Berlin: D.A.A.D. Artist-in-Residence Programme, 1993.

Goodman, Susan Tumarkin, ed. *The Emergence of Jewish Artists in Nineteenth-Century Europe*. Exh. cat. New York: The Jewish Museum, 2001.

———, ed. *From the Inside Out: Eight Contemporary Artists*. New York: The Jewish Museum, 1993.

———, ed. *Marc Chagall: Early Works from Russian Collections*. Surrey, England: Third Millennium, 2001.

———, ed. *Russian Jewish Artists in a Century of Change 1890–1990*. Exh. cat. New York: Jewish Museum, 1995.

Gordon, Mel. *Voluptuous Panic: The Erotic World of Weimar Berlin*. Venice, Calif.: Veral House, 2000.

Gostelow, Mary. *Art of Embroidery: Great Needlework Collections of Britain and the United States*. New York: E. P. Dutton, 1979.

Grafman, Rafi, and Vivian B. Mann. *Crowning Glory: Silver Torah Ornaments of the Jewish Museum, New York*. Boston: David R. Godine, 1996.

Greenberg, Clement. "Review of Exhibitions of American Abstract Artists, Jacques Lipchitz, and Jackson Pollock." In *The Collected Essays and Criticism, Volume 2: Arrogant Purpose, 1945–1949*. Ed. John O'Brian. Chicago: University of Chicago Press, 1986. Pp. 72–75.

Greenfield, Howard. *Ben Shahn: An Artist's Life*. New York: Random House, 1998.

Greenough, Sarah, ed. *Modern Art and America: Alfred Stieglitz and His New York Galleries*. Washington, D.C.: National Gallery of Art and Bulfinch Press, 2001.

Greenough, Sarah, and Juan Hamilton. *Alfred Stieglitz: Photography and Writings*. Exh. cat. Washington, D.C.: National Gallery of Art, 1983.

Grey Art Gallery and Study Center. *Elaine Reichek: Native Intelligence*. Exh. cat. New York: New York University, 1992.

Grimwade, A. G. "Anglo-Jewish Silver." *The Jewish Historical Society of England Transactions* 18 (1953–55): 113–25.

Grossman, Cissy. "Restructuring and Rediscovering a Woman's Oeuvre: Chana Orloff, Sculptor in the School of Paris, 1910 to 1920." Ph.D. diss., City University of New York, 1998.

Guggenheim Museum. *Marc Chagall and the Jewish Theater*. New York, 1992.

Guggenheim, Siegfried. *Rudolf Koch: His Work and the Offenbach Workshop*. Woodstock, Vt.: William Edwin Rudge, 1947.

Gumpert, Lynn. *Christian Boltanski*. Paris: Flammarion, 1994.

Gumpert, Lynn, and Mary Jane Jacob. *Christian Boltanski: Lessons of Darkness*. Exh. cat. Chicago: Museum of Contemporary Art, 1988.

Haam, Achad. "Ueber die Kultur." *Ost und West* 10 (1902): 655–62.

Hackett, Pat, ed. *The Andy Warhol Diaries*. New York: Warner, 1989.

Haertig, Evelyn. *Antique Combs and Purses*. Carmel, Calif.: Gallery Graphics, 1993.

Hambourg, Maria Morris, Mia Fineman, and Richard Avedon. *Richard Avedon: Portraits*. Exh. cat. New York: Metropolitan Museum of Art, 2002.

Handler, Beth. *Elaine Reichek: Projects*. Exh. cat. New York: Museum of Modern Art, 1999.

Harnsberger, R. Scott. *Ten Precisionist Artists: Annotated Bibliographies*. Westport, Conn.: Greenwood, 1992.

Harrison, Helen A. *Larry Rivers*. New York: Artnews Books, 1984.

Harshav, Benjamin. *Moshe Kupferman: The Rift in Time*. Tel Aviv: Givon galeryah le-omanut, 2000.

Haskell, Barbara. *Elie Nadelman: Sculptor of Modern Life*. Exh. cat. New York: Whitney Museum of American Art and Harry N. Abrams, 2003.

Hausner, Gideon. *Justice in Jerusalem*. New York: Harper and Row, 1966.

Heuberger, Georg, and Anton Merk, eds. *Moritz Daniel Oppenheim: Die Entdeckung des jüdischen Selbstbewußtseins in der Kunst / Jewish Identity in Nineteenth-Century Art*. Exh. cat. Frankfurt: Jüdisches Museum der Stadt Frankfurt am Main, 1999. In German and English.

Hilton, Allison. *Russian Folk Art*. Bloomington: Indiana University Press, 1995.

Hirsch, Sanford. *Adolph Gottlieb: A Survey Exhibition: IVAM Centre Julio González*. Exh. cat. Valencia, Spain: Generalitat Valenciana Conselleria de Cultura, Educació Ciéncia, 2001.

———. *The Pictographs of Adolph Gottlieb*. Exh. cat. New York: Adolph and Esther Gottlieb Foundation, 1994.

Hoberman, J., and Jeffrey Shandler. *Entertaining America: Jews, Movies, and Broadcasting.* Exh. cat. New York: The Jewish Museum; Princeton, N.J.: Princeton University Press, 2003.

Homer, William Innes. *Alfred Stieglitz and the American Avant-Garde.* Boston: Secker and Warburg, 1977.

Edwynn Houk Gallery. *Ilse Bing, Vision of a Century.* New York, 1998.

Hunter, Sam. *Rivers.* New York: Harry N. Abrams, 1972.

Hunter, Sam, and Don Hawthorne. *George Segal.* New York: Rizzoli, 1984.

The Israel Museum. *In a Single Statement: Works by Zelig Segal.* Exh. cat. Jerusalem, 1992.

———. *Towers of Spice: The Tower-Shape Tradition in Havdalah Spice Boxes.* Exh. cat. Jerusalem, 1982.

Jaffe, Irma B. *The Sculpture of Leonard Baskin.* New York: Viking, 1980.

The Jewish Museum. *Annual Report 1982–83.* New York, 1984.

———. *Artists of Israel: 1920–1980.* Exh. cat. Detroit: Wayne State University for the Jewish Museum, New York, 1981.

———. *Ceramics: An Exhibit, Gertrud and Otto Natzler.* Exh. cat. New York: The Jewish Museum, 1958.

———. *Fabric of Jewish Life: Textiles from the Jewish Museum Collection.* Exh. cat. New York: The Jewish Museum, 1977.

———. *Ludwig Yehuda Wolpert: A Retrospective.* Exh. cat. New York: The Jewish Museum, 1976.

———. *Perpetual Well: Contemporary Art from the Collection of the Jewish Museum.* Exh. cat. New York: The Jewish Museum, 1999.

———. *A Postcolonial Kinderhood: An Installation by Elaine Reichek.* Exh. cat. New York, 1994.

Jewish Museum, San Francisco. *Making Change: 100 Artists Interpret the Tzedakah Box.* Exh. cat. San Francisco, 1999.

Kalina, Richard. "William Anastasi: Deadpan Conceptualist." *Art in America* 78, no. 1 (January 1990): 144–49.

Kampf, Avram. *Contemporary Synagogue Art: Developments in the United States, 1945–1965.* New York: Union of American Hebrew Congregations, 1966.

Kanof, Abram. *Jewish Ceremonial Art and Religious Observance.* New York: Harry N. Abrams, 1970.

Kao, Deborah Martin, Laura Katzman, and Jenna Webster. *Ben Shahn's New York: The Photography of Modern Times.* Cambridge, Mass.: Fogg Art Museum, Harvard University Art Museums; New Haven, Conn.: Yale University Press, 2000.

Kardon, Janet. *Gertrud and Otto Natzler: Collaboration/ Solitude.* Exh. cat. New York: American Craft Museum, 1993.

Katalog der alten jüdischen Kultusgegenstände Gieldzinski-Stiftung in der neuen Synagoge zu Danzig. Danzig, 1904.

Kayser, Stephen S. "A Polish Torah Crown," *Hebrew Union College Annual* 18 (1950–51): 493–501.

Kayser, Stephen S., and Guido Schoenberger. *Jewish Ceremonial Art: A Guide to the Appreciation of Art Objects Used in Synagogue and Home.* Philadelphia: Jewish Publication Society, 1955.

Kennedy Galleries. *Leonard Baskin, Recent Work.* Exh. cat. New York, 1989.

Kirstein, Lincoln. *Elie Nadelman.* New York: Eakins, 1973.

Kitaj, R. B. *First Diasporist Manifesto.* London: Thames and Hudson, 1989.

Kleeblatt, Norman L. "The Black Banner." In *Bilder sind nicht verboten.* Ed. Jürgen Harten. Exh. cat. Düsseldorf: Städtische Kunsthalle, 1982.

———. "Persistence of Memory." *Art in America* 88, no. 6 (June 2000): 96–103.

———. *Too Jewish?: Challenging Traditional Identities.* Exh. cat. New York: The Jewish Museum; New Brunswick, N.J.: Rutgers University Press, 1996.

Kleeblatt, Norman L., and Susan Chevlowe. *Painting a Place in America: Jewish Artists in New York, 1900–1945.* New York: The Jewish Museum; Bloomington: Indiana University Press, 1991.

Kleeblatt, Norman L., and Vivian B. Mann. *Treasures of the Jewish Museum.* Exh. cat. New York: The Jewish Museum and Universe Books, 1986.

Kleeblatt, Norman L., and Gerard C. Wertkin. *The Jewish Heritage in American Folk Art.* Exh. cat. New York: The Jewish Museum; Museum of American Folk Art; Universe Books, 1984.

Köhler, Michael, ed. *Constructed Realities: The Art of Staged Photography.* Zurich: Edition Stemmle, 1995.

Kotik, Charlotta. *With Paper, About Paper.* Exh. cat. Buffalo: Albright-Knox Art Gallery, 1980.

Kozloff, Max. *New York: Capital of Photography.* New Haven, Conn.: Yale University Press; New York: The Jewish Museum, 2002.

Kreuzer, Stephanie, ed. *Hannah Wilke: 1940–1993.* Berlin: Neue Gesellschaft für Bildende Kunst, 2000.

Kuspit, Donald. "Meyer Schapiro's Jewish Unconscious." *Prospects* 5, no. 21 (1996): 491–508.

Landsberger, F. "Old Time Torah Curtains." *Hebrew Union College Annual* 19 (1945–46): 353–89.

Lauren, Stacey. "Inner Life." *Metroland* 22, no. 3 (January 21, 1999).

Levin, Elaine. *The History of American Ceramics.* New York: Harry N. Abrams, 1988.

LeWitt, Sol. "Paragraphs on Conceptual Art." *Artforum* 5, no. 10 (June 1967): 79–83.

Lipchitz, Jacques, with H. H. Arnason. *My Life in Sculpture.* New York: Viking, 1972.

Lipschutz-Villa, Eduardo, ed. *Wallace Berman: Support the Revolution* (Amsterdam: Institute of Contemporary Art, 1992).

Lipstadt, Deborah. "Feminism and American Judaism: Looking Back at the Turn of the Century." In *Women and American Judaism: Historical Perspectives.* Ed. Pamela S. Nadell and Jonathan D. Sarna. Hanover, N.H.: University Press of New England, 2001. Pp. 291–308.

Livingston, Jane. *The New York School: Photographs, 1936–1963.* New York: Stewart, Tabori and Chang, 1992.

Livingston, Jane, and Adam Gopnik. *Richard Avedon: Evidence 1944–1994.* Exh. cat. New York: Whitney Museum, 1994.

Livingstone, Marco. *George Segal Retrospective: Sculptures, Paintings, Drawings.* Montreal Museum of Fine Arts, 1997.

———. *Pop Art: A Continuing History.* London: Thames and Hudson, 1990.

London, Hannah R. *Portraits of Jews by Gilbert Stuart and Other Early American Artists.* 1927. Reprint, Rutland, Vt.: Charles E. Tuttle, 1969.

Los Angeles County Museum of Art. *Today: Contemporary Ceramists and Their Work.* Los Angeles, 1990.

MacDonald, J. Fred. *Television and the Red Menace: The Video Road to Vietnam.* New York: Praeger, 1985.

Makover, S. J. *The Jewish Patrons of Venice.* Exh. brochure. New York: The Jewish Museum,. 1985.

Mann, Vivian B. "A Carved Mohel's Box of the Eighteenth Century and Its Antecedents." *Proceedings of the Eighth World Congress of Jewish Studies.* Jerusalem, 1982.

———, ed. *Gardens and Ghettos: The Art of Jewish Life in Italy.* Berkeley: University of California Press, 1989.

———. "The Golden Age of Jewish Ceremonial Art in Frankfurt: Metalwork of the Eighteenth Century." *Leo Baeck Institute Year Book* 31 (1986).

———. "Gospels Covers, the *Tik* and the Koran Box." In *Art and Ceremony.* London: Pindar, forthcoming.

———. *Jewish Texts on the Visual Arts.* Cambridge: Cambridge University Press, 2000.

———, ed. *Morocco: Jews and Art in a Muslim Land.* London: Merrell, 2000.

———. " 'New' Examples of Jewish Ceremonial Art from Medieval Ashkenaz." *Artibus et Historiae* 17 (1988): 13–24.

———. "The Recovery of a Known Work." *Journal of Jewish Art* 12–13 (1986/87): 269–78.

———. "A Sixteenth-Century Box in the New York Jewish Museum and Its Transformation." *Journal of Jewish Art* 9 (1983): 54–60.

———. *A Tale of Two Cities: Jewish Life in Frankfurt and Istanbul 1750–1870.* Exh. cat. New York: The Jewish Museum, 1982.

Mann, Vivian B., with Emily D. Bilski. *The Jewish Museum, New York.* London: Scala; New York: The Jewish Museum, 1993.

Mann, Vivian B., and J. Gutmann. *Danzig 1939: Treasures of a Destroyed Community.* New York: The Jewish Museum, 1980.

Marcilhac, Felix. *Chana Orloff.* Paris: Éditions de l'Amateur, 1991.

Marmer, Nancy. "Boltanski: The Uses of Contradiction." *Art in America* 77, no. 10 (October 1989): 169–81, 233–35.

Marshall, Nancy Rose, and Malcolm Warner. *James Tissot: Victorian Life, Modern Love.* New Haven: Yale University Press, 1999.

McEvilley, Thomas. *William Anastasi: A Selection of Works from 1960 to 1989.* New York: Scott Hanson Gallery, 1989.

Merhav, Rivka, et al. *A Glimpse into the Past: The Joseph Ternbach Collection.* Jerusalem: Israel Museum, 1981.

Meyer, Franz. *Marc Chagall.* New York: Harry N. Abrams, 1964.

Miller, Julie, and Richard Cohen. "A Collision of Cultures: The Jewish Museum and the Jewish Theological Seminary, 1904–1971." In *Tradition Renewed: A History of the Jewish Theological Seminary of America.* Ed. Jack Wertheimer. Vol. 2. New York: Jewish Theological Seminary, 1997. Pp. 311–61.

Miller-Keller, Andrea. *Sol LeWitt: Twenty-Five Years of Wall Drawings, 1968–1993.* Exh. cat. Andover, Mass.: Addison Gallery of American Art; Seattle: University of Washington Press, 1993.

Montclair Museum of Art. *Precisionism in America 1915–1941: Reordering Reality.* Exh. cat. New York: Harry N. Abrams, 1994.

Morphet, Richard. *R. B. Kitaj: A Retrospective.* London: Tate Gallery, 1994.

Nathan, Harriet, and Signe Mayfield. "Kay Sekimachi, the Weaver's Weaver: Explorations in Multiple Layers and Three-Dimensional Fiber Art." Regional Oral History Office, University of California, Berkeley, 1996.

Natter, G. Tobias, ed. *Rabbiner-Bocher-Talmudschüler: Bilder des Wiener Malers Isidor Kaufmann, 1853–1921.* Exh. cat. Vienna: Jüdisches Museum der Stadt Wien, 1995. In German and English.

North, Percy. *Max Weber: American Modern.* Exh. cat. New York: The Jewish Museum, 1982.

North, Percy, and Susan Krane. *Max Weber: The Cubist Decade, 1910–1920.* Atlanta: High Museum of Art, 1991.

Notizblatt der Gesellschaft zur Erforschung jüdischer Kunstdenkmäler 23 (1939).

O'Doherty, Brian. *Inside the White Cube: The Ideology of the Gallery Space.* Santa Monica, Calif.: Lapis, 1986.

Ofrat, Gideon. *One Hundred Years of Art in Israel.* Boulder, Colo.: Westview, 1998.

Oklahoma Museum of Art. *Songs of Glory: Medieval Art from 900–1500.* Exh. cat. Oklahoma City, 1985.

The Open Museum. *Chana Orloff: Line and Substance 1912–1968.* Exh. cat. Tefen, Israel: Arieli, 1993.

Ormond, Richard. "The Diploma Paintings from 1840 Onwards." *Apollo* 89 (1969): 56–57.

Parke-Bernet Galleries. *The Michael M. Zagayski Collection of Rare Judaica.* Sales cat. New York, 1964.

Piechotka, Maria and Kazimierz Piechotka. *Wooden Synagogues.* Warsaw: Arkady, 1959.

Pincus-Witten, Robert. "The Neustein Papers." *Arts Magazine* 52, no. 2 (October 1977): 102–15.

Polcari, Stephen. *Abstract Expressionism and the Modern Experience.* Cambridge: Cambridge University Press, 1991.

Pool, David de Sola. *Portraits Etched in Stone: Early Jewish Settlers 1682–1831.* New York: Columbia University Press, 1952.

Rachum, Stephanie. *David Bomberg in Palestine, 1923–27.* Jerusalem: Israel Museum, 1983.

Ramljak, Suzanne. *Elie Nadelman: Classical Folk.* New York: American Federation of Arts, 2001.

Ray, D. J. "Happy Jack: King of the Eskimo Carvers." *American Indian Art* 10, no. 1 (winter 1984): 32–47.

Rivers, Larry, with Carol Brightman. *Drawings and Digressions.* New York: Clarkson N. Potter, 1979.

Rivers, Larry, with Arnold Weinstein. *What Did I Do?: The Unauthorized Autobiography.* New York: HarperCollins, 1992.

Rodman, Selden. *Portrait of the Artist as an American: Ben Shahn, A Biography with Pictures.* New York: Harper and Brothers, 1951.

Rosenberg, Barry A. "The City Influence." In *The City Influence: Ross Bleckner, Peter Halley, Jonathan Lasker.* Exh. cat. Dayton, Ohio: Dayton Art Institute, 1992. Pp. 4–9.

Rosenberg, Harold. "Portraits: A Meditation on Likeness." In Richard Avedon, *Portraits.* New York: Farrar, Straus and Giroux, 1976.

Rosenzweig, Phyllis. *Larry Rivers.* Exh. cat. Washington, D.C.: Smithsonian Institution Press, 1981.

Roth, Cecil. "Stemmi di famiglie ebraiche italiane." In *Scritti in memoria di Leone Carpi.* Ed. Alexander Rofé. Jerusalem: Fondazione Sally Mayer, 1967. Pp. 165–84.

————. "The Lord Mayor Salvers." *The Connoisseur* 96 (May 1935): 296–99.

————, ed. *Jewish Art: An Illustrated History*, rev. ed. by Bezalel Narkiss. Greenwich, Conn.: New York Graphic Society, 1971.

Rubin, Reuven. *My Life, My Art.* New York: Funk and Wagnalls, 1969.

————. *Rubin: Retrospective Exhibition.* Jerusalem: Israel Museum, 1966.

Rutgers, Leonard Victor. *The Jews in Late Ancient Rome.* Leiden: E. J. Brill, 1995.

Sabar, Shalom. *Ketubbah: The Art of the Jewish Marriage Contract.* Jerusalem and New York: Israel Museum and Rizzoli, 2000.

————. *Ketubbah: Jewish Marriage Contracts of the Hebrew Union College Skirball Museum and Klau Library.* Philadelphia: Jewish Publication Society, 1990.

————. "The Origins of the Illustrated Ketubbah in Iran and Afghanistan" (Hebrew). *Pe'amim: Studies in Oriental Jewry* 79 (spring 1999): 129–58.

————. "The Use and Meaning of Christian Motifs in Illustrations of Jewish Marriage Contracts in Italy." *Journal of Jewish Art* 10 (1984): 47–63.

Sammlung jüdischer Kunstgegenstände der Synagogen-Gemeinde zu Danzig. Danzig, 1933.

Sandel, Joseph. "Samuel Hirszenberg" (pamphlet). Warsaw, 1952.

Sandler, Irving. *The New York School: The Painters and Sculptors of the Fifties.* New York: Harper and Row, 1978.

Sarshar, Houman, ed. *Esther's Children: A Portrait of Iranian Jews.* Beverly Hills, Calif., and Philadelphia: Center for Iranian Jewish Oral History in association with the Jewish Publication Society, 2002.

Schiff, Gert. "Tissot's Illustrations for the Hebrew Bible." In *Biblical Paintings: J. James Tissot.* Exh. cat. New York: The Jewish Museum, 1982. Pp. 19–50.

Schoenberger, G. "A Silver Sabbath Lamp from Frankfurt-on-the-Main." In *Essays in Honor of Georg Swarzenski.* Ed. Oswald Goetz. Chicago: Henry Regnery, 1951.

Schwabe, M., and A. Reifenberg. "Ein jüdisches Goldglas mit Sepulcralinschrift aus Rom." *Rivista de Archeologia Cristiana* 12, nos. 3–4 (1935): 341–46.

Semin, Didier, Tamar Garb, and Donald Kuspit. *Christian Boltanski.* London: Phaidon, 1997.

Shachar, I. "Feast and Rejoice in Brotherly Love: Burial Society Glasses and Jugs from Bohemia and Moravia." *Israel Museum News* 9 (1972).

Shadur, Joseph, and Yehudit Shadur. *Jewish Papercuts: A History and Guide.* Berkeley, Calif., and Jerusalem: Judah L. Magnes Museum and Gefen, 1994.

————. *Traditional Jewish Papercuts: An Inner World of Art and Symbol.* Hanover, N.H.: University Press of New England, 2001.

Shahn, Ben. "Imagination and Intention." *Review of Existential Psychology and Psychiatry* (winter 1967). Reprint, John D. Morse, ed., *Ben Shahn.* New York: Praeger, 1972.

Shandler, Jeffrey. "At Home on the Small Screen: Television's New York Jews." In *Entertaining America: Jews, Movies, and Broadcasting.* Ed. J. Hoberman and Jeffrey Shandler. Exh. cat. New York: The Jewish Museum; Princeton, N.J.: Princeton University Press, 2003. Pp. 244–57.

————. *While America Watches: Televising the Holocaust.* New York: Oxford University Press, 1999.

Shilo-Cohen, Nurit., ed. *Bezalel of Schatz, 1906–29.* Exh. cat. Jerusalem: Israel Museum, 1982.

Shyer, Laurence. *Robert Wilson and His Collaborators.* New York: Theatre Communications Group, 1989.

"Sie Wandern." *Ost und West* 10 (1904): 554–62.

Silver, Kenneth E., and Romy Golan. *The Circle of Montparnasse: Jewish Artists in Paris, 1905–1945.* Exh. cat. New York: Universe Books, 1985.

Singer, Susanna, et al. *Sol LeWitt Wall Drawings 1968–1984.* Exh. cat. Amsterdam: Stedelijk Museum, 1984; *Sol LeWitt Wall Drawings 1984–1992.* Bern: Die Kunsthalle, 1992.

Solomon-Godeau, Abigail. "Mourning or Melancholia: Christian Boltanski's 'Missing House.'" *Oxford Art Journal* 21, no. 2 (1998): 1–20.

Spector, Ronald. *Admiral of the New Empire: The Life and Career of George Dewey.* Baton Rouge: Louisiana State University Press, 1974.

Spencer, Charles. "Anglo-Jewish Artists: The Migrant Generations." In *The Immigrant Generations: Jewish Artists in Britain, 1900–1945.* Ed. Charles Spencer. New York: The Jewish Museum, 1982.

Spertus, Maurice. "Ludwig Yehuda Wolpert, 1900–1981." *Journal of Jewish Art* 8 (1981): 86.

Stearns, Robert. *Robert Wilson: From a Theater of Images.* Cincinnati: Contemporary Arts Center, 1980.

Steyn, Juliet. "The Complexities of Assimilation in the 1906 Whitechapel Art Gallery Exhibition 'Jewish Art and Antiquities.'" *Oxford Art Journal* 13, no. 2 (1990): 44–51.

Sussman, Elizabeth. *Nan Goldin: I'll Be Your Mirror.* Ed. Nan Goldin, David Armstrong, and Hans Werner Holzwarth Exh. cat. New York: Whitney Museum of American Art; Zurich: Scalo, 1996.

Sylvester, David. *Bomberg: Paintings, Drawings, Watercolours, and Lithographs.* Exh. cat. London: Fischer Fine Art Limited, 1973.

Taylor, Alice. *Book Arts of Isfahan: Diversity and Identity in Seventeenth-Century Persia.* Malibu, Calif.: J. Paul Getty Museum, 1995.

Temkin, Ann. *Alice Neel.* Exh. cat. Philadelphia: Philadelphia Museum of Art, 2000.

Thompson, Dorothy Abbott. *Hyman Bloom: The Spirits of Hyman Bloom, the Sources of His Imagery.* New York: Chameleon Books, in association with the Fuller Museum of Art, 1996.

Trapp, Frank Anderson. *Peter Blume.* New York: Rizzoli, 1987.

Tsujimoto, Karen. *Images of America: Precisionist Painting and Modern Photography.* Exh. cat. Seattle: San Francisco Museum of Modern Art by University of Washington Press, 1982.

Tuchman, Morris, ed. *Art in Los Angeles: Seventeen Artists in the Sixties.* Exh. cat. Los Angeles County Museum of Art, 1981.

Tuchman, Phyllis. *George Segal.* New York: Abbeville, 1983.

Tucker, Anne Wilkes. *Louis Faurer.* Exh cat. London: Merrell; Houston: Museum of Fine Arts, 2002.

Ulmer Museum. *Nancy Spero: Woman Breathing.* Exh cat. Ulm: Ulmer Museum, 1992.

Umansky, Ellen M. "Spiritual Expressions." In *Jewish Women in Historical Perspective*, 2nd rev. ed. Ed. Judith R. Baskin. Detroit: Wayne State University Press, 1998. Pp. 337–63.

Vetrocq, Marcia E. "Minimalia: A Matter of the Mind." *Art in America* 88, no. 1 (January 2000): 88–95.

Victoria and Albert Museum. *Anglo-Jewish Art and History in Commemoration of the Tercentenary of the Resettlement of the Jews in the British Isles.* Exh. cat. London: East and West Library for the Tercentenary Council, 1956.

———. *Berthold Wolpe: A Retrospective Survey.* Exh. cat. London: Victoria and Albert Museum; Faber and Faber, 1980.

Vidler, Anthony. *The Architectural Unconscious: James Casebere and Glen Seator.* Andover, Mass.: Addison Gallery of American Art, 2000.

Vidler, Anthony, Christopher Chang, and Jeffrey Eugenides. *James Casebere: The Spacial Uncanny.* Milan: Charta; New York: Sean Kelly Gallery, 2001.

Vilnay, Zev. *The Holy Land in Old Prints and Maps.* Trans. Esther Vilnay and Max Nurock. Jerusalem: R. Mass, 1965.

Vishny, Michele. *Mordecai Ardon.* New York: Harry N. Abrams, 1974.

Vitali, Christoph, ed. *Marc Chagall: The Early Years 1906–1922.* Frankfurt: Schirn Kunsthalle, 1991.

Von Wiese, Stephan. *Gert H. Wollheim 1894–1974: Monographie und Werkverzeichnis.* Köln: Wienand, 1993.

———. *Gert H. Wollheim: Phantast und Rebell.* Bonn: Verein August Macke Haus; Stollfuss, 2000.

Wadsworth Atheneum Museum of Art. *Noncomposition: Fifteen Case Studies.* Exh. cat. Hartford, Conn.: 2001.

Weber, Annette. "Splendid Bridal Gifts from a Sumptuous Wedding Ceremony of 1681 in the Frankfurt Judengasse." *Jewish Art* 19–20 (1993–94): 175.

Weber, Donald. "Goldberg Variations: The Achievements of Gertrude Berg." In *Entertaining America: Jews, Movies, and Broadcasting.* Ed. J. Hoberman and Jeffrey Shandler. Exh. cat. New York: The Jewish Museum; Princeton, N.J.: Princeton University Press, 2003. Pp. 113–23.

Weber, Nicholas F. *Anni Albers.* New York: Guggenheim Museum, 1999.

Wei, Lilly. "Talking Abstract, Part One." *Art in America* 75, no. 7 (July 1987): 84–85.

Whitehall Flagler Museum. *Tradition Today: Modern Judaica and Folk Art.* Exh. cat. Palm Beach, Fla.: Jewish Arts Foundation, 1990.

Whiteman, Maxwell. *Copper for America: The Hendricks Family and a National Industry 1755–1939.* New Brunswick, N.J.: Rutgers University Press, 1971.

Wiesel, Elie. *A Jew Today.* New York: Random House, 1978.

Wilke, Hannah. *Intra-Venus.* New York: Ronald Feldman Fine Arts, 1995.

Wilkinson, Alan. *Jacques Lipchitz: A Life in Sculpture.* Toronto: Art Gallery of Ontario, 1989.

———. *The Sculpture of Jacques Lipchitz: A Catalogue Raisonné.* New York: Thames and Hudson, 1996.

Wingler, Hans M. *Das Bauhaus, 1919–1933 Weimar, Dessau, Berlin und die Nachfolge in Chicago seit 1937* (Bramsche, Germany: Rasch, 1975).

Wischnitzer, Rachel. *The Architecture of the European Synagogue.* Philadelphia: Jewish Publication Society, 1964.

Wolf, Edwin II, and Maxwell Whiteman. *The History of the Jews of Philadelphia from Colonial Times to the Age of Jackson.* Philadelphia: Jewish Publication Society, 1957.

Wolfsfeld, Gadi. *Media and Political Conflict: News from the Middle East.* Cambridge: Cambridge University Press, 1997.

Wong, Janay Jadine. "Synagogue Art of the 1950s: A New Context for Abstraction." *Art Journal* (winter 1994): 37–43.

Worringer, Wilhelm. *Abstraction and Empathy: A Contribution to the Psychology of Style.* Chicago: Ivan R. Dee, 1997.

Young, James E., ed. *The Art of Memory: Holocaust Memorials in History.* Exh. cat. New York: The Jewish Museum; Munich: Prestel, 1994.

———. *At Memory's Edge: After-Images of the Holocaust in Contemporary Art and Architecture.* New Haven: Yale University Press, 2000.

Ziegler, A. "Jewish Artists in England." *Studio International* 153 (1957): 1–2.

Photography Credits

Numerals in **boldface** refer to pages.

Abbreviations

ARS   © 2004 Artists Rights Society, New York

NJAB   National Jewish Archive of Broadcasting, The Jewish Museum, New York

TJM   Archives of The Jewish Museum, New York

VAGA   Licensed by VAGA, New York

Front cover: © 2004 Andy Warhol Foundation for the Visual Arts/ARS/Ronald Feldman Fine Arts, New York.
Frontispiece: Courtesy of Kevin Roche, John Dinkeloo and Associates
Back cover: First row: Courtesy of the Sidney Finkel Memorial Scholarship Fund of the Jewish Vocational Service, East Orange, New Jersey (left), © Estate of Ben Shahn/VAGA (right); second row: © Estate of Elie Nadelman (left), © Weegee/International Center of Photography/Getty Images (second from right); third row: Courtesy of the Marian Goodman Gallery, New York (right); bottom: Courtesy of the family of Ludwig Y. Wolpert.

The Jewish Museum and Its History

10 Jewish Theological Seminary of America. **11** TJM. **12** TJM (left and center), From Edward M. M. Warburg, *As I Recall: Some Memoirs* (privately published by author), p. 16 (right). **13–14** TJM. **15** TJM (top left and bottom), From Warburg, *As I Recall*, pp. 5 and 73 (top center and right). **16–17** TJM.

Museum Without Walls

20 Courtesy of Michael David (top left). **21** Courtesy of the family of Max Weber. **28** © Aaron Siskind Foundation. **29** Courtesy of the Estate of Diane Arbus.

Memory and History

41 Courtesy of the Sidney Finkel Memorial Scholarship Fund of the Jewish Vocational Service, East Orange, New Jersey. **49** Courtesy of the Georgia O'Keeffe Foundation. **51** Courtesy of the family of Reuven Rubin. **53** © ARS/ADAGP, Paris. **54** Courtesy of the Israel Museum/Estate of Tim Gidal. **55** © Estate of Louis Faurer/VAGA. **57** © Adolph and Esther Gottlieb Foundation/VAGA. **59** © Estate of Ben Shahn/VAGA. **61** Courtesy of Couturier Gallery, Los Angeles. **63** Courtesy of the family of Mordecai Ardon. **65** © 2003 The Josef and Anni Albers Foundation/ARS. **66** Courtesy of Fabio Mauri. **67** Courtesy of the family of Wallace Berman. **68** Courtesy of the Estate of Moshe Kupferman. **69** Courtesy of Joshua Neustein. **71** © The George and Helen Segal Foundation/VAGA. **73** Courtesy of James Casebere. **75** Courtesy of Shimon Attie. **79** Courtesy of Nancy Spero. **80–81**

© 2004 Sol LeWitt/ARS. **83** Courtesy of the Marian Goodman Gallery, New York. **84–85** NJAB. **86** Photofest. **87** NJAB.

Spirituality and Faith

137 Courtesy of the family of Max Weber. **145** Courtesy of the family of Ludwig Y. Wolpert. **147** Courtesy of Hyman Bloom. **149** © Estate of Jacques Lipchitz, courtesy of Marlborough Gallery, New York. **151** © Adolph and Esther Gottlieb Foundation/VAGA. **153** Courtesy of the family of Ludwig Y. Wolpert. **155** Courtesy of Moshe Zabari. **157** Courtesy of the family of Leonard Baskin. **158** Courtesy of Zelig Segal. **159** Courtesy of Harley Swedler. **160** Courtesy of Carl Solway Gallery, Cincinnati. **161** Courtesy of Amy Klein Reichert. **162** Courtesy of Kay Sekimachi. **163** Courtesy of Michael Berkowitz. **165** Courtesy of Matthew McCaslin.

Society and Politics

Frontispiece © Estate of Peter Blume/VAGA. **181** © 2004 ARS/VG Bild-Kunst, Bonn. **183** © Estate of Peter Blume/VAGA. **185** © Weegee/International Center of Photography/Getty Images. **187** Courtesy of the Alfred Bloch Foundation. **189** Courtesy of William Anastasi and Sandra Gering Gallery. **191** Courtesy of William Kentridge. **193** Courtesy of Tina Barney. **195** Courtesy of R. B. Kitaj. **196** NJAB (left), Photofest (right). **197** NJAB (left and center), Photofest (right). **198–201** Photofest.

Portraiture and Identity

Frontispiece Courtesy of the Estate of Ilse Bing. **215** © Estate of Elie Nadelman. **217** Courtesy of Justman-Tamir. **219** Courtesy of the Estate of Wilhelmine Loeb Wollheim. **221** Courtesy of the Estate of Ilse Bing. **223** Courtesy of the Estate of David Bomberg. **225** © Estate of Larry Rivers/VAGA. **227** Courtesy of Richard Avedon. **229** Courtesy of Nan Goldin and Matthew Marks Gallery, New York. **230–31** © 2004 Andy Warhol Foundation for the Visual Arts/ARS/Ronald Feldman Fine Arts, New York. **233** © Marsie, Emanuelle, Damon, and Andrew Scharlatt. **235** © Estate of Alice Neel, courtesy of Robert Miller Gallery, New York. **237** Courtesy of Robert Wilson. **239** Courtesy of Ross Bleckner. **240–41** Courtesy of Nicole Klagsbrun Gallery, New York.

Index

Page numbers in italics refer to illustrations.